HAYNES CLASSIC MAKES SERIES

BMW

DRIVEN TO SUCCEED

GRAHAM ROBSON

First published in November 2005

A catalogue record for this book is available
from the British Library

ISBN 1 85960 870 1

Library of Congress catalog card no. 2005926146

Published by Haynes Publishing, Sparkford,
Yeovil, Somerset BA22 7JJ, UK
Tel: 01963 442030 Fax: 01963 440001
Int. tel: +44 1963 442030 Int. fax: +44 1963 440001
E-mail: sales@haynes.co.uk
Website: www.haynes.co.uk

Haynes North America, Inc.,
861 Lawrence Drive, Newbury Park,
California 91320, USA

All illustrations are courtesy BMW *except where credited separately.*

Page build by G&M Designs Limited,
Raunds, Northamptonshire

Printed and bound in Great Britain by
J. H. Haynes & Co. Ltd, Sparkford

contents

Introduction
BMW – *growth of a giant*

Ten very different types and ages of BMW, grouped in front of the Mobile Tradition building in Munich.

Searching for the true origins of a famous industrial enterprise is rather like seeking the source of a great river. In the same way that a river grows from any number of small streams, so a big business has many founding influences. Today's BMW is easy enough to understand as an independent car manufacturer, but in 1916, when those famous initials were first brought together, there was much less to observe. The company, which is now the most important business in Germany's Bavaria, was unknown in that part of the world until then.

Nearly a century ago, in fact, BMW was no more than a small concern, whose strategy was to build bigger, better and more powerful aircraft engines for military use. The first BMW-made cars were badged as Dixis, for it was not until 1929 that the original BMW model – the Austin Seven-based/Dixi-based 3/15 – went on sale.

First of all in 1916, therefore, there was the *Bayerische Flugzeugwerke* AG (Bavarian Airplane Works), and a year later that became the *Bayerische Motoren Werke GmbH* (Bavarian Motor Works), which was a more accurate description of what the company engaged in at the time. Not only did one of the world's most famous abbreviations – BMW – come into existence, but before long the equally famous blue-and-white 'spinning propeller' badge and trademark joined it. Thus, at the end of the 20th century, by when BMW was building a million vehicles every year, the company was 83 years old.

Except that the devastation caused by the Second World War changed everything, BMW spent most of that time expanding – steadily, logically and successfully. The original factories were in Munich and Eisenach, but later more automotive plants were established in Germany, and by the beginning of the present century there were massive BMW factories in Austria, South Africa, North America and Great Britain.

Not only that, but along the way BMW had absorbed Glas (and closed it down), Rover and Land Rover (but spat it out), and the Rolls-Royce car operation. It had also built up (and lost, due to bombing) its own aero engine operation, while continuing to make some of the world's best motorcycles. An aircraft gas turbine operation was re-established in the 1990s.

By the early 2000s, suitors had knocked on the door (and been beaten off), business mergers had been proposed (and rejected), and at a time when most of the world's car makers were already huddling together to help them stay afloat, BMW was still proudly independent, financially stable, and looking to handle its own future. All the signs were that this situation would persist beyond the company's first centenary.

The birth of BMW

Three important personalities can take most of the credit for ushering BMW into existence – two of them Austrian, and one from Swabia (the province of Germany which includes Stuttgart). Vienna-born Franz Joseph Popp was a graduate engineer, Dr Ing. Max Friz was an experienced engine designer, and Camillo Castiglioni was a Trieste-based banker.

It was Popp who started by building Austro-Daimler aero engines under

licence at the Rapp Motor Works in Munich, Popp who hired Max Friz to provide engineering expertise, and Popp who consulted Camillo Castiglioni on financial matters when the time came to float the new company. The Rapp influence then gradually faded away as BMW grew up, and a better-financed company, the *Bayerische Motoren Werke* AG, came into existence in August 1918.

By then, new factories had been commissioned on the edge of Munich's airport, but after the end of the First World War in November 1918, the entire business was in peril. Germany, the defeated nation, was banned from making aero engines of any type, and the company had to look around for other activities. Thus it was that BMW began to build engines for trucks, boats and for stationary or auxiliary use. The first BMW motorcycles (which even in those days had shaft-drive transmission) followed in 1923; it was not until 1924 that the international community once again allowed aero engines to be produced in Germany.

By the late 1920s, the Munich-based business was still afloat, but not always profitable. Even so, in 1928 BMW made the momentous move which would finally underpin its future. From 1 October 1928 BMW acquired the Dixi business, whose 19th century factory complex at Eisenach had been building motor cars since 1889 – first of all Wartburg cars, and later the Dixi marque itself. In 1928, Dixi's greatest asset was that it was building British Austin Sevens

Ancestors – Wartburg

Way back in 1898, the first cars to be produced at Eisenach were the Wartburgs, but these machines were a good deal more distinguished than the awful 'Iron Curtain' peoples' cars which followed after the Second World War.

In the beginning, Wartburg produced military vehicles and then

pedal cycles, before launching a (French) Decauville-based small car in 1898. This made Wartburg the fifth motor car brand to be established in Germany. The original models had single-cylinder or two-cylinder engines, with the first larger-engined Wartburgs appearing in 1902. However, after the founder,

Heinrich Ehrhardt, resigned from the company in 1903, he took the Decauville licensing agreement with him.

This brought Wartburg production to an end, after about 250 vehicles had been produced and it was then succeeded by the more significant Dixi brand.

under licence – no fewer than 6,120 in that year alone.

Incidentally, don't be fooled by the glib truism that Eisenach was situated far into Eastern Europe although it did end up in East Germany after the carnage of the Second World War. Politically, this was true enough, but the false 'border' of 1945 had a sinuous character and in fact, this manufacturing town, which was well to the *north* of Munich, was geographically much closer to Frankfurt than it was to Berlin.

Before the war the Eisenach factory was the centre of automotive production, not only for cars, but, at first, motorcycles also. Eventually, however, BMW motorcycles were built in Berlin. In Munich the Milbertshofen works was joined by a vast new camouflaged aero-engine facility at Allach, a north-west suburb of the city, instigated in response to the Nazi Government's requirement that BMW concentrate on the manufacture of air-cooled radial engines.

For the next decade, BMW built up its reputation, and its experience, in automotive manufacture, while relying on its aero-engine business to bring in the profits. Though it was by no means Germany's most important car maker – Mercedes-Benz was much more prestigious, while Ford and Opel (owned by GM) sold many more cars – it rapidly built a sporty reputation which was to survive for the rest of the century.

There were obvious parallels with Rolls-Royce in the UK. By 1939 both companies would be famous – legendary, even – not only for their road transport, but for their aircraft engines. At BMW, huge radial engines would go on to power aircraft as diverse as the Junkers Ju52 transport plane, the Ju88 bomber and the formidable Focke-Wulf Fw190 fighter plane. BMW also became involved in early rocket and gas turbine engine work too. If things had turned out differently the company might even have concentrated on these products to the exclusion of private cars.

It was going to take time to build the private car image. First of all, from

1929, there was the BMW version of the Austin Seven, then a more radical 3/20 of 1932, but it was not until 1933 that the first of the 300-Series six-cylinder BMWs, the 303, came along. From then until 1941, when the Eisenach assembly lines were completely turned over to military projects, both cars and engines grew, not only in size and weight, but in status too.

From a standing start in 1929, when much of the German motor industry considered the tiny Dixi to be a bit of a joke, BMW built up a formidable reputation, not only for engineering, but for marketing, and for that indefinable feature – image. In addition to the consistent use of the blue-and-white 'spinner' badge, the evolution of the 'kidney' grille style, all helped. In twelve short years, engines had leapt from 15bhp/749cc to 90bhp/3,485cc – but the sports versions could still not win major international races at any level.

Annual sales in this period never exceeded 9,000 cars, but as the years passed, these were faster, more luxurious, and therefore more profitable machines. In 1929, BMW's automotive sales were 40 million Reichmarks, but by the time the last private car was built in 1941 this had rocketed to 385 million Reichmarks.

Devastation and rebirth

When Hitler's armies marched into Poland on 1 September 1939, the world changed – for ever. BMW soon began to concentrate on making aero engines, a variety of soft-skinned military transport vehicles, and motorcycles. Production facilities were progressively moved away from Munich. Even though allied bombing – by the RAF and the USAAF – intensified as the war dragged on, neither Allach nor Eisenach was much damaged, while the downtown Munich factory in Milbertshofen was devastated.

When American forces marched into BMW's various factories in April

1945, they found premises which were no longer producing much military material, and a work-force which, although defiant, was now on its knees, ready for reconstruction and redemption to begin. For BMW, all would have been well if the Russian occupation zone had not already been allocated Thuringen, which included the Eisenach factory. Although General Patton's US Third Army had originally liberated it, within weeks the American forces were obliged to draw back to previously agreed Zone boundaries. The Russian Autovelo operation took over the works, and before long cars to pre-war BMW design were again being made.

From that day forward, the pride and joy of BMW's empire, the factory which had done so much to establish the reputation of their cars, was lost to them for ever. Not a car, an engine, or even the tooling, the drawings and archive of the already-legendary 300-Series cars would ever again be available to the West.

For BMW this was a shattering blow. In West Germany its factories were in ruins, in East Germany they were permanently out of reach – so, was there a business that could be rebuilt? Amazingly, through the squalor, near poverty, and much humiliation, there was. Allied orders, originally issued in July 1945, were that BMW's entire facilities were to be confiscated and shipped out as 'war reparations'. Whether this was legal or not, the USA didn't care – they had won the war, after all – but somehow or other these orders came to be much modified.

Before long, the Allach factory was turned into a massive US military vehicle repair operation. Elsewhere in Munich, BMW produced cooking utensils, building fittings, bicycles, baking equipment and agricultural machines. By late 1948, motorcycles were once again in production – but not cars.

BMW arch-enthusiasts such as Ernst Loof and Alex von Falkenhausen set up their own post-war operations, to build up cars around reconditioned BMW 328 material, but the BMW

Ancestors – Dixi

The original Eisenach-built Dixi was announced in 1904, and over the next 25 years more than 8,000 Dixis of a bewildering variety were produced, some with engines as large as 7,320cc, with some rated at up to 75hp. Except that these cars allowed Eisenach to expand, and to provide work for thousands of skilled men in the region, they had no technical influence on the BMWs which were to follow from the same factory.

Although Dixi gradually expanded, the post-war slump of the early 1920s hit the company hard. It was no longer allowed to make military vehicles and by the middle of the decade, the company was in the hands of stock exchange speculator Jakob Schapiro. It was he who concluded the deal with Sir Herbert Austin, whereby the Austin Seven would become the Dixi 3/15hp, and be assembled at Eisenach. This was the last of the Dixis, becoming the first BMW-badged car (the BMW 3/15) in 1929, and so this is where the romance of the BMW motor car marque actually began.

Announced in 1927, the Dixi 3/15 was actually a British-type Austin Seven built under licence at Eisenach. This particular car has a Buhne drop-head coupé style.

Seventy years apart – the BMW 328 of the 1930s compared with the Z4 of the early 2000s.

business itself struggled to stay alive, and it was not until 1951 that the first post-war model – the 501, or 'Baroque Angel' – was put on show.

At a time when Germany was still war-torn and struggling to get back on its feet, the population really needed small cars (VW Beetles, for example), and not luxurious machines like the 501, but BMW had no alternative as they really only knew how to make big cars.

It did seem as if BMW had a death wish at this time though. Not only was the 'Baroque Angel' big, bulbous, and derived from the Type 332 prototype of 1941, but from 1954 it was given an all-new V8 engine (the first post-war German V8, incidentally) and called the 502. If it had been difficult to sell the expensive 501, then selling the even more costly 502 would be more demanding still. To sell *any* numbers of the coachbuilt 503 and 507 types which followed was a real achievement, and losses on the automotive side continued to build up.

However, the company at least once again had a toe-hold in the automotive market and, with its motorcycles continuing to sell well, the business could, albeit rather precariously, stay afloat.

Bubbles – and near-bankruptcy

Then came a radical change of direction. Looking for ways to fill up the Munich factories (where the wartime damage and destruction had long since been repaired), BMW struck an unlikely deal with the Italian concern, Iso, to modify then build their own version of a tiny two-seater bubblecar, dubbed the Isetta.

Sublime to ridiculous? Maybe. Damaging to BMW's image? Very likely. An unconvincing move? BMW thought not. Not only could they see that the company needed to sell smaller cars – *lots* of smaller cars – to stay alive, but they could also sense that the post-war boom in motorcycle sales was about to end.

Call it how you will, but the Isetta certainly set the numbers game spinning. Whereas BMW had only been selling about 3,000–4,000 of the

501 'Baroque Angels' a year, they soon began to make 30,000 Isettas annually, and added to this with the four-seater 600s – no fewer than 27,187 of them in 1958.

Even so, the Isetta/600 range only bought BMW one thing – time. For the 501 generation continued to lose money with almost every example which rolled out of the door. In marketing terms there was a colossal gap between the tiny bubblecar, and the massive, overblown, 500-Series machines. BMW knew what they needed to do to fill that gap – first of all they wanted to build the Michelotti-styled 700s, and then to follow this up with an all-new medium-sized machine (the 'New Class' which would become the original 1500) – but the money was simply not available to make this possible.

Worse, at a time when huge amounts of capital were needed to tool up for these two ranges, BMW's finances were still in an awful state. By late 1959, the situation was so bad that the local Bavarian government became thoroughly alarmed, and offered to invest heavily in the business to keep it alive.

Even more major financial support was still needed and to quote that eminent historian, Halwart Schrader: 'Around this time, rumours of a merger or takeover involving a German or foreign company were heard often. From America and England, so it went, potential buyers or investors were visiting Munich in rapid succession. True enough, there were signs of interest, but serious negotiations never took place. BMW's management still believed, as incredible as it may seem, that it would be able to pull the company up by its own bootstraps...'

The crunch came in December 1959, after BMW's Board had proposed writing down the existing shares, and issuing new shares, which were to be available only to participating banks – and to Daimler-Benz of Stuttgart!

Everyone *except* the Board and Daimler-Benz objected to this proposal, which was thrown out, a cataclysm which caused Chairman Dr Richter-Brohm (who had only been in a position of real power since 1955) to resign. As a result, the proposals were much-diluted, the existing capital was written down by only 25 per cent, and this was the point, too, in which multi-millionaire Herbert Quandt took a major shareholding. Along with the backing from the major banks the company gradually – very gradually – began to turn round and, miraculously, began to look as if it would survive.

1500 – and a new beginning

Amazingly, it did just that. First of all the sharply styled 700s – saloons, coupés and convertibles – held the line successfully from 1959 to 1962, and from that date the totally new-generation 1500 began to take over.

BMW's production figures tell their own story: 17,478 cars, some of them Isettas, had been built in 1955, and 51,081 (mostly Isettas and 600s) were produced in 1958. The following year there was a slump to 36,609, but 53,888 followed in 1960, after which all the trends began to point upwards.

Although the 1500 was new from end to end, smart, crisply styled and technologically advanced, it took time for it to be accepted. Fortune, however, stepped in at this point when one of Germany's long-established companies, Borgward, collapsed. Borgward's Isabella range included a popular 1.5-litre range of middle-class saloons which the 1500 could replace at once – if only the public would accept it.

In fact the new BMW was a perfect replacement in the same price bracket. BMW's new management, now steadfastly backed by Herbert Quandt (who wanted to see a return on his investment) was confident and soon market sentiment turned in

Fifty years of BMW coupés, with the 645Ci in front of historic ancestors.

Who are the Quandts?

In their own way, the German Quandt family is as important to the world of motoring as the Agnellis of Italy, but with less desire for publicity and the high life. First involved with BMW after the near bankruptcy of the company in 1959, the Quandts became major shareholders in BMW, effectively with a controlling interest, and remain so after almost 50 eventful years.

The Quandts are descendants of a Dutch rope-making family, and in spite of having to start again from scratch in 1945 following the destruction, confiscation and dispersal of their

Herbert Quandt, centre, became a major shareholder at BMW in 1959. His family still has major interests in the company today.

industrial possessions in the chaos resulting from Germany's defeat, they were once again numbered amongst the country's 'super-rich' by the 1960s.

Herbert Quandt, afflicted by eyesight problems, was nevertheless a formidable businessman who sat on the board of the rival Daimler-Benz concern. He approached the Bavarian Finance Minister in 1960, offering to take a majority stake in the Munich company, if the Bavarian state would support him for the next few years.

The authorities swiftly agreed to this proposal, Quandt provided finance to rescue the concern, and joined the Board of Trustees, although he would never be involved as an executive director. In the years

which followed, no major financial decision was ever taken without consulting the Quandt family.

Even after Herbert Quandt himself died at the end of the 1970s, his widow Johanna, the matriarch of the family, continued to exercise their influence with a rod of iron, and had much say over the appointment of top managers to 'their' firm. By the 1990s the Quandt shareholding was just below the 50 per cent mark, but Stefan Quandt had become a deputy chairman and his decision was vital when the time came to buy Rover in 1994, and then sell it again in 2000.

To this day, it would be unwise of any important BMW personality to fall foul of the Quandt family, as several have found out to their cost...

BMW's favour. For the first time since 1939, from 1962 BMW had a coherent range of products, starting with the Isetta, moving up through the 700 range, on to the new and exciting 1500, all topped out by the very last of the 'Baroque Angel' series. To this one could add the motorcycles, and a reborn aviation division.

For the first time in years, too, no panic imperatives were required, and the company could carry on developing a coherent strategy. Sales edged upwards – they passed 60,000 for the first time in 1964, and would reach 88,000 only three years later. Not only that, but the company had settled on a well-defined engineering theme – in future the structures would feature unit-construction bodyshells, engines would all be based on the new overhead-camshaft layout, suspension would be all-independent (with that characteristic semi-trailing layout at the rear) – and each type would demonstrably be related to another.

It was also a period in which the product mix changed quite radically. The last Isetta was produced in 1962, the last of the 'Baroque Angel' generation of saloons (the 2600/3200 types) were built in 1963. The last of the cute rear-engined 700 range followed in 1965. On the other hand, the 1500 grew up, becoming an 1800 in 1963, developing into a 1600 in 1964, and with a smart coupé derivative added in 1965. And there was more to follow.

1966 – 50th anniversary

Among all this activity, it would have been easy to have missed an important anniversary, but BMW was not about to do that. Not only did the original 1600-2 two-door saloon appear in 1966, but the first of what would become the celebrated 1,990cc versions of the overhead-camshaft engine also arrived. From this point, BMW seemed to do no wrong, and could always generate enough money

to finance its own steady growth, and expand its range.

The days of producing marginal-motoring mini-cars was now long gone. Whereas the new 1500 saloon had been the most advanced BMW of 1962, within five years that engine was in the smallest of all the cars in the range. Production was about to exceed 100,000 cars a year, which sounded impressive in 1968, but would be dwarfed by future achievements. This was the point at which the first of a new family of six-cylinder-engined cars – the 2500/2800 saloons – went on sale.

BMW was now firmly set on the expansion trail, and was already looking for additional space. Bertone of Italy and Karmann of Osnabrück, West Germany, had already begun the supply of sporty derivatives, but this was only a palliative.

The breakthrough came in 1966 when a neighbouring car company, Hans Glas, hit financial trouble. Based in Dingolfing, not too far north-east of Munich, this was a business worth buying up, so BMW speedily absorbed it, modernised and expanded the premises, and therefore gained a second car assembly plant. Originally only a CKD assembly plant, a South African factory also began to build cars on its own account – and there was more to come.

In 1972, not only did Munich host the Olympic Games, but BMW found time to complete its now-famous and visually distinctive new headquarters building (then, and later, to be nicknamed the 'four-cylinder' building because of its unique shape), and at the same time introduce the very first of a brand-new model family – the original 5-Series.

By the mid-1970s, it seemed, the thoroughly revived BMW could tackle everything, and achieve anything. Not even the impact of the Arab-Israeli War and the Energy Crisis which followed could stop it, apparently. After one short setback in 1974, sales were booming again – the first 200,000/year figure would be notched up in 1975 – for new models included the vitally important 3-Series range,

and the smart 6-Series coupés. Along the way, BMW had built up an enviable motor sport record, not only with saloon cars (some of them turbocharged), and the flamboyant 3.0CSL coupés, but with highly tuned engines for Formula 2 single-seater racing.

M-Sport, and new-generation cars

By this time, there truly seemed to be no end to BMW's ambitions. Not only did the company slot itself comfortably into regular renewals of the series-production cars – 2500/2800 became 7-Series in 1977, a new-generation 'small' six-cylinder engine appeared in the same year, 3-Series and 5-Series types were both renewed with the 1980s in mind, but more ambitious products appeared along the way.

The mid-engined Turbo prototype of 1972 was shown as an 'experimental safety vehicle', but could have been so much more if the Energy Crisis had not intervened, as could the outrageously styled 2002 Turbo which followed it. After a suitable interval, though, BMW then followed up with the M1 project – which was a very specialised, very limited-production mid-engined coupé whose *raison-d'être* was as a publicity vehicle for the company. A high-profile one-make racing series, held at F1 events all round Europe, brought inestimable benefits – and indirectly projected BMW towards providing specialised turbocharged engines for F1 cars in the 1980s.

At a time when many car makers were rushing to join forces with other concerns, BMW stayed peacefully aloof of all such mergers. By the end of the 1980s, in fact, they appeared to be so large, so stable, so profitable, and so capable, that they came to be seen as possible empire-builders on their own.

By 1986, for instance (70 years after formation) BMW was already building nearly half a million cars a year,

The 'four-cylinder' HQ building took shape close to the traditional Milbertshofen factory in downtown Munich. The BMW logo is painted atop the museum display.

including those from its three major German factories, Regensburg having been added to the group by that time. The product range included 3-Series, 5-Series and 7-Series saloons and 3-Series convertibles, 6-Series coupés, and the Z1 Roadster, plus the glamorous M3 sports saloon, and the supply of turbocharged F1 engines to Formula 1 teams such as Brabham. Mixed into this were petrol and diesel engines (some built in Austria), four-wheel-drive variants, and local assembly in South Africa. This was typical of what was to follow, but by no means unique for the period.

Then came the 1990s, when the directors seemed to take a deep breath, to look firmly over the horizon into the future, and to plan firmly for million-a-year sales. If not officially, then as a definite spur to these ambitions, there was the chance to match Daimler-Benz and become Germany's most profitable, and most prestigious, car maker. And, in case we forget, BMW was still strong in the motorcycle business (its products mainly assembled in Berlin), and it was about to re-enter the civil aircraft gas turbine engine business, in a project jointly funded and developed with Rolls-Royce plc of the UK.

The truly big move – for this was BMW's first takeover move since buying up Hans Glas in 1966 – came in 1994 when the company absorbed the Rover Group in the UK. Not that Rover (or even MG or Mini, which were existing brands within that group) were truly vital to the takeover, for it was the Land Rover brand, which had its own peerless store of 4x4 expertise, which was the real prize. From the outset, BMW tried to breathe new life into this ailing British conglomerate (which was, after all, the rather seedy remnants of British Leyland), spending hugely on new-model investment. Without BMW's backing, for sure, Rover could not have afforded to bring forward so many brand-new Rover, MG and Land Rover models to the market place.

At the same time, BMW took its long-awaited step into North American manufacturing, by electing to build a modern plant at Spartanburg, South Carolina. Originally intended for the manufacture of sports cars (the Z3 was the first such model, previewed in 1995, and seen spectacularly in the latest James Bond film), and for BMW to build new four-wheel-drive X5 SUVs (Sport Utility Vehicles, in North American parlance), Spartanburg also assembled 3-Series saloons, and was both large enough and flexible enough to tackle other such jobs in the foreseeable future. Far from being a mere 'spanner plant' (the term applied to factories which manufactured from ready-to-assemble parts supplied by a larger plant), Spartanburg was an important new operation in its own right.

In the same period, BMW also expanded their Port Elizabeth factory in South Africa, so that many 3-Series cars sold in Europe were actually produced in that faraway nation, with much local content. The build quality was so high by that time, that new-car customers rarely knew where their 3-Series had been built, unless they could decipher the hieroglyphics of the VIN code!

There was another acquisition, made in 1998, which partially reflected the aero-engine links which already existed with Rolls-Royce plc. When Vickers of the UK came to sell the Rolls-Royce/Bentley car-making business, VW thought they had snapped up both brands in a brisk bidding battle with BMW. However, as explained later, Rolls-Royce plc had other ideas, the result being that the legendary British brand was transferred to BMW and the first BMW-inspired Rolls-Royce car was unveiled in 2003.

Into a new century

But it wasn't all good news. By 2000, it had become clear that BMW's purchase of Rover/Land Rover had not

worked out, for that ancient concern was beginning to look like a money pit which the German concern had little chance of filling in completely. No amount of German management time and strategy could stem the losses which continued to build, so early in that year the company cut loose, and walked away from its six-year experiment.

Not that it was all that simple, for by that time the company had commissioned a brand-new engine manufacturing plant at Hams Hall, on the eastern fringes of Birmingham, and as part of the terms of the 'divorce' it had also decided to keep the Mini brand, for which a factory at Oxford was thoroughly rebuilt and modernised. This traumatic experience was speedily shrugged off, corporate profits recovered very quickly indeed, and BMW faced up to the 2000s with more confidence than ever before.

Ninety years after BMW was originally set up in Bavaria, therefore, the company had become one of the largest and most prestigious in the world. With an impressive and closely related array of BMW model ranges – stretching from small (1-Series) all the way to massive 4x4s (X5) – it also embraced Mini and Rolls-Royce, not forgetting the motorcycles and aero-engine businesses too. With annual global car sales hovering around the million mark (more than a quarter of them from the Spartanburg factory in the USA, and 180,000 Minis from the UK), the business was looking very healthy.

And according to all the forecasts, there was more to come…

BMW's X5, *built at Spartanburg, USA, which was officially opened in 1995, was an instant success, with the 100,000th example being built in 2001.*

BMW
to 1945

The BMW 303, launched in 1933, was the first of the '300 Series' cars, which not only had a very smart and distinguished body style, but was the first BMW to use what became the familiar 'double kidney' grille, and the first to use an own-design of six-cylinder engine.

What a contrast. Today's BMWs have twin overhead camshaft engines, five- or six-speed transmissions, anti-lock brakes, all-independent suspension, air conditioning, and enough electronic controls to keep a computer boffin happy until he retires. In the 1920s, however, the very first BMWs had side-valve engines, a three-speed gearbox and a top speed of little more than 45mph. In three-quarters of a century, *the Bayerische Motoren Werke* has come a long way…

For BMW, it all stemmed from the acquisition of the Dixi marque of Eisenach, in 1928. Before then Dixi had stayed rather precariously independent, while Munich-based BMW was a rising star in the aero-engine and motorcycle manufacturing business, but with no involvement in making cars. 'Dixi', incidentally, was Latin-based, and meant 'It's the last word' – a good and whimsical way to sell such cars, if not by any means true.

However, when the BMW management team took control of

Dixi 3/15 and BMW-Dixi 3/15
1927–1929

ENGINE:
Four cylinders in line, iron block, iron head

Capacity	749cc
Bore x stroke	56mm x 76mm
Compression ratio	5.6:1
Maximum power	15bhp at 3,000rpm
Valve gear	Two valves per cylinder, side operated
Fuelling	One side-draught Solex or Zenith carburettor

TRANSMISSION:
Three-speed manual, no synchromesh

SUSPENSION:
Front: Beam axle, transverse leaf spring, friction dampers
Rear: Live (beam) axle, cantilever quarter-elliptic leaf springs, friction dampers

STEERING:
Cam-and-roller

BRAKES:
Mechanical, front drum/rear drum

WHEELS/TYRES:
Bolt-on wire; 26 x 3.50 cross-ply

BODY/CHASSIS:
Separate chassis with cross-bracing, saloon or optional coachbuilt tourer/drop-head styles

DIMENSIONS:

Length	8ft 10in
Width	3ft 10in
Height	5ft 4in
Wheelbase	7ft 4in
Track, front	3ft 4in
Track, rear	3ft 5.2in

WEIGHT:
946lb

PERFORMANCE/ECONOMY:

Max speed	46mph approx
Fuel consumption	typically 45–50mpg

UK PRICE WHEN NEW incl. tax:
Not sold in UK – equivalent to £220 in Germany

NUMBER BUILT:

Dixi	6,162
BMW-Dixi	3,146

326
1936–1941

ENGINE:
Six cylinders in line, iron block, iron head

Capacity	1,971cc
Bore x stroke	66mm x 96mm
Compression ratio	6.0:1
Maximum power	50bhp at 3,750rpm
Valve gear	Two valves per cylinder, pushrod overhead
Fuelling	Two Solex side-draught carburettors

TRANSMISSION:
Four-speed manual, synchromesh on top and third gears

SUSPENSION:
Front: Independent, transverse leaf spring, wishbones, hydraulic lever-arm dampers
Rear: Live (beam) axle, longitudinal torsion bars, hydraulic lever-arm dampers

STEERING:
Rack-and-pinion

BRAKES:
Hydraulic, front drum/rear drum

WHEELS /TYRES:
Steel disc; 5.25-17in cross-ply

BODY/CHASSIS:
Separate ladder-style chassis with cruciform cross-bracing, various coachbuilt styles by specialists, on wood or metal framing, with aluminium or steel panelling

DIMENSIONS:

Length	15ft 1in
Width	5ft 3in
Height	4ft 1in
Wheelbase	9ft 5in
Track, front	4ft 3.2in
Track, rear	4ft 3.2in

WEIGHT:
2,480lb

PERFORMANCE/ECONOMY:

Max speed	71mph approx
Acceleration	0–60mph in approx 32sec
Fuel consumption	typically 23mpg

UK PRICE WHEN NEW incl. tax:
£475

NUMBER BUILT:
15,949

328
1936–1940

ENGINE:
Six cylinders in line, iron block, iron head

Capacity	1,971cc
Bore x stroke	66mm x 96mm
Compression ratio	7.5:1
Maximum power	80bhp at 5,000rpm
Valve gear	Two valves per cylinder, pushrod and cross-pushrod overhead
Fuelling	Three downdraught Solex carburettors

TRANSMISSION:
Four-speed manual, synchromesh on top and third gears

SUSPENSION:
Front: Independent, transverse leaf spring, wishbones, hydraulic lever-arm dampers
Rear: Live (beam) axle, half-elliptic leaf springs, hydraulic lever-arm dampers

STEERING:
Rack-and-pinion

BRAKES:
Hydraulic, front drum/rear drum

WHEELS/TYRES:
Steel disc; 5.25/5.50-16in cross-ply

BODY/CHASSIS:
Separate ladder-style chassis with tubular side and cross-bracing, two-door coachbuilt sports car style

DIMENSIONS:

Length	12ft 9.5in
Width	5ft 1in
Height	4ft 7in
Wheelbase	7ft 10.4in
Track, front	3ft 9.4in
Track, rear	4ft 0in

WEIGHT:
1,830lb

PERFORMANCE/ECONOMY:

Max speed	100mph approx
Acceleration	0–60mph in 9.5sec
Fuel consumption	typically 20mpg

UK PRICE WHEN NEW incl. tax:
£695

NUMBER BUILT:
464

At the end of the 1920s, BMW started in the car-building business by joining forces with the Dixi concern, and building Austin Sevens under licence. This is a Dixi 3/15 – to all intents and purposes identical to the Austin Seven. The BMW 3/15 which followed in 1929 had coupled brakes but was otherwise very similar.

their new acquisition, located 250 miles north of Munich, they found a thriving business which was at the heart of the town, and an assembly line already full of stubby little cars which were really no more or no less than rebadged Austin Sevens. Every week, more than 150 of these modest little machines, known as Dixi 3/15s – many of them with open-top bodywork – would roll out of the gates.

Maybe this car was not glamorous, but it was the right car at the right time, selling in the lowest of all bargain basements in a country which was still recovering from the hyperinflation of the early-1920s – and one which was about to dive into the Depression. Those were the days when prices started at RM2,750 (about £220), the major domestic competition coming from DKW, Hanomag and Opel.

Although BMW engineers, led by Max Friz, were not at all impressed by what they saw, it would take time, and capital, to start afresh. Accordingly, BMW's first pragmatic move was to turn the Dixi 3/15 into the BMW-Dixi 3/15 – no technical changes of any nature – then to introduce a modified car, which dropped the Dixi name, from July 1929.

This was the BMW 3/15, and was really the source of all later BMW motor cars. It was a model range very similar to the original Dixi, but with larger and more capacious bodies, modified front grilles, a choice of coachwork (including an all-steel saloon shell from Ambi-Budd of

This was the first BMW-badged car to be completed – a 3/15 model of 1929 – it being a slightly evolved version of the Dixi 3/15, which had started the entire process rolling.

Berlin), and coupled brakes. Prices were down – they started at RM2,200 (about £176) – but BMW's ambitions were clear. Interestingly, in 1930 there was a Type DA3 version of this car, with 18bhp instead of 15bhp, a two-seater sports body, and the model name of 'Wartburg'. This was of course a generation earlier than the awful, smoky, East German 'peoples' cars' which would carry the same name from the 1950s onwards – and in its day it was a capable little machine.

Happily, the 3/15 kept BMW's production lines busy until 1932, by which time no fewer than 9,308 Dixis and 15,948 BMWs had been produced. These cars, however, had never been seen as BMW's future, but as its modest little beginning – and the 3/20 which took over in 1932 was very different indeed.

Except that the general styles were similar, the 3/20 was almost entirely different from the Austin-based 3/15, easily shrugging off its British parentage. Although it was still a tiny 3hp car (according to contemporary German taxation rules), and cost from only RM2,650 (£212), it showed the way that BMW's engineers were thinking. The chassis was a sturdy backbone, the front and rear suspension was now all-independent (the latter by transverse leaf springs and swing axles), but most important of all, the engine was a brand-new overhead-valve four-cylinder type of 782cc which developed 20bhp. Sales ticked over steadily, with 7,215 sold before the car was dropped in mid-1934.

On its own, this engine was not significant, but a six-cylinder version already figured in Eisenach's master plans. Although the Depression hit Germany with a rare ferocity in 1931/32, BMW pressed ahead with yet another new car – the 303, which appeared in February 1933.

Shortly after this, from the summer of 1933, an important new automotive personality, Dipl Eng Fritz Fiedler arrived at Eisenach, to become chief designer. Already known for his work at Stoewer and then Horch, he was much respected, and would have

influence on all BMW cars produced over the next 30 years. Immediately after the Second World War, he would also be noted for his work, in England, on the original Bristol cars and engines, which were clearly BMW-based.

The first of the smooth 'sixes'

For the next eight years, BMW would build only three types of chassis for their private cars, but each entirely different, with all setting standards that their rivals could often not match. These chassis featured independent front suspension by transverse leaf springs.

The original 303-generation cars (1933–37) all used one or other

version of a tubular chassis frame, with a beam rear axle which rode on half-elliptic springs. Later cars – the 320-generation types of 1937–41, had more sturdy box-section chassis frames and, depending on the model, either half-elliptics or longitudinal torsion bars to support their rear axles. Finally, and most significantly as far as BMW's sporting reputation was concerned, the 328 was one on its own, with a tubular frame, which was matched to half-elliptic rear leaf springs.

Apart from the constantly developing style, which featured flowing wing lines and fluid contours quite unlike any other German vehicle

Elegant where the original Dixi 3/15 had been stumpy, and rounded where the badged 3/15 had been angular, the 303 was the first of the truly stylish BMWs of the 1930s.

F76 and F79 delivery tricycles

BMW commercial vehicles? Whatever next? Yet in 1932, when Europe was in the depths of Depression, it seemed to make commercial sense. Anxious to keep its Eisenach factory busy, BMW cobbled together an odd-looking three-wheeler delivery van, complete with an air-

Anything to keep the factory busy ... these strange three-wheelers were built between 1932 and 1934.

cooled motorcycle engine mounted at the front, the loading platform on top of that, and a tiny cabin behind it.

The chassis frame had tubular members, and the front axle was rigid. Early F76 trucks had 6bhp/200cc engines, while later examples (F79s) had 14bhp/400cc units and all had three-speed gearboxes and shaft drive to the single rear wheel, which had swinging

arm suspension. BMW claimed a possible payload of 650kg (1,433lb), but performance was absolutely negligible.

It was all an irrelevance, for these trucks could not compete with competition from Tempo and Goliath. Between 1932 and 1934, only 250 F76s and 350 F79s were produced. This was the first and last time BMW attempted to break into this down-market sector.

of the period, these cars first established, then evolved, the 'twin kidney' type of radiator grille which is such a familiar feature of BMWs all over the world today.

Most important of all, though, was the engine, the smooth long-stroke 'six', which would give such sturdy and reliable service, being extensively modified and developed, until the mid-1950s. Although it all started as an innocuously specified 30bhp power unit, by the 1950s it had grown in size, and had tripled its peak output.

The story of this engine's development is best told in a simple table:

Year introduced (and BMW model)	Capacity (cc)	Bore and stroke (mm)	Peak power bhp/rpm
1933 (303)	1,173	56 x 80	30/4,000
1934 (315)	1,490	58 x 94	34/4,000
1935 (319)	1,911	65 x 96	45/3,750
1936 (326)	1,971	66 x 96	50/3,750
1936 (328)	1,971	66 x 96	80/5,000
1955 (501/3)	2,077	68 x 96	72/4,500

It is fascinating to work out how the capacity 'stretch' was achieved. Over the years, the cylinder bore dimension went up by 12mm, while that of the stroke went up by 16mm, and the capacity increased by 77 per cent – but all derivatives were long-stroke power units.

It was from 1935 onwards that BMW began to catch the enthusiasts' eyes. Where previous models had been worthy, but rather staid, from the launch of the 315/1 and 319/1 Roadsters of 1935, not only was the

BMW's *technology advanced by leaps and bounds in the 1930s. This, the 315 of 1934, not only had transverse leaf-spring independent front suspension, but a 34bhp/1,490cc overhead-valve six-cylinder engine – all available in a variety of body styles.*

engine beginning to look, feel and sound sporty, but the style was attractive too. Look at a 315/1 and you will certainly see styling cues carried on to the 328 which followed it.

The 326 of 1936 – saloons and cabriolets – were fine cars with box-section ladder-type chassis, and 50bhp/1,971cc engines (Autenrieth of Darmstadt produced the open-top and closed saloon shells, as they

The 326 of 1936 had a 50bhp/1,971cc engine, with a rounded front-end style featuring the twin-kidney grille. Many cars were built with this cabriolet body by Autenrieth.

When newly revealed, the six-cylinder engine of the 328 featured a cross-pushrod valve gear layout, downdraught inlet ports, and three carburettors. Impressive and bulky, it was also a very efficient power unit. This 2-litre engine was developed from an earlier BMW 'six'. (LAT)

would do for later-1930s BMWs too), but it was the splendid 328 two-seater which caused such a stir.

Looking back today, one wonders why an 80bhp/1,971cc-engined sports car should have caused such a fuss, but the fact is that this was the best-handling, best-looking, and somehow the 'purest' BMW motor car yet made. The earlier 315/319 pedigree combination of a tubular chassis frame with transverse leaf independent front suspension was carried forward, the weight was trimmed as far as possible, the style was even more advanced – the nose

This was the 328's instrument display, simply laid out, with large matching speedometer and rev-counter dials in front of the driver. (LAT)

Fast, compact and technically advanced by any standards, the two-seater 328 started a new trend in sports car design. Semi-recessed headlamps, knock-off steel wheels and wrap-around front wings were all ahead of their time. A well set up 328 could reach 100mph. (LAT)

Frazer Nash BMWs

By the early 1930s, Britain's London-based AFN business (which manufactured 'chain gang' Frazer Nash cars) was finding its cars defeated by BMW sports machines in international motorsport. To meet this threat, AFN's Bill Aldington approached BMW in 1934 asking if AFN could perhaps manufacture BMW cars under licence in the UK.

Although BMW did not agree to this proposal, it suggested that AFN should become the British BMW importers, an arrangement which took effect for 1935 and after. At the same time it was agreed that *for the British market only* these imports should be marketed as Frazer Nash BMWs.

The first such cars sold in Britain were Type 315s, but before long, Type 319s, 327s and in particular 328s, were all added to the range. Indeed, from late 1936, no fewer than 46 Type 328s were brought into the country. At the same time, AFN also imported an increasing number of high-tech BMW motorcycles.

Except that these cars were treated to a different badge (with a Frazer Nash-BMW roundel surrounding the familiar 'propeller'), and the

AFN imported BMWs to the UK in the 1930s, and although these were mechanically standard, BMW allowed them to be rebadged as Frazer Nash-BMWs. Here is the evidence, on a 328 hub spinner. (LAT)

Aldington family gave them different model names, no other technical or style changes were ever made to the German-built cars. One effect, however, was that as FN-BMW imports rose, sales of domestic Frazer Nash cars died away. Quite a few 315s and 319s were available with British-built coachwork: 37 had Abbott saloon or dhc bodies (315 and 319), 19 had Whittingham & Mitchell bodies (all 319s), and Wendover, Bertelli and Freestone & Webb each did a car, while Tanner Bros did three 319/40 sports two-seaters.

Immediately before the outbreak of the Second World War, AFN was about to start providing its own body styles on the 328 chassis, but this fascinating Anglo-German accord came to an abrupt close; the six chassis imported were bodied by Frazer Nash after the war.

Immediately after the war, of course, AFN re-established links with

BMW, by 'liberating' the 328-style engine, so that it could be manufactured by Bristol, for use in both Bristol and Frazer Nash cars.

This Bertelli-bodied 328 was built for Aston Martin founder Lionel Martin.

The 327 of 1937–41 was a truly elegant BMW – expensive, but undeniably beautiful. With its 55bhp/1,971cc six-cylinder engine, it could reach nearly 80mph and was therefore very suitable indeed for use on Germany's new autobahns. In four years, BMW sold no less than 1,396 cars – and the style definitely inspired the shape of the early post-war Bristol 400 too!

The 335 of 1939–41 was at once the largest, the fastest and the most expensive of all BMW saloons of this period. The 3,485cc six-cylinder engine delivered a top speed of 90mph – quite outstanding for its day – but only 410 such machines, including prototypes, were produced before the war intervened.

being altogether sleeker than before – and the 1,971cc engine's performance had been quite transformed.

It was the engine, complete with its new cylinder head, part-spherical combustion chambers, and the complex cross-pushrod valve actuation, which caught everyone's attention. Even before the outbreak of war, BMW found that they could coax more than 120bhp from this high-revving jewel – and as we now know, in the late 1940s/early 1950s, Bristol improved significantly on that.

Like the Jaguar XK120 of the late 1940s, the BMW 328 seemed to

change the way that people looked at sports cars, and altered their perception of what they really wanted. Maybe the 328 was expensive: the complete Roadster retailed at RM7,400 in Germany – the equivalent of about £590 – and by the time British imports began it cost £695 to buy one from the importers, AFN. But that didn't matter, for the 328 had the soft ride, the hydraulic brakes, the independent front suspension and the near-100mph top speed that its rivals mostly seemed to lack.

For BMW, the tragedy was that this car, the 55bhp 327 coupés and roadsters which followed in 1937, and the excellent 327/28 of 1938 (the secret being in the use of the 80bhp engine), had not really got into their stride when the Second World War broke out.

If Germany had carried on peacefully, the all-new 335 of 1939 might have made its mark and pushed BMW further up-market to compete with Mercedes-Benz. Larger than any previous BMW, the 335 used a new six-cylinder 3,485cc engine, offered a 90mph top speed, had a sturdy box-section chassis frame, and located its rear axle with longitudinal torsion bars and links. For a six-light four-door saloon, all this was for only RM6,700 (£540), offering great style and comfort. Unhappily, the 335 was orphaned almost from birth, and a very promising career was killed off in 1941, after only 410 examples had been built, including prototypes. The last hundred cars or so were sent off for use as VIP military transports.

Thereafter BMW turned itself into a massive, efficient, and proficient weapon of war, not only by producing thousands of magnificent air-cooled radial aero-engines, but by building four-wheel-drive 325s for the German army. When the last of the 335s left Eisenach in 1941, it was the last private car to be built by BMW on that site. Between 1928 and 1941, nearly 79,000 BMW-badged cars had left that plant, which sounds creditable enough – although that figure would eventually be dwarfed by post-war achievements.

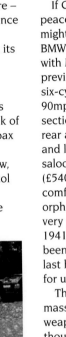

Mille Miglia 328s

Even after the outbreak of the Second World War, BMW still found time to design and develop several special-bodied 328-based racing two-seaters, which were then entered in the 1940 Mille Miglia race that took place in Italy.

Nine laps of a 165km (103-mile) closed road circuit near Brescia, this 1,485km (923-mile) race was closely

A historic occasion – three special-bodied 328 race cars ready to compete in the 1940 Mille Miglia, an event won by Huschke von Hanstein and Walter Baumer in the coupé-bodied car in the centre.

contested by these BMWs and Alfa Romeo 2500SSs. Three open and two closed BMWs started the race, all with unique styles, each built around a chassis frame with a Duralumin-framed bodyshell, with none weighing more than 650kg (1,433lb). The cross-pushrod 328 engines had been developed so far that they produced no less than 135bhp at 5,500rpm.

Driving the Touring of Milan-styled coupé, Huschke von Hanstein and Walter Baumer won the race, with the three open-top cars finishing third, fifth and sixth. Although neither coupé survived the war, all three

For the 1940 Mille Miglia race, BMW built special-bodied 328s, which used race-tuned versions of the celebrated engine in a near-standard chassis, but with this attractive two-seater style. The shape later influenced the appearance of the immediate post-war British Frazer Nash too. (LAT)

open-top models did so. One of them came to the UK in 1945, 'liberated' by the Aldingtons, and became the prototype style for the post-war Frazer Nash. Later owned by 'Gillie' Tyrer, and then journalist Michael Bowler, it was eventually returned to the BMW Museum in Munich.

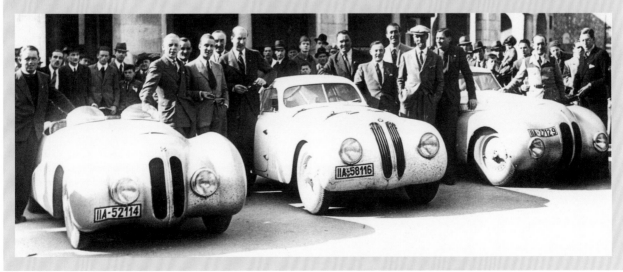

Post-war
rebirth – the
'Baroque Angel'

BMW's first new model after the Second World War was the 501. The original cars had six-cylinder engines, but a new, 2.6-litre V8 unit soon followed. (LAT)

After 1945, it took seven long years before BMW delivered its first post-war cars, and the build up thereafter was painfully slow. Even then, only 50 cars left the rebuilt Munich factory in 1952, with 1,645 following in 1953. At this rate the business would always struggle to be viable.

The delay was understandable. Not only had BMW's factories been devastated by Allied bombing during the Second World War, but its operating economy was in ruins and its markets no longer existed. In addition, after 1945 its previous car-making factory – at Eisenach – found itself behind the Iron Curtain.

501
1952–1958

ENGINE:
Six cylinders in line, iron block, iron head
Capacity — 1,971cc/2,077cc
Bore x stroke — 66mm x 96mm/
68mm x 96mm
Compression ratio — 6.8:1/7.1:1
Maximum power — 65bhp at 4,400rpm/
72bhp at 4,400rpm/
72bhp at 4,500rpm
Valve gear — Two valves per cylinder,
pushrod overhead
Fuelling — One downdraught Solex
carburettor

TRANSMISSION:
Four-speed manual, all-synchromesh

SUSPENSION:
Front: Independent, torsion bars, wishbones,
telescopic dampers
Rear: Live (beam) axle, torsion bars, telescopic
dampers

STEERING:
Bevel gear

BRAKES:
Hydraulic, front drum/rear drum

WHEELS/TYRES:
Steel disc; 5.50-16in cross-ply

BODY/CHASSIS:
Separate ladder-style chassis with box-section
main and tubular cross-bracing; pressed-steel
four-door saloon

DIMENSIONS:
Length — 15ft 6in
Width — 5ft 10in
Height — 5ft 0in
Wheelbase — 9ft 3.6in
Track, front — 4ft 3.3in
Track, rear — 4ft 7.4in

WEIGHT:
2,955lb

PERFORMANCE/ECONOMY:
Max speed — 84mph approx
Acceleration — 0–60mph in 25sec approx
Fuel consumption — typically 20–23mpg

UK PRICE WHEN NEW incl. tax:
Special Order

NUMBER BUILT:
8,936

501 V8, 502
1954–1963

ENGINE:
V8, iron block, alloy heads
Capacity — 2,580cc/3,168cc
Bore x stroke — 74mm x 75mm/
82mm x 75mm
Compression ratio — 7.0:1–7.3:1
Maximum power — 90bhp at 4,800rpm
140bhp at 4,800rpm
Valve gear — Two valves per cylinder,
pushrod overhead
Fuelling — One downdraught Solex
or Zenith/two
downdraught Zenith
carburettors

TRANSMISSION:
Four-speed manual, all-synchromesh

SUSPENSION:
Front: Independent, torsion bars, wishbones,
telescopic dampers
Rear: Live (beam) axle, torsion bars, telescopic
dampers

STEERING:
Bevel gear

BRAKES:
Hydraulic, front drum/rear drum (front disc/rear
drum, to order, from 1959)

WHEELS/TYRES:
Steel disc; 6.40-15in cross-ply

BODY/CHASSIS:
Separate ladder-style chassis with box-section
main and tubular cross-bracing; pressed-steel
four-door saloon

DIMENSIONS:
Length — 15ft 6in
Width — 5ft 10in
Height — 5ft 0in
Wheelbase — 9ft 3.6in
Track, front — 4ft 4.4in
Track, rear — 4ft 7.7in

WEIGHT:
3,153–3,308lb

PERFORMANCE/ECONOMY:
Max speed — 100mph approx
Acceleration — 0–60mph in 15.2sec approx
Fuel consumption — typically 18–20mpg

UK PRICE WHEN NEW incl. tax:
£2,458

NUMBER BUILT:
9,109/3,935

507
1956–1959

ENGINE:
V8, iron block, alloy heads
Capacity — 3,168cc
Bore x stroke — 82mm x 75mm
Compression ratio — 7.8:1
Maximum power — 150bhp at 5,000rpm
Valve gear — Two valves per cylinder,
pushrod overhead
Fuelling — Two downdraught Zenith
carburettors

TRANSMISSION:
Four-speed manual, all-synchromesh

SUSPENSION:
Front: Independent, torsion bars, wishbones,
anti-roll bar, telescopic dampers
Rear: Live (beam) axle, torsion bars, telescopic
dampers

STEERING:
Bevel gear

BRAKES:
Hydraulic, front drum/rear drum (front disc/rear
drum from 1958)

WHEELS/TYRES:
Steel disc; 6.00-16in cross-ply

BODY/CHASSIS:
Separate ladder-style chassis with box-
sections, and tubular cross-bracing; pressed-
steel/aluminium two-door sports tourer

DIMENSIONS:
Length — 14ft 4.4in
Width — 5ft 5in
Height — 4ft 3.2in
Wheelbase — 8ft 1.6in
Track, front — 4ft 8.9in
Track, rear — 4ft 8.1in

WEIGHT:
2,933lb

PERFORMANCE/ECONOMY:
Max speed — 124–136mph approx
Acceleration — 0–60mph in 9.5sec approx
Fuel consumption — typically 15–18mpg

UK PRICE WHEN NEW incl. tax:
£4,201

NUMBER BUILT:
252

3200CS
1961–1963

ENGINE:
V8, iron block, alloy heads
Capacity	3,168cc
Bore x stroke	82mm x 75mm
Compression ratio	9.0:1
Maximum power	160bhp at 5,600rpm
Valve gear	Two valves per cylinder, pushrod overhead
Fuelling	Two downdraught Zenith carburettors

TRANSMISSION:
Four-speed manual, all-synchromesh

SUSPENSION:
Front: Independent, torsion bars, wishbones, telescopic dampers
Rear: Live (beam) axle, torsion bars, telescopic dampers

STEERING:
Bevel gear

BRAKES:
Hydraulic, front disc/rear drum

WHEELS/TYRES:
Steel disc; 6.00-15in cross-ply

BODY/CHASSIS:
Separate ladder-style chassis with box-sections, and tubular cross-bracing; pressed-steel two-door/four-seater coupé

DIMENSIONS:
Length	14ft 4.4in
Width	5ft 7.7in
Height	4ft 9.5in
Wheelbase	9ft 3.6in
Track, front	4ft 4.3in
Track, rear	4ft 7.7in

Weight:
3,308lb

PERFORMANCE/ECONOMY:
Max speed	124mph approx
Acceleration	0–60mph in 13.0sec approx
Fuel consumption	typically 16–19mpg

UK PRICE WHEN NEW incl. tax:
Special Order

NUMBER BUILT:
538

Perhaps worse than that, once the Russian forces had marched into Eisenach, all the factory manufacturing facilities had been impounded, and the drawings (along with the priceless expertise of Fritz Fiedler) had been moved to Britain (rather unofficially, as 'war reparations') to help Bristol set up its new car-making enterprise. The two BMW factories situated in or close to Munich had previously concentrated on producing aircraft engines and motorcycles, so there was absolutely no car-building expertise in the Bavarian city. Much enthusiasm was available, as was the personal dedication and experience of individual engineers and managers, but for the time being they were powerless to do anything about it.

Although new cars badged 'BMW' were soon being made at Eisenach, these were no more than cloned examples of 1930s-type BMWs, produced by consulting stolen drawings and using requisitioned tooling, which the Russian occupying forces decided to build to raise cash. BMW's lawyers weren't able to stop production of BMW-derived cars, but they prevented the BMW name from being used, and from 1952 Eisenach vehicles were known as EMWs.

Having struggled through the hand-to-mouth years of the late 1940s, BMW eventually got the R24 motorcycle (an evolution of the pre-war R23) back into the showrooms, but even though the assembly halls in Munich had then been rebuilt and were yawningly empty, there was still no sign of a new car.

With the Eisenach pedigree seemingly out of reach, if BMW wanted to build cars again, it was seemingly going to have to start from scratch. For some time this appeared to be the case, though when a badly damaged workshop in the Milbertshofen (Munich) factory was eventually cleared out in 1946, this revealed a rather battered prototype of the BMW 332.

This was a sizeable car which Fritz Fiedler had inspired in 1939, intended

The BMW 501 was soon nicknamed the 'Baroque Angel' because of its curvaceous lines. Although there was a family resemblance to 1930s BMWs, most of the engineering was new. When the 501 was unveiled in 1951, it featured a very rounded body style, which made it immediately recognisable. This later V8 saloon displays the larger rear window introduced on all models in 1954. This was the only change of any significance to the 'Baroque Angel' bodywork.

EMW – BMW's unwanted 'love child'

Once the 'Iron Curtain' descended in 1945, BMW's Eisenach factory found itself in Eastern Germany, and real BMW cars were never again made there. After the Russian juggernaut marched in, a new company called Autovelo was set up to start building motorcycles, then motor cars, at Eisenach. In both cases these were little more than remanufactured BMWs (the press tools and many other facilities having survived) – although the communists never offered to recognise trademark rights, or to make any financial recompense!

However, it was not until 1952 that legal action in the West obliged Autovelo to change all this. From that point, the cars they produced would be badged as EMW (Eisenacher Motoren Werke), and would have a 'whirling propeller' in red-and-white instead of black-and-white.

The Eisenach cars were initially the 321, followed by the 327. The 321 was replaced in 1949 by the 340, in essence a 321 with a 326 four-door saloon body – only with a clumsily revised frontal treatment. Two attempts at a modernised design, called the 342 and 343, were despairingly ungainly, and never made it past the prototype stage, and in 1955 EMW production stopped; henceforth Eisenach's mainstay was to be the two-stroke Wartburg, derived from a pre-war DKW design.

BMW, for sure, would not have been proud of the style of this EMW 340, photographed at the Eisenach factory in 2002. (Jon Pressnell)

to update the 'modular' range of 1930s types even further, but it had always been thought the prototypes had been bombed out of existence, Here was a car which used the existing 1,971cc engine, in a six-window/four-door saloon style, and which featured a steering column gearchange. Although the current chief designer, Alfred Böning, immediately latched on to this car as the start, at least, of post-war enterprise, he knew it would still be years before a new BMW could go on sale. Having restored the damaged car, measured everything (all the drawings had disappeared – either to Bristol, or to Moscow!), this seemed to be the only way forward, and after a modicum of test running, the long wait began.

Once Managing Director Kurt Donath could even begin to think of the future, he and Ing. Böning had to choose what sort of car to build. The problem was that there appeared to be a gulf between what they *ought* to build, and what they thought they *could* build. With Germany's post-war economy still in such a fragile state, the home market was only really

Bristol and BMW

Originally, the British link with BMW was forged by the Aldington family and their AFN concern, which produced Frazer Nash sports cars. Their enterprise in selling British –marketed 'Frazer Nash-BMW' cars was steadily growing until the Second World War brought an end to it all.

In 1945, 'Bill' Aldington somehow winkled out samples of the 328

This study shows the clear visual relationship between immediate post-war BMWs (the 501, right) and the Bristol 401 (left). There was much near-common engineering under the skin too. (LAT)

engine from BMW, and all the surviving documentation, along with its talented engineer Fritz Fiedler, were taken back to the UK for post-war use. At the same time, he encouraged the Bristol Aeroplane Co. to set up a car-making subsidiary, established in close co-operation with Frazer Nash – and the rest, as they say, is history.

Bristol further developed the engine, and put it into production in the UK for their own use, while also supplying to Frazer Nash, AC, and several racing car manufacturers. The original Bristol motor car (Type 400) was launched in 1947, this being a

clever amalgam of late-1930s BMW features (the style, for instance, was very close to that of the 327, for instance), and the company prospered by selling small numbers of very expensive machines.

Although Bristol cars gradually became more Anglicised, the ex-BMW engine powered every single model until it was finally dropped in favour of big Chrysler V8 power units in the early 1960s. Amazingly enough, post-war BMW 501s also used developed versions of this same old engine (without the cross-pushrod head though), that power unit being manufactured in West Germany!

capable of supporting small, economy, cars – but BMW only knew how to build fast and expensive cars.

Since they already had the 332 as the basis of a new machine, this was what would have to be developed, and with Donath hoping that the export market would take up much of the demand, work went ahead. If BMW was to produce a credible type of new car, it needed to be an upper-class product, one which could face up to Mercedes-Benz, could be produced in relatively small numbers, and one which would not call for costly manufacturing tooling. Even so, this car would need to use all-steel bodywork, which would require modern jigging facilities.

Although none of the old Eisenach tooling was available, amazingly enough, BMW discovered some pre-war 2-litre engine casting moulds close to Munich, which at least gave the team a flying start. Maybe this 1,971cc engine (which would initially be rated at just 65bhp) was a little too weak-kneed for its task, but there was no other viable option.

By mid-1950, chassis design was complete and three prototype bodies had been completed for assessment – a coupé from Autenrieth of Darmstadt, a saloon shell from Farina, and a rather bulbous four-door saloon from BMW itself in Munich. Although BMW soon took the pragmatic decision to adopt their own design, a new car called the Type 501 was not seen in public until April 1951. Almost from that day, there were critics of the style, which certainly harked back to the 1930s, and it was not long before the new car got itself a nickname – 'Baroque Angel'.

The launch proved to be premature as the first cars did not reach their customers until the end of 1952, and even then, the early deliveries were only made possible by the sterling efforts of the body builders Baur of Stuttgart, who helped BMW by supplying the first 1,870 bodyshells while steel body pressing and assembly facilities were painstakingly completed in Munich.

Here was a boldly designed new car, for apart from the engine, every other

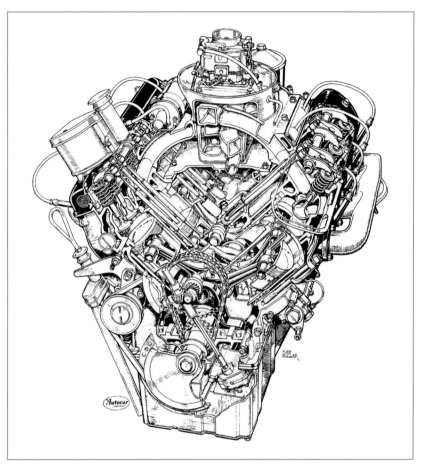

In 1954, BMW introduced its first-ever V8 engine, initially a 2.6-litre unit. Originally used in the 502 saloon, this would power several other models until the early 1960s.

aspect of the chassis, running gear and bodyshell was new. At the time, glowing references were made to the engineering influence of the pre-war 326, but these were somewhat tenuous as the two cars were not at all closely linked.

The six-window/four-door saloon style was conventional enough – and naturally the nose was dominated by the familiar BMW 'kidney' grille, flanked by recessed headlamps – but under the skin there was innovation, bravery even, from end to end. As with late-model pre-war BMWs, the centre-piece of the layout was a sturdy chassis frame, a mixture of box-section and tubular members, running on a 111.6in wheelbase and supporting a large and spacious cabin.

In this new-generation car (whose descendants would be built until the last 3200CS left Munich in 1965), the 1,971cc six-cylinder engine was

mounted well forward, but the four-speed gearbox was separate from it, and positioned between the front seats. This was the first BMW to be offered with a steering column gearchange – fashion, and North American buyers' wishes, made that inevitable.

Although the demand for 501s was certainly evident – there was still a world-wide shortage of new private cars at this time – this fascinating new car had two major faults. One was that its 65bhp engine could not deliver the performance that its style suggested, and the other was its price. Originally it sold for 15,150 Deutschmarks (or about £1,260). When sold in the UK from late 1953, the 501 cost £1,984, compared, for

Although sales were always limited, BMW made sure a drop-top cabriolet version of the 502 was available. In many ways, its style harked back to similar BMWs of the late 1930s.

There was plenty of space inside the cabin of the V8-engined 502. Introduced in 1954, this car rode on a stately 111.6in wheelbase. (LAT)

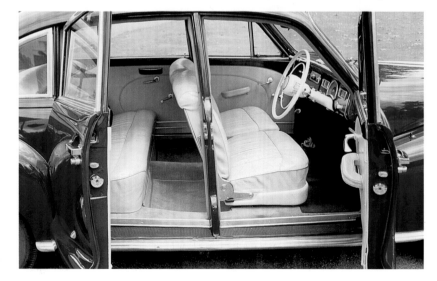

instance, with the £1,616 price of a Jaguar Mk VII.

Independent front suspension was by longitudinal torsion bars (had BMW, like other teams, been looking at the Citroën *Traction Avant*, perhaps?) and wishbones, while the beam rear axle was sprung on longitudinal torsion bars with suitable locating links. The real novelty was in the steering, which was not at all conventional. Instead of a normal steering box there was a sizeable casting containing a carefully machined part-circular bevel gear, which almost doubled as a rack, to which a steering pinion was meshed. Expensive, for sure, but beautifully made, and reminiscent of the way BMW had once built aircraft engines…

The easy way to describe the character of the original 501 was by using the descriptive German word *gemutlich* (which translates as 'pleasant and comfortable'), for here was a car with plenty of space, comfortable seating, high-grade equipment, a Becker radio as standard (still a rarity in the 1950s), and a soft ride. For some customers, however, it was too heavy and lacking in performance, so for the next few years BMW would concentrate on dealing with that problem.

More power was squeezed out of the original engine, and one final stretch (to 2,077cc) was also made available. Since the original 501 was,

Veritas

Veritas was founded in 1946, by former employees of BMW who could see no future for their expertise and enthusiasm at the shattered remnants of their old business. The intention was to build cars based on the pre-war 328 sports car. Originally located at Messkirch/Baden, before moving to Rastatt in 1949, and on to a factory at the Nürburgring in 1950, this enterprise always led a glamorous, but hand-to-mouth existence.

The first Veritas cars were powered by recycled and rebuilt examples of the famous cross-pushrod 328-type engine and using the chassis of reclaimed BMW 328s, with special, sleek, modern-looking two-seater body styles. BMW's styling expert, Ernst Loof, was involved for a time, which gave Veritas an impressive public image. Even so, Veritas's ongoing problem was of finding supplies of appropriate materials and keeping down costs (as much of the car was hand-crafted), so sales were always slow.

In spite of diversifying with the use of a new engine supplied by Heinkel and in making a small Dyna-Panhard based car, Veritas plunged not once, but twice, into bankruptcy, and in 1953 it was all over. BMW took over the remnants of Veritas-Nürburgring, Ernst Loof returned to BMW, which he had been obliged to leave after the war, and the Veritas episode was soon forgotten.

The Veritas formula was to link a modern style to the running gear of a 1930s-type 328. (Karl Ludvigsen, Ludvigsen Library)

frankly, rather a stodgy car, no-one could ever have expected that three fine sporty versions – 503, 507 and 3200CS – would eventually grow out of this layout.

As it was, six-cylinder 500-Series types would be on sale for six years, with the 72bhp 501A/503B becoming available from 1954, with the 501/3 (a more torquey, 72bhp/2,077cc-engined, version) type taking over in 1955. Even the last of these cars could only reach 90mph after a long run in, so no-one was ever excited by their performance. Production of the 501 fell to just 1,080 cars in 1956, to 611 in 1957, and dribbled to a close in 1958.

In the meantime, BMW engineers were back to their resourceful and optimistic best, for while the 501 was struggling into the showrooms, they had engineered a totally new 90° V8 engine, which was going to restore their cars to the top of the performance league. Structurally it was conventional, with one camshaft buried in the centre of the cylinder block's 'vee', cross-flow cylinder head breathing, and a deep sump.

Look carefully at this engine today, though, and you must surely see a resemblance to the latest technology which was then flooding out of Detroit but, no matter. The BMW engine also had aluminium cylinder block and head castings, very efficient looking overhead-valve porting and breathing, along with the sort of power and torque figures which brought a sparkle to engineers' eyes.

Without question, this was a turning point in BMW's post-war fortunes, for once there was an engine to be proud of, then sporty styling would surely follow and, who knows, maybe a return to motorsport was no longer out of the question? BMW was delighted to trumpet the several 'firsts' which this engine signalled – not only a 'first' from BMW, but Germany's original post-war V8, and the trail-blazing unit to use aluminium for *all* its major castings. In particular, BMW was thumbing its nose at

Although big and expensive to build, the V8 engine, as used in the 502, 503, 507 and later models, was a very effective unit. BMW was always proud of it, especially as their deadly rival, Mercedes-Benz, could not match it until the mid-1960s. To a casual observer, the 1950s-style V8 engine looks complicated, but to engineers who had been used to building ultra-powerful radial aircraft engines in the 1940s, this was easy stuff. It started life as a 2.6-litre unit, but grew to 3.2 litres before the end of its career.

Mercedes-Benz, who would have nothing quite like this until the end of the 1960s.

The first V8-engined BMW road car was the 502 of 1954 (effectively a re-engined 501 saloon), when the original 2,580cc power unit produced 100bhp – which was a whole lot better than the 72bhp of the contemporary 501/3, and this was only a start. The 3.2 model was unveiled only a year later at the 1955 Frankfurt Motor Show. Originally titled 502 3.2-litre, this had a 120bhp/3,168cc version of the engine, and two years later the 'Super' derivative had no less than 140bhp, which in 1959 needed front-wheel disc brakes to keep the 110mph top speed in check.

The 502 became the BMW 2600 in 1961, while the 3.2 became the 3200 at the same time – and in one case (3200S) the engine was boosted still further, to produce a rousing and reliable 160bhp. To achieve 118mph with this original body style was something that Ing. Böning cannot even have dreamed about in 1949 when the 500-Series cars were originally being designed.

Such development was enough to keep this ageing model line on sale until 1963, when it finally gave way to make space for more of the new-type four-cylinder cars.

Coupé elegance in the 503

By the mid-1950s, BMW's North American importer, Max Hoffman, had begun to agitate for BMW to produce more sporty cars. The lumpy 500-Series saloons had not sold well in the USA, but he thought that V8-engined sporty cars would do the trick. BMW eventually agreed with him, and shaped up their own idea of a sports coupé, but Hoffman was not happy with this and sought artistic advice from Count Albrecht Goertz, who lived in New York and had once worked with the famed Loewy Studio.

In the end, Hoffman's patronage of Goertz helped to produce not one, but three different sporty BMWs – a 503 coupé, a 503 cabriolet, and a short-wheelbase 507 roadster. Although none of these cars sold in big numbers, and they certainly did not contribute any profits to the company, they did at least raise BMW's profile when it most needed it.

Based on the same rolling chassis as the 502, the new 503 had a version of the 3,168cc V8 engine developing 140bhp, and there were two closely related but intriguingly different two-door body styles. Below the waistline these cars were essentially the same, with light-alloy panels and a graceful, straight-through wing crown line from the headlamps to the vestigial fins above the rear lamps. The coupé had a smart but rather constricting roofline, which meant that the close-coupled rear seats were best occupied by shorter people, while the cabriolet had a smart, but manually folded, soft top over the same seating package.

The initial cars, built in 1956 and '57, were not nearly sporting enough, for they were still afflicted with a steering column gearchange. However, from September 1957, BMW rejigged the chassis, moving the gearbox well forward to be in unit with the engine, and finally specified a central gearchange.

Here, at least, was a car worthy of its looks, and of the V8 engine which powered it. With a top speed of nearly 120mph, it could beat up most cars on German autobahns and North American freeways, but even though it now felt more sporty than before, its major problem was one of price. Launched at 29,500DM ($7,020 in the USA, and the equivalent of £2,500, plus taxes, in the UK), it meant the customer was the sort of person who was already in the market for an Aston Martin or something equally exotic. For sure, this BMW was much more expensive than the twin-cam engined Jaguars of the period.

Such a car, attractive-looking or not, cannot possibly have been profitable for BMW, as only 412 examples of the 503 were produced between 1955 and 1959, with 102 sold in 1956, the first full year of production.

The 507 – Goertz's masterpiece

Perhaps it was no surprise that the 503 was always struggling to make its

Built on the same rolling chassis as that of the 502, the 503 coupé featured a 140bhp/ 3.2-litre V8 engine, could carry four passengers, and reach more than 115mph. Recognisable from any angle the 503 was launched in 1956 and was available in coupé or drop-head coupé form. As with the 507, the 503's style was created by Count Albrecht Goertz. (LAT)

Over the years, BMW coupés have grown faster, sleeker and more powerful, but the 503 of the mid-1950s is still a very handsome machine, of which stylist Count Albrecht Goertz could be proud. In the late 1950s, 503s were available either as coupés or very smartly equipped cabriolets. This period advertising shot showed models decked out in the appropriate high fashion of the period.

Count Albrecht Goertz

Although Count Goertz never had more than a marginal influence on BMW's fortunes in the 1950s, his design work on the 503 coupé and cabriolet and 507 sports car (and later, on the original Datsun 240Z sports coupé) made him an icon with the enthusiast car movement.

Born in Hanover, Germany, he had taken up US citizenship well before the outbreak of war, and had worked with the American industrial designer Raymond Loewy, whose styling services were sold to many companies, including Studebaker, Austin and Hillman-Humber.

By the 1950s, however, he was

Many years after he had styled the 507 two-seater, Count Albrecht Goertz was reunited with a preserved example.

already flying solo, with a prolific one-man design consultancy, and was working mainly in New York. His original introduction to BMW came via an acquaintance with that controversial American motor trader, Max Hoffman, who was not only the BMW importer to the USA at the time, but had been the prime mover behind the birth of sporting versions of the 502 'Baroque Angel' in the first place.

Whatever the merits of Hoffman's claim to have influenced the style of the 503 and 507, it was only the wide-ranging expertise of Goertz and his feel for the North American lifestyle and tastes, and his knowledge of working up a three-dimensional body style, which made these cars possible.

In any case, as an earlier BMW historian has confirmed: 'Before the Goertz final design went into production, a good deal of honing, refining and haggling among Hoffman, Munich management and Goertz himself was to take place…'

BMW, however, was eventually bruised by the trauma of trying to sell expensive 507 types with much money lost on this project, and made no attempt to secure Goertz's services on a long term basis for its next consultancy deal was with Giovanni Michelotti of Italy.

Goertz did not seem to mind this too much, or try to sell himself to every other motor company in the business. Indeed it was getting on for a decade before his name cropped up again – at Nissan.

mark, as in the same period it was always overshadowed by the magnificent, though dynamically flawed, 507 Roadster. This, no question, was Count Goertz's enduring masterpiece, more sinuous than the 503 with which it shared development effort (and factory space), and sexier by far than the Datsun 240Z for which he would become famous more than ten years down the road.

As with the 503, the 507 was inspired by Max Hoffman of the USA, but Goertz's original proposals were not liked ('too high, too angular, more like a Thunderbird than any fundamentally new design' is what Hoffman is reputed to have said of it), but after more than one re-work it was much more satisfactory and this amazingly slinky two-seater made its bow at the Frankfurt Motor Show in September 1955.

Once again, this was a car whose chassis was based on that of the 502, and was in fact very similar to that of the 503, although in this case the wheelbase had been cropped to just 96.5in – a reduction of no less than 14in. There was absolutely no space for more than two seats and the gearbox was in unit with the engine, with a central gearchange.

Looking more Italianate than German, the front-end featured a full-width grille, with little trace of the expected, now traditional, BMW 'double kidney' shape, and in open-top Roadster form or with the optional removable hardtop, the 507 was a masterpiece.

Sensational in its day, and still looking good half a century later, the two-seater 507 was BMW's flagship roadster in the 1950s. With a 150bhp/3.2-litre V8, it could reach speeds of up to 130mph. (LAT)

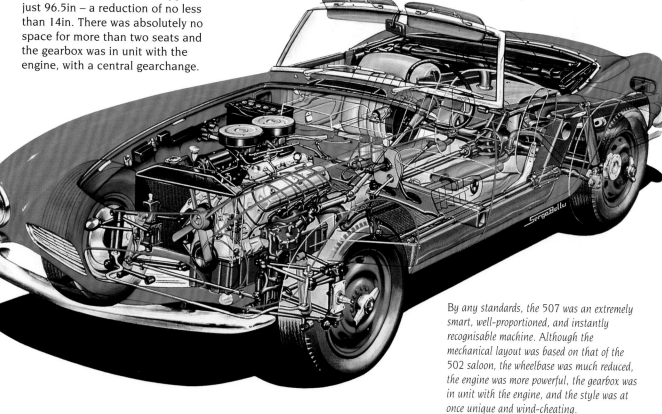

By any standards, the 507 was an extremely smart, well-proportioned, and instantly recognisable machine. Although the mechanical layout was based on that of the 502 saloon, the wheelbase was much reduced, the engine was more powerful, the gearbox was in unit with the engine, and the style was at once unique and wind-cheating.

As sold into the USA, the 507 had a 160mph speedometer. Maybe its true top speed was no more than 130–135mph, but it made a real talking point in the showrooms!

How many other BMW styles were eventually influenced by the splendid 507 of the mid-1950s? It was the sort of car which made almost all others look rather dowdy.

The abiding mystery though is why BMW did not sell more 507s. After all, with such stylish looks, a 150bhp engine, and with a top speed of up to 135mph, depending on gearing, plus a price of 26,500DM (which was considerably less than the 503), it should have found a ready market. But it never did. From November 1956 to May 1959, only 252 cars were ever built, and annual production never exceeded 100.

In later years, it goes without saying, of course, that the 507 immediately joined the ranks of the most desirable BMWs, and today a survivor is worth a king's ransom.

3200CS – Bertone's battle-cruiser

When the new 3200CS model appeared in 1961, it almost counted as an afterthought, for the 502/503 chassis on which it was based was now looking dated, and BMW's management was devoting most of its attention to the new, four-cylinder cars which had proved to be such a success.

It was not as if BMW needed the diversion of yet another limited-production car, as the share capital had only recently been increased, and stable profits were being made for the first time in years. Yet here it was, a smart four-seater coupé, effectively the 503's successor, and one which cost even more – 29,850DM at launch.

This time around, the long-wheelbase 503 chassis ran on a

160bhp version of the 3.2-litre V8 engine, and with front-wheel disc brakes now standard, it was a fast and stable machine. The body was by Bertone of Turin, and not only incorporated the double-kidney front grille, but would lend some of its styling cues to the next-generation BMW coupé, the 2000CS, which followed in 1965.

Bertone provided all the bodyshells for production – trucking them over the Alps at a rate which never exceeded five cars a week – and BMW treated the machine as an indulgence, or attention raiser. Rarely in the limelight, but rarely criticised for a lack of style or elegance, the 3200CS pottered on until the mid-1960s, and was only displaced when Karmann was ready to start supplying visually similar monocoques for the 2000CS model, after 603 cars had been produced.

The 3200CS was the last, the very last, production BMW to be built on the sturdy separate chassis frame which Ing. Böning's team had conceived at the end of the 1940s, and which Alex von Falkenhausen's technical enthusiasms had done so much to nurture in the 1950s.

According to latter-day cynics (of

which there were many), BMW lost money on almost every 500-Series car it sold (certainly the company needed the 'Bubbles' which are described next, merely to stay afloat), for they never seemed to sell enough of the cars in any particular year. All in all, just 23,185 500-Series were sold between 1952 and 1965, with peak production of 4,554 being achieved in 1955.

Complete with twin Zenith carburettors, the BMW 507's 3.2-litre V8 engine was an impressive piece of kit. (LAT)

The last, and most completely equipped of all the sporting 500-Series cars was the 3200CS of 1962–65. Bertone of Turin was responsible for the coupé body style, although final assembly was always in Munich. Just 603 of these 160bhp/3.2-litre V8-powered cars were produced.

Bubbles
for survival

If the 'Baroque Angel' had been selling better, and if BMW was making more consistent profits, the cute little Isetta/600/700 model ranges might never have appeared. Looking back *and* looking forward, these little cars had no relationship with any other BMWs.

The story began in 1953, when the Italian concern, Iso, introduced a tiny but appealing two-seater bubble car which they called the Isetta. This featured a front-opening door, ovoid body styling (which included a fold-back fabric roof) and had an air-cooled two-stroke engine behind the seats, tucked over to the right side of the chassis, with a very narrow rear axle. In March 1954, BMW engineer Eberhard Wolff saw this car on display at the Geneva Motor Show, alerted his bosses to its potential, and left them to consider putting it on sale in Germany.

At first, BMW was appalled, but the prospect of filling up the vast empty assembly halls at Munich won them round. In Germany, in any case, there was already competition on the streets, from the likes of Messerschmitt and Fuldamobil, so the market was obviously there for the taking.

Mechanically simple – the chassis was basic, with box and tubular members, there was leading-arm coil spring independent front suspension, and the car's overall length was no more than 90in. This was a quirky machine in which function came first, and high style nowhere. The bench seat was strictly for two, and when the door was swung open the steering wheel and column came up with it.

But there were important compensations. Not only was Iso ready to conclude a licence-building agreement, but it was also willing to sell its own body presses for BMW to build these machines in numbers. BMW, for their own part, studied the Iso's 9bhp two-stroke engine,

In the 1950s, BMW needed a mass-market product to help keep the factories busy, and the business afloat. Commercially, therefore, it was a stroke of genius to take up the Italian Iso bubble car design, fit a BMW motorcycle engine, and rename it Isetta 250.

Isetta
1955–1962

ENGINE:
One cylinder, iron block, iron head, air-cooled
Capacity	245cc/298cc
Bore x stroke	68mm x 68mm/ 72mm x 73mm
Compression ratio	6.8:1/7.0:1
Maximum power	12bhp at 5,800rpm/ 13bhp at 5,200rpm
Valve gear	Two valves per cylinder, pushrod overhead
Fuelling	One Bing carburettor

TRANSMISSION:
Four-speed manual, no synchromesh

SUSPENSION:
Front: Independent, coil springs, swinging arm, telescopic dampers
Rear: Live (beam) axle, quarter-elliptic leaf springs, telescopic dampers (Note: some versions with single rear wheel)

STEERING:
Worm-and-nut

BRAKES:
Hydraulic, front drum/rear drum

WHEELS/TYRES:
Steel disc; 4.80-10in cross-ply

BODY/CHASSIS:
Separate ladder-style chassis with box and tubular members; pressed-steel two-seater saloon

DIMENSONS:
Length	7ft 6in
Width	4ft 6.3in
Height	4ft 4.8in
Wheelbase	4ft 11in
Track, front	3ft 11.2in
Track, rear	1ft 8.4in

WEIGHT:
794lb

PERFORMANCE/ECONOMY:
Max speed	51mph (245cc)
Acceleration	0–40mph in 22.7sec
Fuel consumption	typically 52–73mpg

UK PRICE WHEN NEW incl. tax:
£415

NUMBER BUILT:
136,367, all types

700/700LS
1959–1964

ENGINE:
Flat two-cylinder, alloy block, alloy heads, air-cooled
Capacity	697cc
Bore x stroke	78mm x 73mm
Compression ratio	7.5:1/9.0:1
Maximum power	30bhp at 5,000rpm/ 40bhp at 5,700rpm
Valve gear	Two valves per cylinder, pushrod overhead
Fuelling	One downdraught Solex/ two downdraught Solex carburettors

TRANSMISSION:
Four-speed manual, all-synchromesh

SUSPENSION:
Front: Independent, coil springs, leading arms, telescopic dampers
Rear: Independent, coil springs, trailing arms, telescopic dampers

STEERING:
Rack-and-pinion

BRAKES:
Hydraulic, front drum/rear drum

WHEELS/TYRES:
Steel disc; 5.50-12in cross-ply

BODY/CHASSIS:
Unit-construction pressed-steel body/chassis unit; two-door saloon, two-door coupé, or two-door cabriolet

DIMENSIONS:
Length	11ft 7.3in/12ft 8.0in
Width	4ft 10.3in
Height	4ft 5.0in
Wheelbase	6ft 11.5in/7ft 5.8in.
Track, front	4ft 2in
Track, rear	3ft 11.2in

WEIGHT:
1,411lb/1,499lb

PERFORMANCE/ECONOMY:
Max speed	(40bhp) 78mph
Acceleration	(40bhp) 0–60mph in 23.4sec
Fuel consumption	typically (40bhp) 34–40mpg

UK PRICE WHEN NEW incl. tax:
(Saloon) £894, (Coupé) £1,040

NUMBER BUILT:
188,121, all 700 types

Anything to make an honest dollar! Famous racing driver Stirling Moss helps a charming model to step out of the BMW Isetta – this showing off the front-opening door, and that a girl could still retain her dignity in high heels while doing so.

discarded it, and fitted their own R25 type 12bhp/245cc four-stroke motorcycle engine instead.

On sale from April 1955, originally at only 2,550DM (about £215) the Isetta was an immediate success, for 12,911 units were delivered in the first full calendar year, which doubled BMW's output at a stroke. In fact, the Isetta went on to sell solidly, for the next eight years. Within two years it had already been given a larger (15bhp/298cc) version of the R25's engine, and the cabin had been restyled with crisper lines, which featured sliding side windows.

For some markets, where tax structures encouraged it, the Isetta could be sold with only a single rear wheel. Although the little Isetta was also built as a Velam in France (through a properly negotiated licence with Iso), scooter manufacturer Hoffmann's plan to build a near-identical machine in Germany was immediately killed off when plagiarism was proved. In Britain, the Isetta was even made under licence in redundant railway premises in Brighton, and because there was no vehicular access to this site – only railway lines – parts were delivered by train, and completed Isettas all had to be delivered by the same method!

So far so, so good, for the little Isetta certainly set the cash registers ringing, even if it did nothing for BMW's previous up-market image. Business, though, was business, and the company then set out to expand on this 'building block' by conceiving an altogether larger, less graceful and (as it transpired) less profitable four-seater car which it called the 600.

The 600 was much more, of course, than a stretched Isetta, for the engine was now mounted in the tail, and was an air-cooled flat-twin 582cc, once again developed from one of BMW's existing motorcycle power units, while

To get in and out of the BMW Isetta, the front (only) door opened forwards, taking the steering wheel and column with it. Simple, for sure, but very effective. (LAT)

This was the tiny single-cylinder, air-cooled, motorcycle-type engine which BMW fitted to the Isetta 250 bubble car, where it drove the rear wheels.

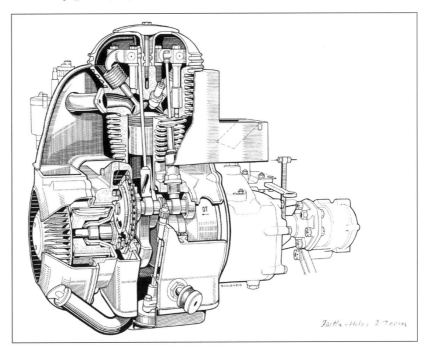

Some Isettas had four wheels, some had three, but all had the single-cylinder air-cooled engine mounted on the side of the chassis, which was accessed by removing a flap in the bodywork. (LAT)

a full-width rear axle had also been standardised.

Not only that, but this was BMW's first, and only, four-seater 'bubble car'. Strangely enough, access to the front seats was still by a forward-opening clamshell door (as with the Isetta, the steering wheel/column folded upwards and forwards as the door was opened), although rear-seat access was by a conventional door in the right (kerb side, on European roads) of the bodyshell.

Not only was the 600 a lot bigger than the Isetta – it was 114in long instead of 90in, but with 19.5bhp it could deliver a top speed of 62mph. Although it was 'more car', it was also more expensive, for it cost 3,985DM (about £330) which brought it perilously close to the price of a good second-hand VW Beetle.

There was, however, one important innovation, for someone at BMW had clearly been looking at Fiat's tiny economy cars, and was learning

lessons. As silly as it might now seem today, the lumpy little 600 was the very first BMW-badged car to use independent rear suspension by semi-trailing arms – and that had originally been seen in the Fiat 600 family car of 1955.

As seen in the BMW 600, this was a simple installation, with coil-over-shock-absorbers at each corner, and with no pretension (or knowledge, even!) of idealising the geometry, but on this limited-performance machine it did a great job. BMW would persist with the development and evolution of semi-trailing arm suspension until the 1980s, and important rivals such as Ford, Opel, Rolls-Royce, Mercedes-Benz and Triumph would all emulate them at some time.

Although BMW sold no fewer than 34,813 600s in three years, it was never a car which took the hearts, either of its board of directors, or the buying public. Too large to be a bubble, too small to be considered a 'real car', and mechanically still too crude to fight it out with other major rivals, but as far as BMW was concerned it had one major advantage – it kept the production lines respectably busy during that time.

The real marketing breakthrough though, followed in 1959, when BMW introduced what was arguably its first modern, truly post-war car, the sharply styled 700. If the company's finances had still not been in such an awful state at this time, maybe the 700 would have reached the market earlier, but in view of the upheavals of this period, the miracle was that it appeared at all.

At this point an immensely talented, mercurial little Italian called Giovanni Michelotti enters the story. Born in Turin, and a stylist from the day he joined the coachbuilders, Farina, in 1937, Michelotti had been freelance since 1949, yet retained strong links with Vignale. By the 1950s he had produced several noted styles and, among his peers, was already famous. Although BMW had already consulted him over the design of a small car in the early 1950s, it was not until 1958 that he was contracted to refine a new style which the Austrian BMW importer, Wolfgang Denzel, had proposed.

The result was the birth of the 700, the outcome being a total change in BMW's image, for here was a range of compact cars with a smart, sharp-edged, style, which was totally different from anything previously seen behind the BMW badge. When Michelotti was revealed as the pencil behind the new generation of Triumphs, the visual links between the 700 and the Triumph Herald (particularly the coupé) were obvious, for the Italian must surely have been working on both those shapes at one and the same time.

Although there were some technical links between the bulbous 600, and the new sharp-edged 700 – the rear-mounted flat-twin air-cooled engine and the front and rear suspensions both being developed from one model to the next – the rest of the car was novel. This, in fact, was the very first BMW to have a pressed-steel unit-construction body/chassis shell, which by definition, meant it cost a great deal of scarce investment capital to put it into production.

That cost was one of the major factors behind BMW's financial crisis, which came to a head in December 1959. Lumber magnate Hermann Krages had already invested heavily in the company, but resigned before the 700 could be launched, and even a proposed loan from the Bavarian government was not enough.

The sequence of events is important. Even though BMW well knew that it was running out of money, and was originally reluctant to put these new cars into production on cost grounds, the original 700 Coupé was launched in August 1959. The financial crisis meeting mentioned in the Introduction occurred in December 1959, and the saloon appeared immediately after that. It was a gamble which soon paid off, for BMW had built 36,609 cars in 1959, but would lift that to 53,888 in 1960, thus turning the corner – at last.

The new 700 range not only had a smart style, but a very rigid unit-body structure, with the enlarged (697cc) flat-twin engine in the tail. As before there was coil spring independent suspension at front and rear, but on this car the installation had been further-refined. Now, for the very first time, BMW's engineers had been able to lay out a range of cars, logically and at minimum cost. There would also be three different body styles, all with two passenger doors, but two wheelbase lengths, and two different power outputs.

Although the core of the range would be the two-door saloon type (originally badged 700 Sedan, but eventually uprated to 700 LS), it was the smart four-seater coupé which was first announced, combining the shorter (83.5 inch) of the two wheelbases with a 30bhp version of the flat twin-engine. This was a smart and very nimble little machine, which soon became a successful 'class' car in motor racing, and it also sold well, for nearly 24,000 were produced in five years.

The Sedan which followed, originally ran on exactly the same floorpan, 30bhp and the 83.5in wheelbase, but it had a more upright passenger cabin, and was considerably cheaper at first: 4,760DM instead of 5,300DM. Straight

As mildly restyled by BMW in 1956, this is the definitive Isetta 300 bubble car, complete with front-opening door and a tiny, single-cylinder air-cooled motorcycle engine mounted behind the seats. More than 160,000 Isettas of all types were produced from 1955 to 1962. (LAT)

Growing up – this was the rear-engined 600 model, a four-seater with a flat-twin air-cooled engine in the extreme tail. As with the Isetta bubble car, there was a door at the front which opened forwards, but there was also a side door for the rear-seat passengers. (LAT)

Racing the 700

In the 1950s, while BMW was struggling to stay in business (and losing money more often than not), factory-financed motorsport was difficult to justify. In any case, BMW was still not making outstanding sports cars, and wasn't going to compete merely to make up the numbers. Even so, stalwarts like Alex von Falkenhausen tried every way to create an interest in motorsport.

With the 700 Series, though, there was a new beginning. At class level, not only were these little cars nimble, but surprisingly fast too. Von Falkenhausen himself won the Tauerning Prize in 1959, while former Grand Prix driver Hans Stuck won hillclimb categories, and many race and rally awards were also gained by

Hans Stuck's BMW 700RS (not a production-line BMW, obviously!) won the Austrian Hillclimb Championship in 1961.

these fleet little cars. In 1959, BMW claimed that 700s had won their category no fewer than 33 times.

In Germany, organisers with much national pride, organised races for cars of less than 700cc. Since the 700 coupé was ideally placed for such events, they also dominated the entry lists – one start-line photograph of

Prince Metternich's BMW 700LS took advantage of a favourable handicap to take tenth place in the 1961 Monte Carlo Rally. Another 700LS finished even higher, in fifth place.

the Nürburgring shows no fewer than 18 BMW 700s on the front five rows of the grid.

away this became BMW's best-selling post-war car so far, for nearly 56,000 Sedans would be built in three years, and the 600 was immediately cancelled to make way for it.

That, though, was just the beginning, for in what we might now call the best 'Product Planning' fashion, there would be several different, faster, and better equipped versions to follow.

Next up was the 700 Sport, a coupé with no less than 40bhp from 697cc (that was enough to deliver an 84mph top speed, which was quite remarkable for the period), and before long, an extremely elegant little cabriolet version (also with 40bhp, and with a bodyshell produced by Baur in Stuttgart) joined in.

All that was enough to set the cash registers ringing, and to put stars in the eyes of BMW's top managers, but what was effectively the 'Mk 2' 700 of 1962 did even more. From that year, the Sedan was displaced by the 700LS, which looked much the same as before, except that the wheelbase had been stretched to 89.8in, which

provided a significantly larger cabin, especially in the rear seats.

Even so, it was not until 1963 that the shorter-wheelbase 700 Sport cars were renamed 700CS, and in mid-1964 the original coupé was revised to run on the lengthened wheelbase platform, and given the same 40bhp as the Sport/CS types. Maybe that car wasn't as sleek as before, but at least the rear-seat passengers, when carried, could not complain about cramp when they got out at the end of the journey.

All in all, the 700 range did a great job for BMW, as it bridged the gap between the bubbles and 'Baroque Angels' of the 1950s, with the unstoppable growth of the New Generation saloons of the 1960s. Particularly in coupé and cabriolet form, these 700s showed that BMW was once again in the business of building attractive-looking machines – desirable, even – and that they once again understood how to combine looks, light weight, performance and handling, and that their self-confidence was returning.

These cars held the line for BMW until the New Class 1500s, 1800s and 2000s could make their own reputation, and they were only withdrawn when the factories were otherwise crammed with the larger, faster and more profitable machines.

Here, for the first time since 1945, BMW could start to boast about production figures – and they duly did so. In six years, no fewer than 188,121 700-family machines were built, of which 36,761 were coupés of one length or another, but only 2,592 were of the more expensive little cabriolets.

Michelotti's reward, by the way, had already been delivered, for he had also been consulted on the shaping of the new 1500 saloon, and would be one of BMW's most favoured consultants in the years which followed.

Assembly of 700 saloons at Munich in the early 1960s. This car neatly filled the gap between the lumpy, dumpy 600 of the late 1950s, and the elegant 'New Class' saloons which would shortly take over.

1500 family
– *the 'New Class'*

During its life, the 'New Class' saloon was built with several different engines and a variety of front-end styles. This very smart German-registered machine was an 1800 of 1964 vintage. All 'New Class' BMWs of the 1960s shared the same basic four-door saloon car body style. With original styling advice from Michelotti in Italy, this shape was refined by BMW themselves, something which other makers had to match if they were to stop it succeeding. They failed. (LAT)

Even before the launch of the sleek Michelotti-styled 700s, and before the financial cataclysm of 1959, BMW had started work on an all-new medium-sized car – not just a car, but the first of a proposed new family of vehicles – but there were months when the mock-ups and a prototype stood sidelined in workshops, and no real progress could be made.

By 1960 the financial reconstruction, and the massive injection of Quandt capital, had changed everything, and work once again forged ahead. Urged on by financial chief Ernst Kampfer, the

technical team made their decisions. The original medium-sized car had been conceived around brand-new engines – a 1.3-litre 'four' and a related 1.8-litre 'six' – but that proposal was thrown out because of the huge investment which would have been needed.

Finally, in 1960, the bare bones of the new car were agreed. In brief, there would be a squat, rather angular, four-door saloon car style – larger than the 700 but considerably smaller than the ageing 500-Series cars. With MacPherson strut independent front suspension, front-

1500
1962–1964

ENGINE:
Four cylinders in line, iron block, alloy head
Capacity	1,499cc
Bore x stroke	82mm x 71mm
Compression ratio	8.8:1
Maximum power	80bhp at 5,700rpm
Valve gear	Two valves per cylinder, single overhead camshaft
Fuelling	One downdraught Solex carburettor

TRANSMISSION:
Four-speed manual, all-synchromesh

SUSPENSION:
Front: Independent, coil springs, MacPherson struts, telescopic dampers
Rear: Independent, coil springs, semi-trailing arms, telescopic dampers

STEERING:
Worm-and-roller

BRAKES:
Hydraulic, front disc/rear drum

WHEELS/TYRES:
Steel disc; 6.00-14in cross-ply

BODY/CHASSIS:
Unit construction, pressed-steel four-door saloon

DIMENSIONS
Length	14ft 9.2in
Width	5ft 7.3in
Height	4ft 9in
Wheelbase	8ft 4.4in
Track, front	4ft 4in
Track, rear	4ft 5.8in

WEIGHT:
2,337lb

PERFORMANCE/ECONOMY:
Max speed	92mph approx
Acceleration	0–60mph in 15sec approx
Fuel consumption	typically 25–27mpg

UK PRICE WHEN NEW incl. tax:
£1,350

NUMBER BUILT:
23,807

2000tii
1969–1972

ENGINE:
Four cylinders in line, iron block, alloy head
Capacity	1,990cc
Bore x stroke	89mm x 80mm
Compression ratio	9.5:1
Maximum power	130bhp at 5,800rpm
Valve gear	Two valves per cylinder, single overhead camshaft
Fuelling	Kugelfischer fuel injection

TRANSMISSION:
Four-speed manual, all-synchromesh

SUSPENSION:
Front: Independent, coil springs, MacPherson struts, anti-roll bar, telescopic dampers
Rear: Independent, coil springs, semi-trailing arms, anti-roll bar, telescopic dampers

STEERING:
Worm-and-roller

BRAKES:
Hydraulic, front disc/rear drum

WHEELS/TYRES:
Steel disc; 175-14in radial-ply

BODY/CHASSIS:
Unit construction, pressed-steel four-door saloon

DIMENSIONS:
Length	14ft 9.2in
Width	5ft 7.3in
Height	4ft 9in
Wheelbase	8ft 4.4in
Track, front	4ft 4.4in
Track, rear	4ft 6.2in

WEIGHT:
2,580lb

PERFORMANCE/ECONOMY:
Max speed	115mph approx
Acceleration	0–60mph in 10.5sec approx
Fuel consumption	typically 20–22mpg

UK PRICE WHEN NEW incl. tax:
Not imported to UK

NUMBER BUILT:
1,952

2000CS/2000C coupés
1965–1969

ENGINE:
Four cylinders in line, iron block, alloy head
Capacity	1,990cc
Bore x stroke	89mm x 80mm
Compression ratio	9.3:1/8.5:1
Maximum power	120bhp at 5,500rpm 100bhp at 5,500rpm
Valve gear	Two valves per cylinder, single overhead camshaft
Fuelling	Two side-draught Solex carburettors/one downdraught Solex carburettor

TRANSMISSION:
Four-speed manual, all-synchromesh/optional automatic transmission on 2000C.

SUSPENSION:
Front: Independent, coil springs, MacPherson struts, anti-roll bar, telescopic dampers
Rear: Independent, coil springs, semi-trailing arms, anti-roll bar, telescopic dampers

STEERING:
Worm-and-roller

BRAKES:
Hydraulic, front disc/rear drum

WHEELS/TYRES:
Steel disc; 175-14in cross-ply

BODY/CHASSIS:
Unit construction, pressed-steel two-door four-seater coupé

DIMENSIONS:
Length	14ft 10.3in
Width	5ft 5.9in
Height	4ft 5.5in
Wheelbase	8ft 4.4in
Track, front	4ft 4.4in
Track, rear	4ft 6.2in

WEIGHT:
2,646lb

PERFORMANCE/ECONOMY:
Max speed	115mph/107mph. approx
Acceleration	0–60mph in 10.4.5/12.5sec approx
Fuel consumption	typically 20–23mpg/20–23mpg

UK PRICE WHEN NEW incl. tax:
(2000C) £3,250/(2000CS) £3,250

NUMBER BUILT:
8,883/2,837

wheel disc brakes, and with a semi-trailing arm independent rear end this was a natural technical advance on the layout of the 700's system.

All this was conventional enough, and it was quite overshadowed by the new engine, the progress of which was masterminded by Alex von Falkenhausen. With a sturdy five-main-bearing cast-iron cylinder block, an aluminium cylinder head, and a single downdraught Solex carburettor, this was a single overhead camshaft design, BMW's first, and the forerunner of many successful engines to come.

As installed, the engine was canted over 30° towards the right side of the engine bay – not, as some people suggested, to provide a lower head-on profile (which was not pronounced), but to allow for ambitious multi-choke carburation and, eventually, fuel injection, to find space alongside it. This canted-over engine philosophy, incidentally, established a BMW

This is the car that changed BMW's prospects – the 1500 'New Class' saloon of 1961. Engineered at great expense, and brand-new from end to end, the 'New Class' featured an overhead camshaft engine and all-independent coil spring suspension.

tradition which would carry on into the next century.

Originally a 1,499cc four-cylinder unit, which meant it was easy to choose the new model's name – 1500 – the new power unit had built-in capacity 'stretch' as even at that point, BMW was planning on it eventually going out to 1,800cc, but in due course they would find that 1,990cc was easily and reliably possible. When previewed, it was rated at 75bhp, but when deliveries began, it produced 80bhp – and guaranteed a top speed of more than 90mph.

Here was an engine which, quite literally, underpinned BMW's future, for lineal developments of this unit would power a multitude of BMWs: saloons, cabriolets, estate cars ('Tourings'), coupés and sporty machines over the next four decades. Not only that, but when BMW turned to turbocharging, motorsport, and eventually to supplying F1 engines, the engineers discovered just how strong this original cylinder block had always been.

It was the 1500, too, which established a real precedent for BMW, as the company did not build its own transmissions, choosing instead to take supplies from capable outsiders

– Getrag for manual boxes and ZF for the automatics, which would follow from 1966 on later models.

Although Italy's Giovanni Michelotti had designed the original 'New Class' body style, this contribution was later played down by BMW management. Before the car met its public, a number of hands at Munich had had an input and, as ever, it was difficult to credit any one person with the finalised shape.

Features which established style and engineering cues for future BMWs of this size included the forward-leaning prow, the use of a full-width front-hinged bonnet panel, the sharply cut-off tail style (later the Triumph 2000, which Michelotti also styled, would look very similar!), the slim screen and door pillars, and the straight-through crease along the flanks.

The 'New Class' 1500 was launched, somewhat prematurely, at the Frankfurt Motor Show in 1961, for although BMW had been thinking of a medium-range car for some while, it was still not ready to start making deliveries – and even when it did, there were teething problems. The German team, though, worked diligently to cure everything, and it was not long before the new car's reputation began to grow. The public, it seemed, was relieved to see what they considered to be a *real* modern BMW – not a bubble car, not a grown-up bubble car, and not an overblown 'Baroque Angel', but a car which could compete on level terms in the market place.

The very first pilot-production cars were built in February 1962, but it was not until October 1962 – a good year after launch – that full production got under way. Initially priced at 8,500DM (or only $2,125/£760), and even though, by the end of 1962 this had leapt to 9,485DM ($2,370/£850), the realistic pricing ensured a healthy demand, and it was not long before the order books back in Munich were swamped.

Compared with 1959, when the company was staggering from financial crisis to financial crisis, the prospects for BMW had changed completely, and those days would

never return. Although the 1500 was not at all fast, for BMW this really was the 'Big Leap Forward'. Before this, BMW had always been looking for ways to sell the cars they could make, but now they were continuously looking for ways to make more cars which where selling themselves. It was the first-ever BMW to be evolved into a real range, with different engines, trim levels, and marketing aspirations.

Not that it was all sweetness and light, for the 1500 was riddled by teething troubles, particularly in getting the quality right, and the transmission sorted out. For those reasons, BMW held back true mass production – only 1,737 1500s would be produced in 1962 – until everything was right, and until new, faster and more capable derivatives could be brought to market.

Diversification, when it came, was all about adding new-type engines, except for the 2000C/2000CS coupés (described at the end of this chapter), and each and every car in this range was built with the same basic four-door saloon shell, although there were differences in front-end style from model to model. In more recent years, BMW has become known for producing up to seven different styles on the same chassis/platform.

The big push to offer faster and more sporty BMWs once again, got under way at the Frankfurt Motor Show in September 1963, when the new 1800 and 1800TI 'twins' appeared (in this case, 'TI' denoted 'Turismo Internationale'). Clearly, this was what the public had been waiting for, as demand and sales for 'New Class' cars rocketed at once. In 1963, just 27,987 cars – most of them original-type 1500s – were produced, while in 1964 that figure leapt to 37,823 (almost all of them 1800s), and surged again to 58,524 in 1965 (again the vast majority being 1800s).

So, how was this success achieved? Partly, of course, it was because ever more modern production facilities at Munich were coming on stream, but otherwise it was because what was basically a worthy but under-powered saloon car was being made a lot more

desirable with more power. By fairly simple increases to the cylinder bore, and crankshaft stroke, the sturdy four-cylinder overhead camshaft engine was enlarged to 1,773cc.

In 'normal' 1800 form this produced 90bhp (and a potential top speed of 101mph). The engine of the 1800TI however, looked – and was – a lot more exciting, for it was equipped with twin dual-choke side-draught

Launched prematurely in 1961, and on sale from 1962, the 1500 soon made its name, and was the first of a long line of BMWs to use the sturdy, tuneable, four-cylinder overhead-cam engine. (LAT)

BMW's legendary four-cylinder overhead-cam engine made its debut in humble, 80bhp/1.5-litre form – but there was much, much, more to follow during the next two decades. (LAT)

Simple instrumentation, but it displayed all you needed to know in the 'New Class' BMW 1500 of the early 1960s. (LAT)

Solex 40 PHH carburettors. Not only did these gobble in a most exciting manner (owners of Ford Lotus-Cortinas, or Alfa Romeo Giulias will know exactly what this means), but they helped to produce no less than 110bhp, and gave the car a top speed

BMW's 2000CS coupé was actually engineered around the platform and running gear of the 2000ti saloon, but with an entirely fresh, two-door superstructure.

of nearly 110mph. There was, however, a big difference between the BMW and its obvious rivals – whereas the Ford was cheap-and-cheerful (cynics once suggested that Lotus, who built these cars, did not employ quality control engineers!), and the Alfa was prone to all manner of build problems brought about by rather casual Italian workmanship, the BMWs were being built with Teutonic precision and dedication.

This was exactly the car that BMW's enthusiastic engineers had always hoped they would be allowed to develop, for the new 1800TI was now the sort of *real* sports saloon, which could rush up and down the de-restricted German autobahns at a most impressive pace, never needing to make excuses.

But there was more to come, for BMW was already finding ways to pump up the new range. In 1964, they announced the 1600 model (which was effectively a 1500 with an 83bhp/1,573cc engine), and there was also the extrovert 1800TI/SA, a no-holds-barred 'homologation special' intended to allow BMW to go motor racing, and to win.

Like the contemporary Ford Lotus-Cortinas and Alfa Romeo Guilia GTAs, the TI/SA (SA = *Sportausfaurung* or sports version) made few compromises to comfort, silence or tractability. These cars had twin dual-choke side-draught Weber 45DCOE carburettors, a 10.5:1 compression ratio and peak torque at 5,250rpm, all matched to a five-speed transmission.

Because BMW only had to build a limited number of cars to achieve sporting homologation, the 1800 TI/SA was only produced in 1965, with just 200 examples produced, all of them being sold to accredited and licensed race car drivers. Even then, the story of that car was not over, for to turn it into a race-winning machine, thousands more Deutschmarks had to be spent on the engine – and BMW was happy to provide those pieces too…

The final 'stretch' of the robust overhead-cam engine followed in 1965, when the 1,990cc version appeared, this producing a lazy 100bhp in single carburettor form, and 120bhp when fitted with the same side-draught Solexes as the 1800TI. This gave BMW the chance to introduce new 2000 (100bhp) and 2000TI (120bhp) versions of the car. Originally it was only the 2000 which was given a new nose style, with rectangular headlamps, but the 2000TI followed suit from 1968.

As far as this amazingly successful range was concerned, BMW still had one big surprise for their clientele. Just before the end of 1969, the 2000Tii was introduced, the extra 'i' indicating that fuel injection had been applied to the engine – and the peak power had been boosted yet again, this time to 130bhp.

Those were the days when fuel injection for private cars was still a rarity, and such models tended to be very expensive. Kugelfischer were world leaders at that time (in the 1970s they would gradually lose out to Bosch) and provided the BMW installation. Here, now, was a car about which BMW could boast in the way that they had once been so proud of the pre-war 328, and of course of the 507 Roadster of the 1950s. Like both those cars, the 2000 Tii was expensive (14,290DM in 1969 – the equivalent of $3,575), and therefore quite rare, for only 1,922 such saloons would be built in three years.

The Glas relationship

Until the takeover of 1966, BMW and Glas were geographical neighbours, but had no formal business relations. BMW was based, of course, in Munich, while Glas's modest factory was in Dingolfing, an hour's drive north east of that city.

In the beginning, Glas built agricultural machinery, but began making Goggo motor-scooters from 1951, and tiny two-stroke Goggomobil cars from 1955. Then, from 1961, a new range of front-engined Glas cars was launched, which had overhead-camshaft four-cylinder engines, and where camshaft drive was by internally cogged belt (a world 'first').

Although the full-size cars offered no competition to BMW, the Goggomobil was definitely a rival for the Isetta bubble cars, so BMW continued to monitor what the Dingolfing-based concern was up to.

By the mid-1960s, Glas was showing real signs of automotive maturity, first with the launch of the 1300GT and 1700GT coupés, but most especially with the ambitious Frua-styled 2.6-litre V8 sports coupé. By that time, there were 4,000 workers at Dingolfing, in what were surprisingly simple and rather cramped conditions.

Unhappily, though, it was only the globular little Goggomobil which made any money for Glas, so when that model finally lost popularity in 1966, the company's finances were immediately put in disarray.

Speedy negotiations with BMW (in which ex-BMW motorcycle racer Georg Meien, by that time a motor trader in Munich, was an important factor) soon saw Glas absorbed by BMW, and the transformation began. Rationalisation began at once. The BMW badge was applied to the coupés, with the 1300GT and its 1700GT sister being replaced by a 1600GT with the BMW 1.6-litre engine and BMW's semi-trailing rear while the 2.6-litre V8 coupé had its existing power unit uprated to 3.0 litres. Neither model lasted long.

Until the mid-1970s, BMW used as much existing, or easily modified, Glas engineering as it could, eventually shipping production tooling out to the BMW concessionaire's plant at Pretoria in South Africa. There, from 1968, the Frua-styled Glas 1700 was made, with a much-modified and (BMW) re-engined machine becoming the BMW 1800SA, and later the 2000SA. These models were eventually updated with a BMW grille, and renamed 1804 and 2004. The last were produced in 1975, after about 12,000 had been assembled in Pretoria.

Apart from propping up Glas in the short term, BMW was most interested in its real estate, and the possibility of expansion. In the next few years vast new factory buildings were erected, quite dwarfing what was already there. From 1972, the original 5-Series was assembled at Dingolfing, and by the end of the 1970s, other mass-market BMWs had also been added to the production lines there.

Model cocktails

Between 1968 and 1972, when the 'New Class' finally bowed out, to be replaced by the very first 5-Series range, there was still time for more to be done to these cars, notably by shuffling engines, power outputs, trim packs, nose treatments, and titles. Those were the years in which the 1800 engine was re-jigged with a larger cylinder bore, shorter stroke and promotion of commonality, and where the 2000tilux took over from the 2000TI, with the aid of the 2000's upmarket rectangular headlamp nose. From 1966, 1800s and 2000s became the first-ever BMWs to have an automatic transmission option, with ZF being the suppliers, and setting up a long-term relationship which shows no signs of flagging, even after 40 years.

Overseas assembly, from Munich-supplied kits, also began in a small way, and in the UK there was even a nostalgic rebirth when the British concern AFN (which had imported BMWs to the UK in the 1930s) started doing this again, with cars rebadged once again as Frazer Nash BMWs. Production, which had peaked early, at 60,614 cars in 1966, sagged after the smaller '02' models joined the range, but was still strong until 1971, after which BMW's facilities were once again torn apart to make space for the new 5-Series to take over.

Although little could be more boring than to list, in turgid detail, all the derivatives of this one design – in fact there were a round dozen of them – it should be pointed out how BMW's marketing experts had filled in every possible corner. Although all except the coupés (see below) were four-door saloons with the same style, hidden

away were five different engine sizes, nine different power outputs and a choice of transmissions, manual or automatic. Prices, too, spanned from 9,485DM to 17,500DM, and this was in a period where cost inflation was very low. It was almost as if staff had been to Detroit to learn how to ring the changes: there would be much more of the same in the 1970s.

Karmann + BMW = 2000 coupés

As the 1960s progressed, BMW's confidence grew and grew. Convinced that they could cut a swathe in the sporty market sector (and, of course, with Mercedes-Benz and the 230SL in their sights), BMW developed a smart coupé version of the 2000, using the existing platform, but with a new two-

'New Class' cars in motorsport

Once the larger-engined versions of the 'New Class' saloons went on sale, they proved to be ideal for motorsport. With all-independent suspension, they already had promising chassis and in 1.8-litre, or especially in 2.0-litre form, they could be power-tuned to match all but the very fastest of twin-overhead-camshaft Alfa Romeos or Ford Lotus-Cortinas.

Initially, in 1965, the most important derivative was the

Hubert Hahne and the latest 1800TI, racing at the Nürburgring in 1964, and well on the way to establishing BMW as a competitive touring car racing marque.

1800TI/SA, a 1,773cc-engined example which had 130bhp in so-called 'standard' tune, but which could be persuaded to produce much more in out-and-out racing form. Often known as 'Tisa' models, these five-speed gearbox-engined models carried initials which denoted 'Touring Internationale', and 'Sonderausfurung' ('Sporting Special'). Driven by such famous racers as Dieter Glemser, Hubert Hahne and Pascal Ickx, these cars were emphatic race winners, especially where endurance had to be added to pace.

Hahne and Glemser went on to win yet more races in 2000TIs, including the gruelling Spa 24-Hour race, and Germany's own prestigious long-distance event at the Nürburgring.

The engine, too, proved to be remarkably sturdy, and a magnificently complex 16-valve twin-cam unit (with engineer Ludwig Apfelbeck designing the valve operation) was raced with success as a 1.6-litre engine in Formula 2. Many years later, of course, the bare bones of this remarkable power unit formed the basis of the turbocharged BMW F1 engine of the early 1980s.

door coupé superstructure. There would be two versions – 2000C with 100bhp, and 2000CS with 120bhp – the 'C' being the only version to be optionally available with automatic transmission.

Although this very elegant 2+2 machine was styled in-house, by Wilhelm Hofmeister's design team,

Karmann of Osnabrück (in north western Germany, to the west of Hanover), got the job of providing press tools and final assembly facilities for these cars. In appearance, there is no doubt that Bertone's work on the now-obsolete 3200CS had been an influence, although there were no common

panels. Structurally, the coupé roof was permanently welded to the rest of the shell, and this was a pillarless design. One feature was a vast rear window; another, even more striking, was the use of complex 'round-the-corner' headlamp pods.

Although feeling a touch over-bodied, this was a machine which

could certainly handle the 120bhp engine of the 2000TI with some aplomb, and it definitely gave BMW's image a further boost in the late 1960s.

Although 2000C/2000CS sales in themselves were not astonishing – 2,837 2000Cs and 8,883 2000CSs in four years – this gave BMW *and* Karmann a graceful start in the sporting coupé business. Their real significance, though, was that they were the true ancestors of their six-cylinder-engined coupés (starting with the 2800CS) which followed from 1968.

Maturity

By the end of the 1960s, in any case, the 'New Class' models were no longer the only BMWs on the block, for they had been joined by two other types, the smaller '02' models, and the much larger six-cylinder range. In less than a decade, without question, BMW had transformed itself from a company staggering from crisis to crisis, and generating cash-flow by producing motorcycle-engined cars with strictly limited performance and a very few high-quality machines that few could afford. It had now become a thriving, modern, industrial machine with annual production exceeding 150,000 a year (three times what it had been in 1960) – with a lot more still to come.

The success of the 'New Class' is a perfect example of what was achieved, for in a 12-year life no fewer than 364,378 of those four-door saloons and coupés had been produced. BMW, clearly, had tapped into rising prosperity and aspirations, world-wide, as 165,335 of those had powerful 2-litre engines.

Even so, in terms of numbers built, the 'New Class' was already on its way to being eclipsed by a smaller, but equally appealing family – the '02' models of the late 1960s...

The easy way to pick one 'New Class' saloon from another was to look closely at the boot lid. This UK-registered car of 1969–70 was an 1800 derivative. (LAT)

By ringing the detail styling changes, BMW evolved an entire range of cars from the original 'New Class' bodyshell. Complete with rectangular headlamps, this was the 2000 model.

'02' Series
– a BMW for everyman

Late-model derivatives of the 02-Series had a smoother tail end, with restyled tail lamps, like this 2002 seen posed alongside Cutty Sark *at Greenwich. (LAT)*

By the mid-1960s, BMW was back in its pomp. Totally recovered from the traumas of the 1940s, and the financial upheavals of the 1950s, it now had a modern factory, a huge order book, ever-increasing sales – and ambition to do a whole lot more.

The next big leap came in 1966, with the launch of a new line, whose rather confusing title (1600-2) sounded familiar, but the structure of

1600-2
1966–1975

ENGINE:
Four cylinders in line, iron block, alloy head
Capacity	1,573cc
Bore x stroke	84mm x 71mm
Compression ratio	8.6:1
Maximum power	85bhp at 5,700rpm
Valve gear	Two valves per cylinder, single overhead camshaft
Fuelling	One downdraught Solex carburettor

TRANSMISSION:
Four-speed manual, all-synchromesh

SUSPENSION:
Front: Independent, coil springs, MacPherson struts, telescopic dampers
Rear: Independent, coil springs, semi-trailing arms, telescopic dampers

STEERING:
Worm-and-roller

BRAKES:
Hydraulic, front disc/rear drum

WHEELS/TYRES:
Steel disc; 6.00-13in cross-ply

BODY/CHASSIS:
Unit-construction, pressed-steel two-door saloon; cabriolet version 1967–71

DIMENSIONS:
Length	13ft 10.5in
Width	5ft 2.6in
Height	4ft 7.5in
Wheelbase	8ft 2.4in
Track, front	4ft 4.4in
Track, rear	4ft 4.4in

WEIGHT:
2,073lb

PERFORMANCE/ECONOMY:
Max speed	102mph
Acceleration	0–60mph in 12.5sec
Fuel consumption	typically 26–30mpg

UK PRICE WHEN NEW incl. tax:
£1,298

NUMBER BUILT:
277,320

2002
1968–1975

ENGINE:
Four cylinders in line, iron block, alloy head
Capacity	1,990cc
Bore x stroke	89mm x 80mm
Compression ratio	8.5:1
Maximum power	100bhp at 5,500rpm
Valve gear	Two valves per cylinder, single overhead camshaft
Fuelling	One downdraught Solex carburettor

TRANSMISSION:
Four-speed manual, all-synchromesh, or five-speed, all-synchromesh; optional automatic transmission

SUSPENSION:
Front: Independent, coil springs, MacPherson struts, anti-roll bar, telescopic dampers
Rear: Independent, coil springs, semi-trailing arms, anti-roll bar, telescopic dampers

STEERING:
Worm-and-roller

BRAKES:
Hydraulic, front disc/rear drum

WHEELS/TYRES:
Steel disc; 165-13in radial-ply

BODY/CHASSIS:
Unit-construction, pressed-steel two-door saloon; optional styles included Touring (estate car), and cabriolet

DIMENSIONS:
Length	13ft 10.5in
Width	5ft 2.6in
Height	4ft 7.5in
Wheelbase	8ft 2.4in
Track, front	4ft 4.4in
Track, rear	4ft 4.4in

WEIGHT:
2,228lb

PERFORMANCE/ECONOMY:
Max speed	107mph
Acceleration	0–60mph in 10.6sec
Fuel consumption	typically 24–27mpg

UK PRICE WHEN NEW incl. tax:
£1,597

NUMBER BUILT:
398,434

2002Tii
1971–1975

ENGINE:
Four cylinders in line, iron block, alloy head
Capacity	1,990cc
Bore x stroke	89mm x 80mm
Compression ratio	9.5:1
Maximum power	130bhp at 5,800rpm
Valve gear	Two valves per cylinder, single overhead camshaft
Fuelling	Kugelfischer fuel injection

TRANSMISSION:
Four-speed manual, all-synchromesh

SUSPENSION:
Front: Independent, coil springs, McPherson struts, anti-roll bar, telescopic dampers
Rear: Independent, coil springs, semi-trailing arms, anti-roll bar, telescopic dampers

STEERING:
Worm-and-roller

BRAKES:
Hydraulic, front disc/rear drum

WHEELS/TYRES:
Steel disc; 65 x 13in radial-ply

BODY/CHASSIS:
Unit-construction, pressed-steel two-door saloon/three-door hatchback ('Touring')

DIMENSIONS:
Length	13ft 10.5in
Width	5ft 2.6in
Height	4ft 7.5in
Wheelbase	8ft 2.4in
Track, front	4ft 4.4in
Track, rear	4ft 4.4in

WEIGHT:
2,227lb

PERFORMANCE/ECONOMY:
Max speed	116mph
Acceleration	0–60mph in 8.3sec
Fuel consumption	typically 26–29mpg

UK PRICE WHEN NEW incl. tax:
£2,299

NUMBER BUILT:
38,703

Five years after the 'New Class' saloons went on sale, BMW introduced a model they originally titled 1600-2. Although it had a new, smaller, two-door platform/shell, this car used much of the same running gear as the 'New Class' cars, including the engine, transmission and rear axle. What became known as the '02-Series' later spawned cabriolet and hatchback ('Touring') models too.

which was completely different. Here, to complement the four-door 'New Class' saloons which were breaking every BMW sales record, was a new, smaller, lighter and altogether more nimble two-door saloon. Merely the first of what would be a rapidly burgeoning range, it showed that BMW intended to make smaller cars, and to sell them at even keener prices.

Because the new car's engine was basically the same as that used in 'New Class' saloons, seasoned BMW-watchers could guess what could – might, even – happen in the future. Indeed, if there was space in the engine bay for a humble 85bhp 1,573cc power unit, then surely a fuel-injected 2-litre 'tii' type should squeeze in there too? Certainly it

could – but at the time no-one even thought that a turbocharged derivative would follow…

New structure

Although the new 1600-2 (the clientele tended to ignore the '-2' part, so BMW eventually gave in themselves) was shorter than the 'New

Class', BMW had not engineered it the easy way, by cutting-and-shutting the floor pan. Instead, a totally new platform had been devised – and for

The 1600-2 was smaller, lighter and more nimble than the original 'New Class' models, but was still a full four-seater. Before the end of production, in the mid-1970s, BMW not only introduced a fuel-injected version, but a turbocharged type also.

the time being all cars were to have two-door saloon structures.

The platform itself was more compact – with a 2in shorter wheelbase and 2in narrower rear track – although the front track, and most of the components in the front suspension were the same as before. The cabin itself only had two passenger doors, and was slightly smaller in all dimensions, for the roof line was down, and the overall width had slimmed down by 4.7 inches.

Unless they had been pigging out on junk food, customers didn't seem to mind any of this, especially as – engine for engine – the new two-door cars were no less than 345lb lighter, that much more economical, and nicer to drive. It was almost as if BMW had set out to design a sports coupé

When the 2002 was introduced in 1968, it re-wrote the definition of a sports saloon, for it was fast, comfortable and reliable without having to be cosseted, or serviced every other week. Smaller in every way, lighter and more nimble, with two-door styles, the '02' cars were a successful complement to the original 'New Class' cars. The two types were built alongside each other for several years. (LAT)

without actually advertising it as such. The 'New Class' cars were sizeable, comfortable, and relatively spacious machines – whereas these new '02' models were compact, brisk, and without too many frills. Not only that, but they were much cheaper too – in Britain, when sales began, a 1600 cost £1,298, while a 'New Class' 1800 cost no less than £1,498. Not that these were bargain-basement prices by any

Here's a rarity. Most 2002s had manual transmission – which was how the majority of customers liked it – yet BMW also offered an automatic transmission option, which became ever more popular as the years passed by. (LAT)

means – for one could buy a Jaguar 2.4 Mk II for £1,342.

With the original 1600-2, whose engine produced only 85bhp, the top

Turbo coupé – the mid-engined project car

In 1972, BMW not only launched the all-new 5-Series family cars, but also showed off a magnificent irrelevance, the mid-engined Turbo coupé. Irrelevant only because it was a two-off, and not even a very practical one at that, this was really a case of BMW engineers thinking aloud, and was studied carefully by BMW's rivals because of that.

Originally the mid-engined chassis, which featured a transversely positioned turbocharged 1,990cc engine, was merely a study, but even while it was being built behind closed doors in Munich, stylist/designer Paul Bracq drew up an exciting two-door coupé bodyshell, and saw the car turned into a running prototype.

Sensing criticism for wasting their team's time, BMW opted to call this car an 'experimental safety vehicle',

Only two examples of the mid-engined Turbo coupé project car were produced. Gull wing door operation was a notable feature. (LAT)

gave the body energy-absorbing front and rear body sections, and fitted a radar device to warn if the Turbo was travelling too close to the car in front. The glass-fibre body featured a fat roll-over bar, and there were extra-strong side-impact bars in the lift-up gull-wing doors.

If, indeed, this was a safety investigation car, it looked a whole lot more graceful than the lumpy horrors being produced by BMW's rivals (notably Mercedes-Benz), so the company reaped much kudos because of that. Although it was quite a compact car – it was 163in long – enthusiastic pundits warmed to the idea of a 'safety' car which had a 200bhp engine and a projected top speed of 155mph.

Lessons for the future were, in any case, incorporated in the engine later found in the 2002 Turbo saloon of 1973, and in the general style/layout of the mid-engined M1 supercar which followed in the late 1970s.

From this angle, it can be see that the style of the Turbo coupé project car was a clear precursor of the M1 supercar. (LAT)

Just two cars were built, and both have survived, with one usually on display in the company's museum.

speed was just about 100mph, much of the charm was in the car's compact size and obvious roadability. In size, this was a car whose performance squared up to British mass-production 'standards' like the Ford Cortina GT, but at a much higher price. Even so, the BMW not only had an overhead cam engine (still a rarity in this market sector), but independent rear suspension, and what was once again becoming a great selling point – the famous BMW 'spinner' badge.

Expanding the range began almost at once – and those who thought that BMW had already pushed out the boundaries with the 'New Class' machines eventually had to think again. Between 1966 (when the original 1600-2 was launched) and 1977, there were 14 distinctly different types. That range, incidentally, included three body types, three engines, eight different power outputs, carburettors, fuel injection *and* turbocharging, and four-speed manual, five-speed manual and automatic transmissions.

In the end, for a customer there was almost as much fun in sitting down in a comfortable chair, with a catalogue (and a stiff drink!), to work out which engine should be chosen, with which transmission, in which body, before marching back to the BMW dealership and placing an order. And if this seemed to be complicated in the 1960s, be assured that it would intensify in future years.

It was the 1600-2 which really underpinned BMW's arrival in the US market, and it is significant that BMW's annual output rose above 100,000 units a year in 1968, when the new '02' cars were truly getting in to their stride. No wonder that in eleven years, BMW built no fewer than 863,203 of all types!

Engines and body styles

BMW's overhead camshaft four-cylinder engine was still a very modern unit when the original 1600-2

A snug fit in a compact engine bay, the fuel-injected engine of the 2002Tii was carefully and efficiently packaged. (LAT)

was laid down, therefore the same family was used in the smaller car. Early thoughts of starting off with a 1.4-litre engine were abandoned when the cost accountants pointed out that the savings would be tiny.

After starting off with the 1600-2, powered by an 85bhp/1,573cc version of this engine, BMW would eventually add new models and engine sizes, all the way up to the 130bhp/1,990cc engine which was used in the 'New Class' 2000Tii. But that was not all, for in 1973 (and in exactly the same season as the first Energy Crisis exploded around the world) there was also the 170bhp/1,990cc turbocharged engine for the short-lived 2002 Turbo.

Maybe we had all thought that BMW only saw the 1600-2 family as one of relatively simply equipped two-door saloons. Within 18 months – actually in September 1967 – we were proved wrong, when the company suddenly revealed the 1600 cabriolet.

Students of unit-construction body engineering will know that it is never easy to convert a saloon shell into a drop-top: BMW knew this, realised

Yet another version of the 02-Series cabriolet; a contemporary, late 1960s view with suitably dressed models.

Introduced in 1967, the 02-Series cabriolet featured this neat body style by the specialist coachbuilders, Baur of Stuttgart. (LAT)

their limitations, and hired the Stuttgart-based Baur company to do the job for them. Baur, of course, had built traditional-style bodyshells for BMW as early as the 1930s, and the 700 Convertibles from 1961, so there was a long-time connection.

Amazingly, Baur not only reinforced the underside of the platform so that the cabriolet structure was stiff enough, but these cars were still full open-top four seaters. Originally these cars were 1600-2s, with 85bhp, but from 1971 there would also be a 100bhp/2002 type, which replaced the 1600, with a built-up roll-over bar behind the doors/front seats. While maybe not as sleek, this was unquestionably elegant and a further aid to body rigidity.

BMW, clearly, was happy to take converted bodies from Baur for many years, and treated them as valued associates. Baur would also be closely involved in building the sensational M1 super car (described more fully in Chapter 9), but meanwhile the cabriolet contract with BMW kept it nicely occupied, as it would not be until the mid-1980s that BMW began to make its own 'in house' cabriolets.

Baur's cabriolet was, at least, conventional by BMW standards, but the next effort, an in-house project by the way, was a complete surprise. Called 'Touring' by BMW, but effectively a cross between a three-door estate car, and a sporting hatchback, this new body style of 1971 was entirely new to the Bavarian concern, which had never before acknowledged that there were BMW customers who might also wish to carry bulky loads as well!

Cleverly, BMW had retained the same pressed steel platform, the complete front end, and the same side passenger doors, and had then grafted on a rather angular roof, and a massive lift-up hatchback. To help load-carrying, the rear seat backrests were also arranged to fold forward and provide a long flat floor. Maybe BMW customers were not the type who would want to sleep in their cars, but in the case of the 02 Tourings they might even have done so, for the flattened loading floor was 74in long.

This, unfortunately, was not a body style which took immediate root at BMW, and sales were always limited. The rather awkward appearance (from some aspects, in particular from three-quarter rear) cannot have helped, but there also seem to have been criticisms about side-wind stability on German autobahns. Production of all such Tourings ended in the summer of 1974.

Building the range

First of all there was the two-door 85bhp/1,573cc engined 1600-2 saloon, then from September 1967 it was joined by the new cabriolet, and at the same time, a more sporting version called the 1600 TI, which had twin dual-choke Solex carburettors, 105bhp/1,573cc, servo-assisted brakes, and front and rear anti-roll bars. This engine could not be 'de-toxed' to meet North American requirements, so it was strictly an interim machine which was only available until the end of 1968, with just 1,259 such cars built.

Next up were the exciting 2-litre engined twins – the 100bhp 2002 and the 120bhp 2002 Ti saloons. Looking virtually identical to the 1600-2, these were the sort of BMWs which brought real sporting performance within reach of tens of thousands of younger drivers, including the author, who ran a 2002 as a business, commuting and pleasure machine for the whole of 1968.

As the range filled out, and as the reputation of the cars spread more widely, production of '02' models had to be raised to meet the demand. In 1966 (the first year), 13,244 were built with 42,546 in 1967 and a very creditable 68,100 in 1968. Even that was not going to be the peak, for in 1972 an amazing 125,123 would be built – an average of about 2,500 02s every working week.

Because BMW had its hands full at the end of the 1960s, with the launch and expansion of the new-generation six-cylinder model range (see Chapter 6), the 02s then stood their ground until 1971, after which more and more changes were introduced. Early in 1971, not only was the Touring body

The Baur-constructed 02-Series cabriolet offered fresh-air motoring, but with a permanent roll-over hoop, for body stiffness and extra protection. (LAT)

BMW's first estate car – although they insisted on calling it a 'Touring' – was the 02-based model of 1971. (LAT)

2002 Turbo – right car, wrong moment

If only the 2002 Turbo had been introduced earlier. If only the first Energy Crisis had not erupted at *exactly* the same time that the 2002 Turbo was launched. If only the front-end style had not been so aggressively 'move over' in character...' If only...

With an engine evolved from those

There was no mistaking the 2002 Turbo of 1973–74. Not only was there a suitably reversed script on the front spoiler (which, of course, read the correct way round when viewed through the rear-view mirror of the car ahead!), but wheelarch extensions were also standard.

fierce units used in European saloon car racing in 1969, and later shown in the Turbo Coupé of 1972, the 1,990cc engine of the 2002 Turbo produced 170bhp at 5,800rpm. Because control mechanism techniques were still in their infancy, this engine did not have the flexibility of later power units, and there was considerable turbo lag. Even so, when driven hard, it certainly delivered – the top speed being 130mph.

Complete with lowered suspension, wider wheels and tyres, front and rear spoilers, flared wheelarches and colourful striping along the flanks, it

certainly made its point. The '2002 turbo' script on the front spoiler – reversed so that it spelt out a message in the rear view mirror of any car it caught – was perhaps the final straw.

Not only were the customers slow to buy such an extrovert machine, but the motoring press, too, was quite hostile. As a result, the 2002 Turbo was dead and buried within a year with only 1,672 such cars ever made. Public opinion, though, is capricious: as the 'classic car' movement developed in the 1980s and 1990s, this rare model became predictably desirable.

Buying an 02-Series

1. Although rust has taken its toll of many cars, there is still a good choice of 02-Series cars on the road. The cheapest cars, naturally, are 1502s and 1602s while 2002s and 2002Tis are the best all-round 'starter classics'. The 2000Tii cars are fast, but their fuel injection may be expensive to keep in order and insurance is costly.

2. 2002 Turbos may be desirable, but they only come in left-hand drive, with turbo characteristics acting like an 'on-off' switch. Running costs, if not restoration costs, may be very high.

3. Cabriolets are rare, and surprisingly rigid, so are desirable. Body supplies are now very limited.

4. Parts supply, in general, is very good for all derivatives, although expensive. BMW recognises its heritage, and has encouraged the remanufacture of many components.

5. These are all now old cars, and bodyshell corrosion may be a problem, but many replacement steel panels are available. Particular rust spots to look out for are around the rear suspension/axle mounting points, and where the rear coil springs are mounted to the shell.

6. Corrosion around the front bulkhead, where it joins the sills, and on the sills themselves, is to be expected. Corrosion may also affect the front of the shell, ahead of the engine, and between the front wings and inner panels.

7. Well-serviced engines last for at least 100,000 miles before they need major attention. After that, notable wear points may involve valve guides/seals, but camshafts don't wear as much as originally feared. Replacement aluminium cylinder heads are available, but they should not be needed unless internal water passage corrosion has taken hold.

8. Four-speed gearboxes were standard when new, but five-speeders were optional, and a number of cars have been converted retrospectively. In old age, both eventually suffer from sloppy linkages, with excessive side-to-side movement. Internally, look for worn splines in transmission output shafts, and – naturally – worn second and third gear synchromesh.

A surprising number of 02s were built with automatic transmission.

9. In old age, MacPherson strut top bearings tend to seize, which leads to ultra-heavy steering. Worm-and-roller steering boxes also wear and develop sloppiness, but this can be adjusted away. Replacement parts are mainly still available.

10. If you buy an 02-Series car, it is advisable to obtain English language repair manuals, which are available (but can be expensive), as they are invaluable for anyone planning to up-date and restore an aged car.

11. No matter which country you live in, join the appropriate BMW owners' club. Such clubs are closely involved with restorers, maintenance topics, and parts provisioning. Your investment in an annual subscription will pay off many times.

---

style introduced (it was versatile, and would eventually be available with most of the mechanical packages, from 85bhp/1.6-litres to 130bhp/2.0-litres), but this was also the season for the launch of the 'gap-filling' 90bhp/1,766cc 1802 model, and the exhilarating Kugelfischer-injected 130bhp/1,990cc 2002Tii.

Almost every motoring enthusiast, and even some of BMW's rivals, now saw this range as offering something for everyone, which brought great satisfaction to a management team which could remember the end of the 1950s when the company's very survival was seen to be in doubt.

Even so, it was not the end, for in September 1973, the extrovert 2002 Turbo appeared, but this version had a short and not at all that successful life (see sidebar). The final derivative of all – the 75bhp/1,573cc 1502 – did not appear until January 1975, and was on sale for less than three years, but in fact, it outlived all other 02-family derivatives.

The 1502 was developed in a hurry, in response to the change in buying patterns after the shock of the 1973–74 Energy Crisis, and was really no more than a stripped out, 'Plain Jane' version of the 1600-2 with a lower-compression-ratio 75bhp/1,573cc engine. Meant to placate those who (temporarily at least) thought that the only way to keep on motoring was to use 'economy' cars, it was a great success. By mid-1975 it had taken over completely from the 1600-2, and by August 1977 it had found no fewer than 72,632 customers.

By any commercial, visual and marketing standards, the 02-range of BMWs was a remarkable, and lasting, success for BMW. Not only did it finally prove just how versatile the Munich-based company had become, but it made so much money for the company that it could afford to invest in a very different type of compact BMW – the first of the 3-Series.

The high-performance variant which most enthusiasts will remember with awe is bound to be the 2002 Turbo, although it was the infinitely more practical and driver friendly 2002 Tii which sold more widely.

The first
silky 'sixes'

With motor racing in mind, BMW developed the very special 3.0CSL from the CSi in the early 1970s. Not only was the bodyshell much lightened, with aluminium panels, but final models had an extrovert, but highly effective, aero package added on. (LAT)

By the mid-1960s BMW was booming. All memory of the trauma of the 1950s was being abandoned to the history books, and the company was looking for every way that it could possibly expand. For years there had been a burning jealousy of Mercedes-Benz, although

no direct rivalry. BMW needed larger and more powerful cars, for its ambition was at least to match Mercedes, if not to humiliate them, with new products.

By the late 1960s it was time for the big push. The 02-Series was breaking all previous sales records. Not only

2500/2800
1968–1977

ENGINE:
Six cylinders in line, iron block, alloy head
Capacity	2,494cc/2,788cc
Bore x stroke	86mm x 71.6mm
	86mm x 80mm
Compression ratio	9.0:1
Maximum power	150bhp at 6,000rpm
	170bhp at 6,000rpm
Valve gear	Two valves per cylinder, single overhead camshaft
Fuelling	Two downdraught Zenith carburettors

TRANSMISSION:
Four-speed manual, all-synchromesh; optional automatic transmission

SUSPENSION:
Front: Independent, coil springs, MacPherson struts, anti-roll bar, telescopic dampers
Rear: Independent, coil springs, semi-trailing arms, anti-roll bar (2800), telescopic dampers

STEERING:
Worm-and-roller, optional power-assistance

BRAKES
Hydraulic, front disc/rear disc

WHEELS/TYRES:
Steel disc; 175-14in radial-ply

BODY/CHASSIS:
Unit-construction, pressed-steel four-door saloon

DIMENSIONS:
Length	15ft 5in
Width	5ft 8.9in
Height	4ft 9.1in
Wheelbase	8ft 10in
Track, front	4ft 8.9in
Track, rear	4ft 9.6in

WEIGHT:
4,035lb

PERFORMANCE/ECONOMY:
Max speed	120mph
Acceleration	0–60mph in 9.3/8.9sec
Fuel consumption	typically 20–23mpg/ 19–22mpg

UK PRICE WHEN NEW incl. tax:
£2,997/£3,447

NUMBER BUILT:
94,206/54,597

2800CS (3.0CSi)
1968–1975

ENGINE:
Six cylinders in line, iron block, alloy head
Capacity	2,788cc (2,985cc)
Bore x stroke	86mm x 80mm
	(89 x 80mm)
Compression ratio	9.0:1
Maximum power	170bhp at 6,000rpm
	(200bhp at 5,500rpm)
Valve gear	Two valves per cylinder, single overhead camshaft
Fuelling	Two downdraught Zenith carburettors (Bosch fuel injection)

TRANSMISSION:
Four-speed manual, all-synchromesh; optional automatic transmission

SUSPENSION:
Front: Independent, coil springs, MacPherson struts, anti-roll bar, telescopic dampers
Rear: Independent, coil springs, semi-trailing arms, anti-roll bar, telescopic dampers

STEERING:
Worm-and-roller, with power-assistance

BRAKES:
Hydraulic, front disc/rear disc

WHEELS/TYRES:
Alloy disc; 195/70-14in radial-ply

BODY/CHASSIS:
Unit construction, pressed-steel two-door four-seater coupé

DIMENSIONS:
Length	15ft 3.5in
Width	5ft 5.7in
Height	4ft 5.9in
Wheelbase	8ft 7.3in
Track, front	4ft 8.9in
Track, rear	4ft 7.2in

WEIGHT:
2,988lb (3,087lb)

PERFORMANCE/ECONOMY:
Max speed	131mph (139mph)
Acceleration	0–60mph in 8.0sec (7.5sec)
Fuel consumption	typically 19–23mpg

UK PRICE WHEN NEW incl. tax:
£4,997 (£6,199)

NUMBER BUILT:
9,399 (8,199)

3.0CSL
1971–1975

ENGINE:
Six cylinders in line, iron block, alloy head
Capacity	2,985cc/3,003cc/3,153cc
Bore x stroke	89mm x 80mm
	89.25mm x 80mm
	89.25mm x 84mm
Compression ratio	9.5:1
Maximum power	200bhp at 5,500rpm
	206bhp at 5,600rpm
Valve gear	Two valves per cylinder, single overhead camshaft
Fuelling	Bosch fuel injection

TRANSMISSION:
Four-speed manual, all-synchromesh

SUSPENSION:
Front: Independent, coil springs, MacPherson struts, anti-roll bar, telescopic dampers
Rear: Independent, coil springs, anti-roll bar, telescopic dampers

STEERING:
Worm-and-roller, with power-assistance

BRAKES:
Hydraulic, front disc/rear disc

WHEELS/TYRES:
Alloy disc; 195/70-14in radial-ply

BODY/CHASSIS:
Unit construction, pressed-steel two-door four-seater coupé. Some aluminium skin panels, some cars with aerodynamic splitters and rear aerofoil

DIMENSIONS:
Length	15ft 3.5in
Width	5ft 5.7in
Height	4ft 5.9in
Wheelbase	8ft 7.3in
Track, front	4ft 9.9in
Track, rear	4ft 8.1in

WEIGHT:
2,800lb

PERFORMANCE/ECONOMY:
Max speed	133mph
Acceleration	0–60mph in 7.3sec
Fuel consumption	typically 15–18mpg

UK PRICE WHEN NEW incl. tax:
£6,399

NUMBER BUILT:
1,039

that, but it was such a money-spinner that BMW could build up reserves, which would allow it to invest in another model range. It was time to re-launch a six-cylinder BMW.

As other historians have already noted, this was not merely a car which could compete, head-to-head, with the latest Mercedes-Benz models, but it was also aimed at high-flyers. Up to that point in the late 1960s, thrusting businessmen with a leaning towards BMW had had to make do with the most powerful 2-litre 02-Series models. Fast, maybe, but still lacking that important cachet of a lengthy bonnet and the thrum of a silky six-cylinder engine under it.

In the meantime, there was a new personality at BMW – Paul Hahnemann, who had joined the company from Auto Union in 1963.

This is the well-equipped fascia/instrument panel layout of the six-cylinder 2500/2800 BMW of the late 1960s. (LAT)

Here was a master salesman/marketer, who had electrified all at BMW who came to know him, and invented what he called the 'Niche Theory', whereby BMW would sell cars, not directly against their competitors, but into a slightly different sector of the same market.

By 1968, with his reputation already set in stone in Munich, his views on BMW's new model range were crucial to the company's success. Now, for the first time since 1945, BMW hoped to fight Mercedes-Benz at its own level. Hahnemann's theory (proven in practice) was that each car BMW sold in the very demanding middle and upper price ranges would be in direct competition with Mercedes-Benz. Even though the Stuttgart colossus had just launched its own 'New Generation' machines, Hahnemann's team was sure that a different type of BMW would give it a real fight. As a spokesman trumpeted about the planning of the new cars when they

were launched in September 1968: 'Our model is neither a muscle-bound body builder, nor a solid citizen. We are thinking more of a field athlete – temperamental, sinewy, fit, nimble-footed, agile, energetic, and entirely youthful.'

Take this 'mission statement' on board, take in the fact that the new cars would have straight-six cylinder engines, and that the style would be a natural progression from the 02-Series, and the marketing stance almost wrote itself. No-one, though, could have forecast that these machines would be so obviously related to the O2s, but so very different in character, and so definitely up-market.

When the new cars were launched in the autumn of 1968, they were seen to be almost exactly the same size as the 'New Generation' Mercedes-Benz models. This was no coincidence, for BMW was spoiling for a fight with the Stuttgart concern. However, although they might have been the same size, they were technically much more advanced. Not only did the BMWs have a more advanced type of six-cylinder engine, but there was a rather more effective chassis and a more sporty character.

'Character' is not a feature which can be conjured up from a computer, or from a book of specifications. It has to reflect what the management team thinks, and wants, of a new car. In the case of the new BMWs, the cars were not aimed at the comfortable, middle-class, expanding-waistline market, but at clients who wanted a lot of sporting feel to blend in with their 120mph-plus straight line performance. And with Alex von Falkenhausen in charge of engine development, and Paul Hahnemann itching to sell the cars, there was never any lack of resolve.

There were to be two new closely related six-cylinder types, badged 2500 and 2800 – these being considerably larger than the 02-Series. Not only in engine size and power output, of course, but in physical presence. Under their spacious five-seater four-door cabins,

Larger in every way than the 'New Class' saloons which had been on sale for six years, the 2500/2800 models had a spacious new structure, and were all powered by overhead-camshaft six-cylinder engines. The family resemblance to 'New Class' and 02-Series cars was obvious. The 2500 was powered by a 150bhp/2.5-litre engine. (LAT)

the new 2500/2800 types ran on a 106.0in wheelbase platform, which was much longer than that of the 02 cars, which used a 98.4in wheelbase.

Power came from a smooth seven-bearing single-overhead-camshaft six-cylinder engine, which was a very close relative of the existing overhead-cam 'four'. Way back in the late 1950s, BMW had always planned that this should be so, and some of the jigging and machine tool facilities in their engine shops took account of this. It wasn't that the new 'six' was a simple 'four-plus-two' (although

Closely related to the existing four-cylinder power unit, BMW's new straight-six of 1968 was an impressive engine. Initially available with twin carburettor induction, it was eventually updated to use fuel injection. (LAT)

BMW-Glas 3000 coupé

After BMW took over Glas in the 1960s, there was an interim period when cross-over models were produced. One was the re-engineered BMW-Glas 1600GT coupé, but more exciting was a sports coupé officially known as the BMW-Glas 3000 V8. However, because Glas had bought in the fastback body style from Frua of Italy (and it bore some resemblance to Frua styles for current Maserati coupés), it soon gained the nickname of 'Glaserati'.

Although BMW applied its own 'whirling propeller' insignia to the bonnet, boot lid and hub caps, it made no important technical changes. The original car was powered by a 2.6-litre Glas V8, which came complete with belt-driven single overhead camshaft, and had transistorised ignition, while the chassis featured de Dion rear suspension and four-wheel disc brakes. The cabin was a full four-seater, looking slightly angular from some aspects, but undeniably

Glas's coupé was soon nicknamed the 'Glaserati'.

attractive: 277 original Glas-badged types were produced.

BMW authorised engine enlargement to 160bhp/2,982cc, which guaranteed a top speed of more than 120mph. Although it was only in production from September 1967 to May 1968 (BMW had its own 2800CS coupé on the way, and would certainly not want to sell two very similar cars side by side), and body-shells were all hand-crafted. BMW-Glas managed to sell 389 of these hand-built coupés. Some still survive.

common machining facilities made this possible), but that the seminal layout of pistons, connecting rods, valve gear and combustion chamber layouts, along with camshaft drive arrangements, were all shared with the 'four', and the engine was also laid over in the engine bay at a similar angle.

Two types were immediately available – a 150bhp/2,494cc engine and a longer-stroke 170bhp/2,788cc unit, both of them fed by twin downdraught Zenith 35/40 carburettors. At the time, BMW was at pains to suggest that these were 'new' engines, for the bore and stroke figures were not yet

standardised, as this little chart
makes clear:

Engine/cylinders	Capacity (cc)	Bore x stroke (mm)
1600-2/4	1,573	84 x 71
2002/4	1,990	89 x 80
2500/6	2,494	86 x 71.6
2800/6	2,788	86 x 80

This seemed conclusive enough, until
the 3-litre engine appeared in 1971:

3.0S	2,985	89 x 80

All was now clear, for this was the
capacity to which von
Falkenhausen's team had been
aiming for so long!

Although the style and structure
of the new car was all new – the
much longer-wheelbase platform
and wider wheel tracks made that
inevitable – to BMW-watchers the
engineering layout was very familiar.
The all-steel four-door saloon shell
incorporated a long, wide and
imposing bonnet with the familiar
double-kidney grille up front, but
this (along with the 2800CS coupé
which was launched at the same

*Introduced in 1968, BMW's big six-cylinder-
engined saloons sold in huge numbers for the
next nine years, without a need to change the
styling. The first cars had 2.5 or 2.8-litre
power units, but by the early 1970s a
3.0-litre engine had become available. This
was the 3.0S model of 1971. (LAT)*

time) featured a four-headlamp
nose, the first ever to be seen on a
BMW production car.

At first glance the MacPherson strut
front suspension looked familiar, but
in this application the struts were
actually leaning back towards the
scuttle, at 14° 30". Not only did this

help provide lighter steering (which BMW trumpeted), but it also helped feed suspension bump loads more efficiently into the front bulkhead/windscreen pillar/door pillar area.

As with the 02-Series and the earlier 'New Class' saloons, independent rear suspension was by coil springs and semi-trailing arms, and these were the first-ever BMW road cars to have disc brakes at front and rear. In addition (but only until

To make the big six-cylinder-engined saloons even more saleable in the 1970s, BMW not only increased the engine size to 3.3 litres, but also introduced a longer-wheelbase version of the car, with more space in the rear seat. (LAT)

1971) on the 2800 there was also the bonus of self-levelling rear suspension and a limited-slip differential. On the 2800, too, ZF power-assisted steering was an optional extra.

Even in their original specification, these were the fastest, the most impressive and the most capable BMWs yet put on sale. Even the 'entry-level' 2500 could reach 120mph, and the engines were so smooth, so silent, and so untroubled that 100mph cruising was easy wherever traffic conditions allowed it.

And this was only the beginning, for this was a range of saloons which would have a life of nine years. Need one say that without altering the style, or the basic engineering, there would

eventually be five different engine sizes, seven different power outputs, carburettors or fuel injection, two different wheelbase lengths, two different makes of optional automatic transmission, and a regular reshuffle of options and features.

Peak production came in 1972, when 43,609 cars were manufactured, and from 1974 four different engine sizes and two different wheelbase lengths were simultaneously available. Was it any wonder that in nine years no fewer than 208,305 of these saloons were built?

After building more than 36,000 cars in the first full year (1969), BMW then set about re-modelling and expanding what they had to offer. It was no coincidence that, in 'marketing-speak', they also richened the mix, gradually pushed up prices, and made more profit too. This was also the period in which specially equipped types for North America were badged as 'Bavaria' models.

From April 1971 there was the 3.0S, now with 180bhp/2,985cc, but still with twin Zenith carburettors, this also being the first BMW to have an optional Borg Warner automatic instead of the usual ZF type. Was this change done on technical grounds, or because ZF was no longer providing the best possible automatic? Memories have now faded, but the fact is that ZF was so distressed by this move that it redoubled its efforts, and would again become the favoured automatic supplier when the succeeding car, the original 7-Series, came along in 1977!

It so happened that the 3.0S, which had power-assisted steering as standard, would only be the company flagship for a matter of months, for yet another derivative, the 3.0Si, appeared in September 1971, this having a 200bhp/2,985cc engine, and Bosch D-Jetronic fuel injection. This, truly, was the year in which BMW embraced Bosch injection as the technology of the future, for the same equipment was also added to the 3-litre coupé *and* the 2002Tii in the same season.

Karmann

By the mid-1960s, BMW was expanding so rapidly that it needed to contract out some of the body building operations for its more specialised cars. Turning to Karmann of Osnabrück, at the other end of West Germany (the train journey was in excess of 400 miles), it used that company's expertise to ease the bottleneck.

Founded as long ago as 1901, Karosseriefabrik Karmann was one of the oldest and most respected coachbuilding firms in Europe, while Wilhelm Karmann had been founded by taking over the coach

manufacturer, Klages.

To their eternal credit, in the 1950s Karmann realised that traditional separate-chassis coachbuilding skills would eventually become redundant, and invested heavily in preparing flexible unit-construction bodyshell production facilities.

Accordingly, when BMW wanted to see the 2000C/2000CS family of coupés built up on the platform of the new-generation car, Karmann was the ideal candidate for that job. After this Karmann also produced the first 6-Series coupés.

Karmann, however, was fiercely independent of *any* major manufacturer, so in the next two decades it also produced Sciroccos and Golf Cabriolets for VW, Escort Cabriolets and Sierra Merkur XR4Tis for Ford, bodies for Porsche, body tooling for the Triumph TR6, and also produced many of its own caravans.

When the time came to start building special coupés in the 1960s, BMW turned to the specialist body manufacturers, Karmann of Osnabrück. It was the beginning of a long and fruitful relationship between the two concerns. (LAT)

As fitted with injection, here was a massively capable autobahn-storming machine, which could reach nearly 130mph, in great comfort, and with uncanny turbine-like smoothness from the engine. Even though the fuel

In 1968, BMW replaced the 2000CS coupé by the six-cylinder 2800CS, and only three years later upgraded that car into this, the 3.0CSi, which had a 200bhp fuel-injected engine. The main cabin and proportions of the 2000CS were carried forward, but the 3.0CSi had a longer wheelbase, a different front-end style, and of course, the powerful new engine. (LAT)

injection was still mechanically controlled and sensed (the L-Jetronic which took over in the late 1970s was electronically controlled), this was a considerable advance over any multi-carburettor installation. It was BMW's good fortune that this precisely-controlled fuel injection system arrived immediately before the Energy Crisis struck, and fuel prices went through the roof.

After two years of stability BMW then made further changes to the range (it was bad luck that larger, heavier and more expensive types appeared just as the Energy Crisis

occurred), and when it introduced the 3.3L BMW watchers only needed to see the title to work out for themselves what had been done, although the engine was a rather odd amalgam.

The six-cylinder engine had been treated to a long-stroke crankshaft – 88.4mm instead of 80mm – which meant that capacity was up to 3,295cc, although BMW retained the twin Zenith carburettor installation, and peak power output was 'only' 190bhp. Automatic transmission was standard, but a manual change was available for any customer who really

The cabin of the 3.0CSi – so typical in every way of the BMWs of the early 1970s. (LAT)

nagged for it! No matter, for the principal USP (unique selling proposition) of this car was its 4in longer wheelbase bodyshell, all that 'stretch' being concentrated in the rear seat area to give more lounging room for the captains of industry who might buy such cars.

From February 1975, the same longer-wheelbase shell was also mated to other existing engines, to produce the 2.8L and the 3.0L. In both cases, the carburetted engines were retained.

Finally, and towards the end of the run of these cars, BMW once again reshuffled its engine specifications. With an eye to rationalisation, and

The rear end of the final series 3.0CSL models featured a massive transverse boot-lid-mounted rear spoiler, and a ring spoiler on the rear of the roof panel itself. The result was increased downforce at high speeds, and a devastating improvement in race-circuit performance. (LAT)

The fully matured version of the 2800CS was the 3.0CSi, which was built from 1971 to 1975, with a 200bhp/3.0-litre engine.

with future models in mind, it changed the 'stroked' engine to 3,210cc (89 x 86mm), fitted Bosch L-Jetronic fuel injection, and therefore created the 3.3Li saloon. This was by far the rarest of all these machines, as it was only in production for six months: all-in-all there were 3,030 3.3L/3.3Lis, of which only 300/400 had fuel injected engines.

These long-wheelbase shells were effectively produced at Munich, by

Not all 3.0CSLs had the aero kit, and not all were stripped out to be as light as possible. This was a more typical example of the type, which was produced in 1972/73. (LAT)

what the industry calls 'knife-and-fork' methods – much hand-carving, stretching and re-welding went on to add those precious four inches, making them very costly to build. Price-conscious historians will want to know that when the long wheelbase cars were introduced in the UK in mid-1974, the 3.3L cost £8,443 compared with £5,301 for the 3.0S – nearly a 60 per cent price hike, equivalent incidentally, to £785 for every extra inch.

Even though sales of these big cars were halved after the Energy Crisis struck so hard – 41,755 were built in 1973, but only 18,820 followed in

1974 – they were still a solid and profitable success. BMW had no doubt that there was a place in their range for such massive and prestigious machines. The last of these cars were produced in Spring 1977, after which the original 7-Series models took over.

2000CS + six-cylinder + 2800CS

As an integral part of BMW's transformation of its up-market image at this time, the engineers also took

Developed specifically for motor racing, the bewinged 3.0CSL 'Batmobile' was a remarkably successful machine. For many years these cars fought a running battle with Ford's equally special Capri RS3100s.

the opportunity to re-engineer the Karmann-built coupés, eventually turning the same basic structure from a 120bhp four-cylinder type to a smooth, desirable, near-140mph machine called the 3.0CSi. Along the way, too, they would allow BMW Motorsport to develop a lightweight, ultra-powerful, bewinged machine called the 3.0CSL which finally became a touring car race winner in 1973 and beyond.

BMW enthusiasts may know that this transformation was neither fast, nor smoothly carried out, for the 2000CS became the 3.0CSi in three stages, and the limited-production 3.0CSL itself was eventually offered with three

The 'Batmobile' version of the 3.0CSL had this fuel-injected 206bhp/3.15-litre version of the celebrated six-cylinder engine. More than 350bhp was available in full race tune. (LAT)

Based on a fully race-prepared 3.0CSL (note the enormous front spoiler, and the vast air intakes on the flanks), Alexander Calder's 'art car' carried a truly striking colour scheme.

different engine sizes, and with an extrovert body kit at the end of the run.

The first big change, seen in the autumn of 1968 (although not yet ready for series production), was that the 2000CS gave way to the 2800CS coupé. Because the 2000CS coupé style had only been on sale for three years, BMW retained the cabin and main structure for the new car, while grafting an entirely new front-end into place. This was made possible by stretching the wheelbase from 100.4in to 103.3in – just enough to make space for the 170bhp/2,788cc six-cylinder engine, along with the new 2500/2800 saloon car's front suspension, and with a four-headlamp nose which had a definite family/style resemblance to that of the big new saloons.

Although this was only a halfway solution to completely new engineering, it looked remarkably integrated. The clientele seemed to forgive the retention of drum brakes from the old 2000CS model, for with a 130mph top speed and acceleration to match, this could certainly spar with Porsche 911s on Germany's autobahns, and have a more comfortable four-seater cabin into the bargain.

The second up-date, to a car called the 3.0CS, followed in April 1971, and although this model looked just the

This profile of an early-1970s 3.0CSi coupé shows the clear family resemblance to the early 2000CS model. Both cars had a 2+2 cabin. (LAT)

same as before, it featured the latest 180bhp/2,985cc engine, a more solidly engineered Getrag manual gearbox, and a Borg Warner (instead of ZF) automatic transmission option, plus the ventilated rear disc brakes which it had always truly warranted.

Even that car was only an interim step, on the way to the final evolution, which came in September 1971, with the launch of the 3.0CSi, the letter 'i' naturally denoting the use of the Bosch fuel-injected engine, and a rousing 200bhp, which delivered a top speed of nearly 140mph.

From 1974, however, BMW went the other way to meet the marketing needs of post-Energy Crisis customers, launching the 2.5CS, which had the 150bhp/2,494cc engine, steel disc wheels and no power-assisted steering, though four-wheel disc brakes were retained. It was really no more than a sop to public opinion, the public virtually ignored it, and only 844 such cars were sold in three years.

All-in-all, however, these were all solidly built, fast, and relatively unstressed sporting coupés, which sold steadily from 1968 to 1977. Karmann, although criticised at times for its failures to keep up the build quality, did a great job in relieving the log-jam at Munich, and manufactured

no fewer than 44,254 of them.

The most astonishing of all these machines, for sure, was the 3.0CSL, a car intended for use in motorsport, and for which the phrase 'homologation special' might have been invented. From 1970, BMW was competing in the European Touring Car Championship (let's not even worry as to how a coupé could even be classed as a 'Touring Car' – but BMW, Ford and Porsche all managed it!), and finding that it was being defeated by limited-production Ford-of-Germany Capri RS2600s, which were by no means as standard as they ought to have been.

The competition, they say, begins when the regulations arrive, and BMW thought that Ford was bending those rules to its own advantage. Concluding that the only way to beat rule-benders was to do the same thing, BMW then evolved the 3.0CSL (and, incidentally, head-hunted Jochen Neerpasch from Ford-of-Germany!) to fight back.

The original 180bhp 3.0CSL (L = *Leicht*, or 'Light' in German) came along in May 1971, kitted out with light-alloy body skin panels, Plexiglas rear quarter windows, a GRP rear bumper, and no front bumper at all – this saving 290lb, but this was just a start.

Next up, from August 1972, the Bosch fuel-injected engine was

Buying 3.0-litre coupés

1. Buy the fastest, best-equipped, and largest-engined version you can afford, for this was a range which improved continually for seven years. Later types were definitely more satisfying than originals.

2. Because of their interim chassis (rear drum brakes, old-type rear suspension), early 2.8-litre types are not recommended. Expect to pay more for a 3.0-litre type.

3. Think carefully before buying a 3.0CSL. Now valued higher than conventional types, they are virtually no faster, and with their aluminium panels they are more vulnerable to minor body damage. The cost of replacement aluminium panels is horrendous.

4. Bodyshell corrosion in all types can be serious. In particular, this can affect the box sections in the inner front wings and front bulkheads, especially close to the windscreen and pillars, and where they meet the sills, which may also have crumbled.

5. The floorpan, the sills, and the splash areas around the rear wheelarch 'boxes' were all vulnerable to corrosion. Karmann, which built these shells, had nothing to be proud of, and these areas may need restoration, especially if the car you choose has been parked outdoors for much of its life.

6. Although the six-cylinder engines are robust, they may suffer camshaft lobe wear from 40,000 miles and upwards. On cars fitted with fuel injection, these are usually reliable, but expensive to rebuild and repair.

7. Six-cylinder heads were originally known for furring up, restricting water flow, and eventually overheating. Be sure that the head on 'your' car is still sound, has never overheated, or needed skimming to restore the gasket face.

8. Manual gearboxes have quite a hard time in these cars, and on higher-mileage cars you can expect the synchromesh to have worn (second and third gears, usually). Worn bearings tell their own story with the noise they emit. Rebuilds are possible, but at a high price.

9. Even on new and low-mileage cars, the suspension was relatively soft. In old age, the damping may have become definitely sloppy. Rebuilds are always possible, and parts are available, but again, this will be costly.

10. Brakes, even the four-disc installation of later cars, may have had a hard time. Look carefully for brake disc cracking, or the contact surfaces being worn or ridged, and be prepared for regular (excessive, some say) pad changes.

11. Electric window lifts in the doors sound luxurious, but have a reputation for slow operation and a tendency to stick. You have to live with this, though – just make sure the doors and 'furniture' themselves are kept clean and dry.

fitted, with a capacity of 3,003cc (a 0.25mm increase in cylinder bore did that trick), this being enough to put the car into the 'over 3-litre class', and then from August 1973 there was the famous 'Batmobile' 3.0CSL,

in which the engine was enlarged still further (to 3,153cc), and where there was a bizarre but effective 'aero' kit which included a transverse rear spoiler on the boot lid, a further ring spoiler on the rear of the roof, and twin vertical strakes on top of the front wings.

Now for the complications! The aero kit could not officially be fitted to German-market cars because of existing protrusion regulations, so it was supplied as a 'kit' in the boot on delivery, while many cars were not actually built with aluminium body skin panels. In the classic era, finding a completely aero-kit equipped 3.0CSL was like searching for the unicorn's horn.

In this respect, BMW were no more or less scrupulous than any of their rivals in claiming how many cars had

been made when far fewer had actually been produced, for it now seems that only 1,039 of all types were produced in four years (instead of 1,000 of each type – and very few of the 3.2-litre types had aero kits)…but Ford, Lancia, Fiat, Alfa Romeo et al. were all cheating just as hard as they could too.

As a road car, the 3.0CSL was distinctly inferior to the 3.0CSi, for it was noisier, less refined, and no faster – but as a motorsport contender it was a real winner. Having defeated Ford in 1973, to win the ETCC title (which was what Neerpasch had planned all along), it then went on to be Europe's most successful touring car for the rest of the decade.

From the end of 1975, this graceful pedigree of coupés was finally retired, replaced by the original 6-Series cars.

3-Series
– the money spinner

During the 1990s, this M3 coupé was the dream car of most enthusiasts from eight to eighty years old. Up front there was an ultra-powerful 3.2-litre six-cylinder engine, and the chassis was very effective too. Later, in the 1990s, cabriolet and four-door saloon types were also made available.

For BMW, the car which would become the icon, the money-spinner, and the car which everyone seemed to aspire to at least once in their lives was born – the 3-Series. Originally produced as a direct replacement for the 02-Series

of 1966–75, it eventually became much more than that.

In the next generation it would be built in larger numbers, in more factories, in different shapes and sizes, than any other BMW. In round figures, once the new century had

First 3-Series (E21)
1975–1982

ENGINE:
Four or six cylinders in line, iron block, alloy heads

Capacity	(4-cyl) 1,573cc/1,766cc/ 1,990cc; (6-cyl) 1,990cc/ 2,315cc
Maximum power	From 75bhp at 5,800rpm to 143bhp at 6,000rpm
Valve gear	Two valves per cylinder, single overhead camshaft
Fuelling	Solex downdraught carburettor, or Bosch K-Jetronic fuel injection

TRANSMISSION:
Four-speed or five-speed manual, all-synchromesh, or optional automatic transmission

SUSPENSION:
Front: Independent, coil springs, MacPherson struts, anti-roll bar, hydraulic telescopic dampers
Rear: Independent, coil springs, semi-trailing arms, anti-roll bar (optional, some models), telescopic dampers

STEERING:
Rack-and-pinion, optional power-assistance on six-cylinder models

BRAKES:
Hydraulic, front disc/rear drum (front disc/rear disc on 323i), servo assistance

WHEELS/TYRES:
Steel disc; 165-13in radial-ply

BODY/CHASSIS:
Unit construction, pressed-steel two-door saloon, and two-door cabriolet

DIMENSIONS:

Length	14ft 3.4in
Width	5ft 3.4in
Height	4ft 6.3in
Wheelbase	8ft 4.9in
Track, front	4ft 5.7in
Track, rear	4ft 6.1in

WEIGHT:
From 2,293lb

PERFORMANCE/ECONOMY:

Max speed	100mph to 126mph
Acceleration	0–60mph from to 12.9 to 8.3sec
Fuel consumption	typically 21–25mpg to 18–22mpg

UK PRICE WHEN NEW incl. tax:
From £2,799

NUMBER BUILT:
1,364,039 (all types)

M3 (and Evolutions)
1986–1991

ENGINE:
Four cylinders, iron block, alloy head

Capacity	2,302cc/2,467cc
Bore x stroke	93.4mm x 84mm 95mm x 87mm
Compression ratio	10.5:1/11.0:1/10.2:1
Maximum power	200bhp at 6,750rpm 215bhp at 6,750rpm 220bhp at 6,750rpm 238bhp at 7,000rpm
Valve gear	Four valves per cylinder, twin overhead camshafts
Fuelling	Bosch Motronic fuel injection

TRANSMISSION:
Five-speed manual, synchromesh on all forward gears

SUSPENSION:
Front: Independent, coil springs, MacPherson struts, anti-roll bar, hydraulic telescopic dampers
Rear: Independent, coil springs, semi-trailing arms, anti-roll bar, hydraulic telescopic dampers

STEERING:
Rack-and-pinion, power-assisted

BRAKES:
Hydraulic, front disc/rear disc, with servo assistance and ABS

WHEELS/TYRES:
Cast alloy disc; 205/55-15in, later 225/45-16in radial-ply

BODY/CHASSIS:
Unit construction, pressed-steel two-door saloon or convertible; with some plastic panelling

DIMENSIONS:

Length	14ft 3.7in
Width	5ft 5.9in
Height	4ft 5.7in
Wheelbase	8ft 4.9in
Track, front	4ft 7.9in
Track, rear	4ft 8.0in

WEIGHT:
2,640lb

PERFORMANCE/ECONOMY;

Max speed	140mph (200bhp)
Acceleration	0–60mph in 7.1sec (200bhp)
Fuel consumption	typically 19–23mpg

UK PRICE WHEN NEW incl. tax:
£22,750

NUMBER BUILT:
17,184 saloons, 786 convertibles, (incl. 505 Evo 1, 501 Evo II, 600 Evo III, Europa Meister 150, Ravaglia/Cecotto 505)

M3 and M3 Evolution (Series E36)
1992–1999

ENGINE:
Six cylinders in line, iron block, alloy head

Capacity	2,990cc/3,201cc
Bore x stroke	86mm x 85.8mm 86.4mm x 91mm
Compression ratio	10.8:1/11.3:1
Maximum power	286bhp at 7,000rpm 295bhp at 7,000rpm 321bhp at 7,400rpm
Valve gear	Four valves per cylinder, twin overhead camshafts
Fuelling	Bosch Motronic (some Siemens) fuel injection

TRANSMISSION:
Five-speed manual (six-speed on Evolution models), all-synchromesh

SUSPENSION:
Front: Independent, coil springs, MacPherson struts, anti-roll bar, telescopic dampers
Rear: Independent, coil springs, multi-link Z-axle, anti-roll bar, telescopic dampers

STEERING:
Rack-and-pinion, power-assisted

BRAKES:
Hydraulic, front disc/rear disc, with servo assistance and ABS

WHEELS/TYRES:
Cast alloy disc; 235/50-17in (Evolution model 225/45-17in front; 245/40-17in rear)

BODY/CHASSIS:
Unit-construction, pressed-steel two-door coupé, convertible, or four-door saloon; some light-alloy panels

DIMENSIONS:

Length	14ft 6.5in
Width	5ft 7.3in
Height	4ft 5.8in
Wheelbase	8ft 10.3in
Track, front	4ft 7.9in
Track, rear	4ft 8.9in

WEIGHT:
3,219lb

PERFORMANCE/ECONOMY:

Max speed	162mph (286bhp)
Acceleration	0–60mph in 5.4sec (286bhp)
Fuel consumption:	typically 25–28mpg

UK PRICE WHEN NEW incl. tax:
M3, £32,450/M3 Evolution £36,550

NUMBER BUILT: 71,242

M3 (E46); (M3 CSL)
2000–2006

ENGINE:
Six cylinders, iron block, alloy head
Capacity	3,245cc
Bore x stroke	87mm x 91mm
Compression ratio	11.5:1
Maximum power	343bhp at 7,900rpm (360bhp at 7,900rpm)
Valve gear	Four valves per cylinder, twin overhead camshafts
Fuelling	Bosch fuel injection

TRANSMISSION:
Six-speed manual, all-synchromesh

SUSPENSION:
Front: Independent, coil springs, MacPherson struts, anti-roll bar, telescopic dampers
Rear: Independent, coil springs, multi-link location, anti-roll bar, telescopic dampers

STEERING:
Rack-and-pinion, power-assisted

BRAKES:
Hydraulic, front disc/rear disc, servo-assisted, with ABS

WHEELS/TYRES:
Alloy disc; 225/45-18in front; 255/40-18in rear radial-ply (235/35-10in front; 265/30-19in rear radial-ply)

BODY/CHASSIS:
Unit-construction, pressed-steel two-door coupé, and convertible (CSKL had aluminium and carbon panels)

DIMENSIONS:
Length	14ft 10.85in
Width	5ft 10.0in
Height	4ft 6.0in
Wheelbase	8ft 11.2in
Track, front	4ft 11.4in
Track, rear	4ft 10.2in

WEIGHT:
3,477lb (3,054lb)

PERFORMANCE/ECONOMY:
Max speed	160mph (161mph)
Acceleration	0–60mph in 4.8sec (4.8sec)
Fuel consumption	typically 20–23mpg (20–23mpg)

UK PRICE WHEN NEW incl. tax:
£38,500 (£58,455)

NUMBER BUILT:
Ongoing

dawned, the existing (fourth-generation) 3-Series was selling at around half-a-million cars a year, and with a fifth-series range already being developed, BMW was hoping for even more in the future.

Along the way, too, BMW also homed in on the obvious sporting potential of such cars, which were of a size and form which might become victorious in many different types of motorsport. And, this time around, they did it properly, for instead of rather apologetically producing a turbocharged machine (such as the 2002 Turbo), they encouraged BMW Motorsport to produce an entire, astonishingly effective, series of M3s, which won World, European and many other national championships.

This is the point at which it makes sense to use BMW's own codes, to delineate one generation of 3-Series from another. The original E21 cars ran from 1975 to 1983 (and there were 1.36 million of them), these being replaced by the second-generation, E30 types from 1982 to 1994 (2.3 million were produced). There was never a clean cut-off between families, as the more specialised models – such as convertibles and 'Touring' (estate car) types – tended to arrive late on the scene, and to leave it even later!

Third generation 3-Series cars were known as E36s (1990–2002), and the first of the fourth-generation cars, dubbed E46, appeared in 1997. Along the way, the E36 provided its platform for BMW's built-in-the-USA Z3 sports car of 1995, and for the radically different, short-tail 3-Series Compact (hatchback).

One had to be patient, well-read and seasoned to know precisely which 3-Series derivatives came first, when, how and where it was marketed! This, in fact, is the point where any BMW marque history has to start taking a company-wide (perhaps global) view, for the figures are almost too complex to summarise.

E21 – the original 3-Series models

By the 1970s, BMW was growing so fast, in so many directions, that there were great difficulties in launching new models without interfering with

Announced in 1975, the original 3-Series, all with two-doors, was an obvious descendant of the long-established 02-Series, although it rode on an entirely fresh platform and suspension units. This is the 320 of 1975, complete with four-cylinder fuel-injected 2-litre engine.

the build-up of others. Accordingly, the six-cylinder cars had appeared in 1968, the first of the 3-litre engines came along in 1971, while the 5-Series arrived in 1972, followed by several 5-Series derivatives in 1973 and 1974.

To seasoned BMW-watchers, therefore, it was no surprise that a long-awaited replacement for the successful 02-Series range did not appear until the 5-Series had been on sale for nearly three years. In fact, the introduction of the new range – the (E21) 3-Series – was in 1975, this being most conveniently in the middle of BMW's annual summer holiday 'shut-down'.

Not merely a reskin, on an old platform, the E21 featured a brand-new platform, and up-dated versions of the now famous overhead-camshaft four-cylinder engine and its related transmission options. What no-one could know at that point, was that BMW was already planning to richen the mix two years further down the road, by adding a new 'small' six-cylinder engine too.

Because BMW had now settled firmly down to a strategic policy of evolution, rather than revolution, in its new-model planning (that 'r' could add hundreds of millions to any

investment decision, and BMW was having none of that!), the pundits could almost have forecast the shape the new car would take, along with the various engine options which might appear in due course!

Although the pundits might have been right in their basic assumptions, they could not have realised just how much extra refinement BMW would build in to the new car. Just as the 5-Series had replaced the 'New Class' by being larger, heavier and smoother than before, so the original 3-Series cars were bigger, roomier in the cabin, more comfortable – and certainly more refined than before.

Compared with the 02-Series, the original 3-Series ran on a 2.5in longer wheelbase, 1.3in wider wheel tracks, and was longer by a full five inches. Most of that extra bulk was concentrated in the cabin area, which made this car more of a comfortable four/five-seater than the 02-Series cars had ever been.

The style itself was really a logical extension of that of the 5-Series, but only with two doors. There was still little attempt to reduce aerodynamic drag (that would come later, after Energy Crisis oil price increases had worked through to petrol prices, and

Continuity? That's what BMW was trying to emphasise here. Furthest from the camera is a late 1920s Dixi, the yellow saloon is a 700 type, and the car closest to the camera is an E30-type 3-Series.

had promoted cost inflation around the world), so the nose still incorporated a lean-forward double-kidney grille, full width intake, and either two or four built-in, but still drag-raising, circular headlamps.

The basic layout was very familiar to all 02-Series drivers (they would, BMW hoped, form the major client base for the new 3-Series) – which is to say that there were four-cylinder single-overhead-camshaft four-cylinder engines up front, manual or automatic transmission choices, MacPherson strut front suspension, and coil spring/semi-trailing arm rear suspension. Disc brakes up front were universal, and for the moment, all models had drum rears.

Technically, the important changes were that BMW had provided a much softer ride/handling package than before (even in Germany, where Herr Typical-Customer drove fast and hard on autobahns), and that these were the first-ever BMWs to have rack-and-pinion steering, with optional power-

Head on: this is the front-end view of the second-generation 3-Series of 1982, with a more wind-cheating nose and four headlamps as seen on all models.

assistance on the larger-engined/more powerful types.

There had even been time for the existing engines to be modified considerably, not only with the latest triple-spherical-segment combustion chamber shapes (the six-cylinder engines had featured this detail for some years already), but with all carburettor-equipped models now having double-barrelled carburettors, more power and lower exhaust emissions. On cars with fuel injection, Bosch know got the nod over Kugelfischer (very shortly, Bosch would become one of BMW's 'favourite sons', and be joined at the hip as far as new developments were concerned), and once again, peak outputs were nudged upwards.

The new cars lined up like this:

Model	Engine (cc)	Power output (bhp at rpm)
316	1,573	90 @ 6,000
318	1,766	98 @ 5,800
320	1,990	109 @ 6,000
320i	1,990	125 @ 5,700

All except the 320i had a double-barrel Solex carburettor.

This, then, was the birth of a phenomenon. Even though it was only available as a two-door saloon, from the day that it was launched the 3-Series became BMW's best-seller, and would remain so for the next 30 years (and five generations!). More than 130,000 such cars were built in the first full year (1976), and this was only the beginning.

No sooner had the new range settled down than big improvements were made. From the summer of 1977,

Although the second-series 3-Series of 1982 looked like no more than a face-lifted original, BMW had changed almost every styling component, including the nose, which was much less thrust-forward than before. Four-door saloon and estate car versions soon followed.

BMW introduced a brand-new 'small' six-cylinder engine coded M60 (see sidebar), which took over from the four-cylinder 2-litre 'fours', and before the end of the year, BMW had also launched the 3-Series cabriolet, whose bodyshells were built by Baur of Stuttgart. Because these bodies were effectively conversions of the saloon (they retained the sturdy steel framing around the side windows, along with a pressed steel brace above and behind the front-seats, they were more 'Targa' than true convertibles.

For the next few years, the 3-Series was such a solid and unspectacular success that it tended to be ignored by the pundits, who found other new BMWs – such as the mid-engined M1, and the second-generation 5-Series – more exciting. The new six-cylinder engined 3-Series cars rapidly settled down, the fuel-injected 323i being a particularly pleasing and versatile family/sports saloon. At the other end of the spectrum, the company

eventually confused almost everybody by rebadging the 1,573cc-engined car as a 315, while the 316 took on a 1,766cc engine instead!

As the 1980s opened, BMW was already selling more than 200,000 3-Series cars every year – which was half of all BMW's annual motor car output – but there was burning ambition at Munich to do more. From the end of 1982, therefore, a new-generation 3-Series would take over.

E30 – the second-generation, and a real range at last

I know of at least two experienced motoring writers who opened BMW's press information pack for the second-generation 3-Series, and blurted out: 'They've sent the wrong pictures! These are for the old car…'

But there was no mistake. Although the second-generation 3-Series (E30 in BMW-speak) looked astonishingly like the E21 types which it was to supersede, there were many differences in detail. Not only that, but this was the first 3-Series for which the company planned several different derivatives – not only a cabriolet, but a four-door saloon, an estate car, a rather different cabriolet of their own, a fiercely successful motorsport version, and even one with four-wheel-drive transmission.

In those days, not as much was made of these things as is done now, but hindsight shows that the new E30 was built on only a lightly-modified version of the E21's platform, while

In 1985, BMW finally announced their own 3-Series cabriolet (previous drop-tops had been by Baur of Stuttgart). It did not have an integral roll-hoop over the passenger compartment. This was the 325i version, complete with 2.5-litre six-cylinder engine.

even some of the inner panels of the superstructure were the same. As one seasoned observer commented at the time: 'If BMW's new 3-Series cars don't look much different from their predecessors it's because they're not meant to be. Call it Germanic conservatism if you like – aerodynamic styling and the current preoccupation with Cd factors may be fashionable, say the Bavarians, but they have no intention of allowing fashion to interfere with the good looks, that sporting, youthful image, of their cars.'

Although there were visual differences between new and old, one really had to stand the two cars side-by-side to see what, and where, they were. All cars now had a smoother, less 'aggressive' nose, with four headlamps, the bonnet was longer and more sloping, while the tail/boot area was higher and slightly more boxy. Flusher-fitting glass all round, and other minor tweaks helped bring the Cd down to 0.38, not sensational by contemporary Audi and Ford (Sierra) standards, but creditable enough. The important advances, though, could not be seen – overall weights had been trimmed, maximum payloads were up (by an average of 65lb), and now there was a six-year anti-corrosion warranty on the structures.

Under the skin, however, everything looked familiar, with four- and six-cylinder engines spanning 90bhp to 139bhp (all but the 316 now having Bosch L-Jetronic fuel injection), four- or five-speed manual

A four-wheel-drive version of the 325i, the 325iX, was launched in the mid-1980s. Intended only for sale in niche markets where winter motoring was often on snow and ice, it had impressive traction. Seeking such weather conditions to launch the car in high-summer, BMW found a high-altitude ski resort in Austria to demonstrate the transmission.

gearboxes, and optional automatic transmission. The basic layout of the independent suspension, and the rack-and-pinion steering, was the same as before, but at the rear the splay angle of the semi-trailing arms had been reduced from 20° to 15°, the coil springs and dampers had been separated (to allow a larger boot space to be provided), and disc brakes had been standardised on all four wheels.

Although BMW hoped that the media would ignore the change to the rear suspension geometry, there was no chance of that. When they were being cornered hard, with a suspension allowing significant rear wheel camber changes, previous models had built up a reputation for sudden rear-end breakaway: the change from E21 to E30 was made to reduce this – although it could not eliminate the habit and only another major change – to the use of the 'Z-axle' on E36 types in the 1990s – would do that.

Over the next four years, BMW expanded this range, launching the four-door saloon derivatives at the end of 1983, more power (150bhp) for the 323i, and announcing the 122bhp/2,693cc 325e model specifically for low-emissions markets. From mid-1985, the 323i gave way to the 170bhp/2,494cc 325i, while the very first 3-Series diesel, the six-cylinder/86bhp /2,443cc appeared at the same time. The first true BMW estate car – a conventional five-door arrangement which the company preferred to be known as a 'Touring' – arrived in the spring of 1988.

Looking back from the early-2000s, where modern turbo diesels often deliver better operating economy *and* higher performance than their petrol-powered equivalents, it's easy to see why 1980s diesels were scorned for their lack of almost everything – power, refinement and low emissions. Not surprisingly, the 324d was not a success, but as an early Steyr-built

BMW power unit it was very significant.

The three truly important launches, however, were the arrival of the 325iX (BMW's first-ever four-wheel-drive private car), the BMW-built cabriolet (a *complete* cabriolet, built in-house, in place of the earlier Baur-bodied model) – and the M3!

M3 – the original race winner

Previewed at the Frankfurt Motor Show in September 1985, but not available until mid-1986, the aggressive-looking M3 was a purpose-built 'homologation special' saloon,

Previewed in 1985, and on sale from 1986, the original M3 was one of the most successful BMW 'homologation specials' of all time. In road-car form it produced 200bhp, and race-prepared versions were World Touring Car Championship contenders for some years.

Driving 'works'-sponsored M3s like this, Roberto Ravaglia became World Touring Car Champion in 1987. Here he is on his way to victory at Jarama, Spain, early in the season.

which BMW Motorsport wanted to be successful in Touring Car racing, not only in Germany and in Europe, but all over the world. History shows that it succeeded, and if Ford's mighty turbocharged Sierra RS500 Cosworth had not also been on the same scene, it might have been truly dominant.

Although it looked superficially like any other two-door 3-Series saloon, the M3 was different in every detail. Not only was it the first-ever 3-Series car to use a four-valve/twin-cam engine, but the only one to use flared front and rear wheelarches, and it also had a different roof/rear window/boot-lid profile to improve the aerodynamic performance. The suspension layout was basically like that of other

3-Series types, but with wider wheels, larger tyres and firmed-up suspension, along with power-assisted steering.

The real breakthrough was with the engine however. Complete with four valves per cylinder, and twin overhead camshafts (with the bottom end bored and stroked to 93.4 x 84mm, 2,302cc), this was a distant relation to the six-cylinder variety used in early M1s and M635 and M5 types, and also to the turbocharged F1 engine of the period. Even in standard, road-going form, this produced a hard and purposeful 200bhp at 6,750rpm, but when fully prepared for motor racing it could push out well over 300bhp, and deliver staggering performance.

Not only that, but the race cars were usually extremely reliable. This figure might have been dwarfed by the 500bhp-plus produced by Ford Sierra RS500 Cosworths, but when they

sometimes blew up in long-distance races, the M3s invariably went hammering on to win.

Although BMW only had to build 5,000 cars to achieve motorsport 'homologation' (approval to compete), the M3 found such a ready market that more than 17,000 cars would be produced in five years. No fewer than 6,396 saloons were assembled in 1987, the year in which the M3s shone so brightly in the World Touring Car Championship.

The original road-going M3, in fact, was a hard-riding but characterful machine, which made every ordinary driver feel fast, and every fast driver unbeatable. Customers loved the noise it made, how it performed, and of course they loved its hewn-from-the-solid build quality. It was no wonder, therefore, that a convertible version appeared in May 1988 (only 786 such cars were ever produced, making them real latter-day collectors' pieces).

In an attempt to keep the M3 competitive in Touring Car racing, no fewer than five special-edition types were eventually put on sale, the fiercest of which being the 'Sport Evolution III' (built only in the winter of 1989/90), which had a 238bhp/2,467cc engine.

By 1991, though, time had marched on so rapidly that the mainstream E30 range had been overtaken by the new-generation E36 3-Series cars, so a new-type M3 had to follow in 1992.

E36 – third-generation 3-series – yet more variety

This time around, and starting in December 1990, there was much change between old and new types. Except for using developed versions of existing engines and transmissions, every aspect of the third-generation (E36) 3-Series was new. Not only that, but by the time the range had been completely fleshed out, there were four-door saloons, fixed-head coupés, estates (Tourings), convertibles, M3s – and a new and rather curious hybrid known as the Compact.

This was the most ambitious, and as it transpired, the most successful, new-model programme that BMW had ever attempted. By the end of the 1990s, 3-Series types would be in production on several sites in Germany, along with manufacture in South Africa and, for a time, assembly from German-supplied kits in the brand-new Spartanburg plant in the USA. By the end of the century, BMW would be making close to half-a-million 3-Series of one type or another every year; all in all, 2,745,773 cars of all types were built.

Except for the use of familiar engines and transmissions, there was much new compared with the old. E36 was evolved on an all-new platform, with an all-new style, a new type of Z-axle rear suspension, and new targets

for the derivatives which eventually appeared. Engines would become larger and more powerful, new generations of diesel engines would become both powerful and creditable with the customers, and BMW somehow convinced the world that its rather awkward, truncated, Compact hatchback was what they had wanted all along…

Compared with the E30, the third-generation E36 was larger, smoother and more versatile. Running on a 106.3in wheelbase, with an overall length of 174.5in, it followed industry trends in being that important bit larger, bulkier, and more roomy in the cabin than its predecessor. Inevitably, too, it was heavier – the four-door saloon weighing in at 2,492lb.

All cars had MacPherson strut front suspension, and servo-assisted four-wheel disc brakes with ABS anti-lock, but technically, the real novelty here was in the independent rear suspension. This was the first 3-Series BMW to use what the company proudly named its 'Z-axle' layout. No

matter how well-developed, or carefully controlled, the old semi-trailing arm layout (it dated from the 1950s) had never been totally satisfactory. In its place, BMW had developed a complex multi-link layout, which had been extensively proved in the public eye, on the limited-production Z1 sports car, and later on the 8-Series coupé, which provided excellent grip and roadholding in all conditions.

The style of the new car was much more wind-cheating than before – on all types there was a smoothly detailed nose with faired-in headlamps and higher but shorter proportions around the tail. Four-door saloons came first, a sleek two-door coupé (almost all exterior panels

This group shot shows how shapes evolve only slowly under BMW – clockwise from top left are a mid-1990s 3-Series Compact, an 02-Series 2002, an E36 generation four-door saloon of the mid-1990s, the red car (front) is the second-series 3-Series, and in the centre is an original-type 3-Series model.

BMW turbo F1 engine

For more than a decade in the 1960s and '70s, F1 racing was dominated by Ford's ubiquitous Cosworth DFV V8 engine – until Renault reread the regulations, decided that they might be able to produce a powerful turbocharged 1.5-litre engine, and eventually developed a reliable race-winning unit. Inspired by this, BMW Motorsport then set out to beat the world with their own engineering, choosing to use the famous and durable 1.5-litre block of the four-cylinder 3-Series and 5-Series types, to develop a new 16-valve cylinder head, and to turbocharge it. Paul Rosche led the design team, but it was sheer, dogged, Teutonic application which eventually produced a magnificent power unit.

BMW's turbo four-cylinder race-engine experience stretched back to the 1960s, but the F1 project of the late 1970s was a new venture. Work began in 1980, an existing F2-type cylinder head was chosen, and by early 1981 (when Brabham first fitted the engines to their chassis) they were producing 570bhp.

This is Nelson Piquet in a Brabham-BMW BT52, on his way to becoming World Champion in 1983.

Much more power was in prospect, once BMW discovered that it was well-used, high-mileage cylinder blocks which were the strongest (so these were used). The first race win came in 1982, and Nelson Piquet won the F1 World Championship for Brabham in 1983. By the following year the engines produced upwards of 850bhp in qualifying trim.

Brabham, Arrows and eventually Benetton used these ever-developing engines with distinction, although by 1986, the latest 'lay-down' installation (where the engines were canted well over to one side) was not at all satisfactory. In 1985, engines regularly started Grands Prix with more than 1,000bhp, and at one stage, BMW is reported to have seen a flash reading of 1,400bhp on a test bed! However, it could not be sure, as its test beds were not calibrated up to such a colossal figure.

When revised F1 regulations hobbled the turbocharged engines, before banning them altogether, BMW withdrew from direct support, and handed over their stock of power units to Heini Mader's tuning shop in Switzerland. It had been a fascinating period, which was of huge marketing value to the BMW marque.

The third-generation 3-Series range, coded E36 within BMW, was introduced in 1989–90 and was slightly larger and faster than the older types, and was equipped with the new-fangled Z-axle independent rear suspension system.

therefore, was best advised to sit down with brochures, a jotting pad, and that stiff drink, before coming to any decision, as the permutations seemed to be endless.

By this time, indeed, the 3-Series had become conventional, mundane even, by its own very high standards. Customers knew what sort of car they might buy, that it would need loading up with costly extras to reach an acceptable level of equipment, that it was costly, that it was now a car to be found on every road, every motorway, and in every car park – but that it would also deliver whatever was promised in the brochures.

Except for the magnificent M3 model (described below) there was, however, an extra model, which broke BMW's own mould. Available in 1994, there was also the Compact,

being different from those of the saloon) and a two-door cabriolet following in late 1992, and an estate (Touring) version in 1994.

Before this range was fully developed in the mid-1990s, no fewer than eight different petrol engines, three M3-type petrol engines, and three high-performance turbo-diesel had been made available, along with five-speed manual gearboxes (all cars), four- or five-speed automatic transmissions (depending on the model), and a huge list of options.

The least powerful 316i used a 100bhp/1.6-litre four-cylinder engine, the 328i a 193bhp/2,793cc six-cylinder engine (BMW phased in aluminium cylinder blocks from the mid-1990s), while diesel power spanned 90bhp/1,665cc/4-cyl to 143bhp/2,498cc/6-cyl. Any customer,

Although the E36-type of 3-Series coupé looked rather like a two-door version of the saloon, in fact almost every exterior panel was different. The 1990s-generation M3 was also based on this car.

effectively BMW's first-ever hatchback (if, that is, we ignore the original 02-Series Touring of the early 1970s).

In some ways this was an oddity, for although it still ran on the 106.3in wheelbase and was a full four-seater, the rear of the chassis/platform was re-jigged to accept the older, less space-occupying, semi-trailing-arm suspension of the E30. From the nose to the screen, the Compact was like other E36s, but aft of that there were two passenger doors, a much shortened tail, and a large sloping hatchback: the rear seats, of course, could be folded forward to increase stowage space.

In many ways, the Compact was always meant to be the 'entry-level' E36, which explains why all but a very few cars had four-cylinder petrol engines of 102–140bhp, or a 90bhp/1,665cc diesel. As an indulgence though, BMW also sold a few 170bhp/2,494cc/six-cylinder-engined cars too.

Because it didn't handle as well as the Z-axle cars, because it didn't look as good as other types, and because it was never intended to be a performance car, the Compact was respected, rather than enjoyed – yet by 2000, when it was displaced by a

new-generation type, more than 400,000 had been sold.

Profitable? For sure – and BMW was proud of that. And there was more, because BMW also used the unique new-plus-old platform of the Compact as the basis of its Z3 sports car (described in Chapter 13).

The M3 and six-cylinders – a formidable combo

There was never any doubt that a second-generation M3 would follow the original – but few of us could have forecast that it would use phenomenally powerful six-cylinder engines, and have such mind-expanding performance. Previewed in October 1992 as a two-door coupé, but with cabriolet and saloon types following up in the next two years, the latest M3 was nothing short of phenomenal. This time around, it was not intended for use in motorsport, but merely to provide wealthy customers with one of the fastest and most assured cars on the world's highways.

Another departure for BMW – the original 3-Series Compact model. With a shorter tail than other 3-Series types of the period, and with the old-style semi-trailing link rear suspension, this hatchback model was a new entry-level BMW.

Although the latest machine was certainly a Supercar, it was smoother in overall character and, unless one knew where to look, was visually much closer to standard than might be expected. Like the brutal early M3s, some aerodynamic improvements had been made, but there were no flared wheelarches, and no big rear spoiler either.

This time, though, there was lots of smooth, high-revving, but very torquey and well-tamed, six-cylinder power, with roadholding and capability to match. The first E36 M3s had 286bhp from 2,990cc, but from late 1995 the 'M3 Evolution' was even fiercer, with 321bhp/3,201cc (which some pundits suggested was really 'half of a McLaren F1 V12 engine').

Because BMW had bowed to environmental pressure over maximum speeds, the M3 was electronically limited to 155mph (250kph), but of course, engineers and enthusiasts soon discovered ways

A new six-cylinder engine

In the 1960s and '70s BMW had relied on one or other of the various four-cylinder and six-cylinder engines which had all evolved from their original unit. Nearly twenty years on – in late 1977 – the company finally launched a new-generation power unit. This was the silky overhead-cam six-cylinder unit which started life at 1,990cc, and was ultimately stretched (for the M3 of the 1990s) to 3.2 litres. Compared with the early 'six', the difference was that the overhead camshaft was now driven by an

internally cogged belt instead of a duplex chain.

By the early 21st century, this engine had not only grown larger, but had been redesigned in almost every detail – with twin overhead camshafts, four valves per cylinder, an aluminium cylinder block, fuel injection, and (very far removed from the original) was available in diesel form too.

In the beginning, the new type had a bore of 80mm and a very short stroke of 66mm. Cast in aluminium alloy, the single-overhead-cam

cylinder head incorporated two lines of valves, both operated by rockers from the camshaft, which was itself driven by a cogged belt from the nose of the cast-iron crankshaft.

But, how things change. In 1977, and fuelled by a single Solex carburettor, the 1,990cc engine produced just 122bhp. By the 2000s, almost every detail, and the casting material, had changed, so that the M3 had Bosch fuel injection, four valves per cylinder, measured 3,245cc and produced up to 360bhp.

of de-coupling that limit, and found that more than 170mph was occasionally possible, even if the manufacturer's warranty was then no longer valid.

From 1998, BMW gradually introduced a range of new-type fourth-generation 3-Series cars, designated E46. This was the four-door saloon version, the original and by far the best selling of all the derivatives.

This was such a monstrously capable machine, not only very fast but extremely refined, that there was a significant demand for open-top and saloon car versions, which BMW was happy to satisfy. By the mid-1990s, BMW was building nearly 12,000 M3 models every year, and rave notices continued to flood in from all round the world. BMW even took the trouble to 'de-tox' the engine

for use in the USA, and although such M3s only had 243bhp they were still staggeringly competent machines. As ever, the company used the high-performance cars to test public reaction to new features – on the M3 Evolution of 1996 it was possible to order the SMG (Sequential M Gearbox).

Time, however, once again caught up with the 3-Series, for a fourth-generation car was launched in 1997.

E46 – the fourth-generation 3-Series

It would be far too easy to be blasé about yet another generation of 3-Series – 'OK, time for another generation to be launched…time to tweak the style a little…' – but BMW was never complacent about its products, or its clientele. When the time came for the E46 to gradually replace the E36 types, it would take three years to do the job, progressively, carefully, and altogether successfully.

Because this was a very early example of the design studio's work under Chris Bangle's control, it was still a conventional shape, slightly more rounded than the E36, but still distinctive. Thousands of hours in company wind-tunnels had allowed the drag coefficient to be forced down to no more than 0.27 – which was little more than half that of the craggy BMWs of the 1950s and early '60s.

As one might have expected, the new car (E46) was that little bit larger, more roomy, and faster than the old car had been. Longer and wider by 1.5in, with a 1in longer wheelbase, it was also slightly heavier. Clearly the need to include air bags, full air conditioning, and much more detail equipment, tended to push up the weight, so BMW had adopted aluminium (instead of steel) for many suspension components in an attempt to stem the increases.

The overall result was a marginally, but definitely, more capacious car which fitted into only a slightly larger envelope. Maybe it might have been even larger, except that this would have put the new car very close to 5-Series territory, and that would never do…

In truth, although BMW's marketing specialists had insisted on the change, the old E36 was not nearly ready for retirement, but because so very many of them had already been sold (in round figures, up to about three million) BMW thought it was time for a change.

This was the time when one of the more excitable British magazines used to publish thumbnail character sketches of cars on the market, and in its 'Against' column, summarised the 3-Series as 'Every man and his dog has one…' (As a 328i owner, was the author of this book that one man, or his dog? No matter – for he was not complaining.)

Once again, here was a range of BMWs which seemed to offer something for everyone. In three years of phased launching there would be four-door saloons, coupés, cabriolets, estate cars, a new-type Compact, and of course a yet-more-formidable M3. And, in due course, but not until 2002, the Z4 sports car would go on sale in North America.

It seems so callous to describe this new car as 'just another 3-Series', especially as up to half-a-million such cars would be manufactured every year. Yet this is exactly what it was – BMW's bread-and-butter, in more ways than one, backed by major new factories all round the world.

The days of building BMWs in one factory were, of course, long gone. We soon learned that seemingly identical E46s would be assembled in Munich, Dingolfing (the ex-Glas factory, much re-developed), Regensburg,

E46 3-Series Tourings (estates) were produced with a whole variety of engines in the late 1990s/early 2000s.

Spartanburg (USA) and Rosslyn in South Africa, with CKD kits being supplied to at least ten other locations around the world. More and more modernised petrol and 'common-rail' diesel engines would flood out of the Steyr factory in Austria, and the brand-new Hams Hall factory in England.

It would be nearly impossible to list every nuance of E46 engineering, for here was another all-can-do BMW. By the time the mainstream range was fully matured, there would be five different petrol engines, four immensely capable turbo-diesels, and two different tunes for the mighty M3. Other, less advanced, less modern engines had already disappeared and things had changed so much that even the Compact had five of those engine options. Five-speed manual and automatic transmissions were freely available on all types.

Because the second-generation Compact, which appeared in March

E46-type M3s of the early 2000s not only had 343bhp engines, but startlingly styled wheels and these functional air outlets in the flanks, to make their marketing point. Except for the contemporary M5, they were the most desirable BMWs of all.

2001, now had the more sophisticated Z-axle rear suspension, it was an altogether more appealing car, although its modified front end style (the four headlamps were enclosed in separate mountings) and the truncated tail/hatchback layout were still a turn-off for some traditional BMW customers. The company rode all the punches, sweetly reminded the pundits of the new specification *and* the increased load space in the tail, and that the Compact was to be available with modern and more effective diesel-engine options, thus demand increased still further.

M3 for the 2000s – approaching perfection?

At the turn of the century, one of BMW's biggest challenges was to make the E46-type M3 a better car than the stupendous E36 variety of 1992–1999. Rumours going around in the months before the new car was introduced in February 2000 suggested that several radical improvements might appear, but in

the event the pundits were mainly disappointed.

As expected, apart from the aggressive front lower spoiler, mild flaring of front and rear wheelarches and the cooling vents in the front wings, along with not two, but four exhaust outlet pipes, the new car was visually very similar to all other E46 types. Originally, only a two-door coupé was made available, but a cabriolet followed in 2001.

Although BMW admitted to dabbling with the idea of making this M3 a V8-engined car ('In fact we got as far as constructing prototypes', said Adolf Prommesberger, head of M-Division), in the end the team opted for the final (and this time it really *was* final) stretch of the six-cylinder engine. By pushing out the cylinder bore from 86.4mm to 87.0mm, the capacity went up from 3,201cc to 3,245cc. This allowed peak power to rise to 343bhp at a spine-tingling 7,900rpm.

The miracle is that the engine had been capable of such a persistent 'stretch'. When this power unit had made its original, rather inoffensive, debut in 1977, it was smaller, less powerful, and only had a single-cam cylinder head. Here is the comparison:

BMW Model	Engine size (cc)	Bore x stroke (mm)	Power output (bhp/rpm)
1977 320-6	1,990	80 x 66	122/6,000
2000 M3	3,245	87 x 91	343/7,900

For enthusiastic BMW watchers, the rest of the chassis was quite predictably arranged. Behind the engine was the six-speed Getrag gearbox of the previous M3 evolution (with an optional SMG change), the road wheels were now of 18in diameter (8J at the front, 9J at the rear), the suspension was subtly stiffer than mainstream E46s, and the cabin carried unmistakeable family resemblance to the latest of the bigger M5 types (see Chapter 8).

This was, of course, a fearsomely capable performer. Even in 'standard' form (the lightweight CSL was still to come, in 2003!), the M3 could rush up to an electronically-limited 155mph,

Buying 3-Series – first and second generations

1. Don't be in any hurry to buy, for there is a lot of choice: good, average and frankly grotty. More than 1.4 million original-type, and 2.0 million second-generation 3-Series types were built. Hundreds of thousands survive to this day, with a choice of engines and body styles. Think carefully whether you want a staid runabout (in which case go for a 316) or a high-performance machine (six-cylinder, up to 325i). You can also have saloons, cabriolets (quite rare) or estate cars (called Tourings). Cabriolets came in two varieties, originally by Baur, but from the mid-1980s by BMW themselves – the latter being just as rigid, and with a fully retractable top.

2. Six-cylinder types (320i, 323i, 325i), from the late 1970s are smooth, other four-cylinder types are more work-a-day. Except for the early 320i, which has its fans, the 316 and 318 types are neither as well-liked, nor as valuable as classics; they are, however, simpler to maintain.

3. The M3, built only from 1986, is the most racey of all. Visually similar to other 3-Series two-door saloons, it is very different in every way. Left-hand drive only, it has different body panels (front and rear wings, roof and rear quarters), a complex 16-valve engine, and a special five-speed gearbox. Although the most revered early-type 3-Series road-burner, it is rare, expensive to run, and equally

expensive to restore. Many cars have been thrashed and over-driven at 'track-days', so beware.

4. On all types, particularly those with more power, look out for oversteering handling, and lack of rear-wheel grip in wet conditions. There is no solution – the problem relates to rear suspension geometry – so it always helps to have the best possible tyres. Caveat emptor – a significant number of 3-Series, even well-loved survivors, have suffered accident damage due to spins or off-road excursions at one time or another.

5. Worn suspension bushes and mounts, particularly at the rear, can significantly harm a car's road-holding, steering and precision. Don't be too depressed if you experience this, for all such mountings are available – and restoration is a good investment.

6. Bodyshell rust can occur in all the conventional places. On these 3-Series, look for corrosion, or bodged-up repairs around the rear suspension sub-frame, coil spring and shock absorber mounting points. This is most likely to be more severe on high-powered types, because of increased torque reversals through all those points.

7. Engines may have had a hard life, and their smoky behaviour may

forecast worn piston rings, valve guides and seals. Aluminium cylinder heads soon overheated and distorted if water levels were allowed to fall – this being known to happen in the early years. Suspect any engine which appears to use (or lose) water, or which has any form of contamination in the cooling water itself.

8. Relatively early camshaft wear was well-known on six-cylinder engines. When shopping for a car, be sure that the performance is well up to what the archives tell you it should be. Change and replacement is possible, of course, but is not cheap.

9. These are costly cars to maintain. Third or fourth owners might have penny-pinched, or not used franchised or specialist dealer help. Suspect any car which does not have an impeccable, or comprehensive, service record. In particular, on six-cylinder cars be sure that the camshaft drive belt has been changed at recommended intervals.

10. Styling and equipment is a matter of choice. However, you will have to pay extra for more recent (late 1980s) types with six-cylinder engines, and any car with five-speed transmission. Alloy wheels (standard on top-of-the-range cars and the M3) were always desirable as options, as is the boot-mounted tool-kit, if still complete.

and make mincemeat of almost every other car on the road.

BMW then astounded everyone by launching the very limited-production M3 CSL (only sold as a two-door coupé), where around 400lb had been trimmed off the overall weight by discarding some so-called 'luxury' equipment adding carbon and other exotic composites in place of steel and aluminium, plus 19in wheels as

standard. Somehow, too, the engine had been slightly massaged to produce 360bhp, and although the top speed was still electronically limited, the entire package felt harder and more purposeful than ever. This, by any standards, was the nearest that BMW could provide to full-on sports car behaviour and character, and in the UK it was put on offer at £58,455, a staggering price for such a car.

All in all, in the early 2000s, it was no wonder that BMW could sell more than that (planned-for) half-a-million 3-Series cars every year. By 2003, though, the range was already fully mature, and rumours had already begun to spread about a replacement. In the winter of 2004–2005, indeed, the first of that fifth-generation range, coded E60, would go on sale.

5-Series – *a vast and successful family*

The M5 of 1999 often caused motoring writers to go into orgasmic detail, for many people found it one of the most complete and most capable of all BMW models ever produced. With a 400bhp/5.0-litre V8 engine, it provided almost limitless performance – really more than could ever be used on the public highway.

When the first of the mighty 5-Series cars was launched in 1972 it signalled another stage in BMW's expansion. Not only was it the very first BMW to carry a 'number' title (the '02-Series' only picked up that title retrospectively, many years later, while the first of the 3-Series cars appeared in 1975), but it was the first new BMW to be assembled at the much-modernised and expanded former Glas factory at Dingolfing.

The new 5-Series was a direct replacement for the original company-saving 'New Class' model range, which had been on sale for the previous ten years. Like that range, the 5-Series was meant to be an infinitely versatile four-door saloon into which all manner of engines, trim and mechanical packs could be installed. On this occasion, the big breakthrough was that the engine bay was so shaped that BMW could not only use the familiar four-cylinder engines, but could also squeeze into the same space the latest straight-six overhead camshaft power units.

Original 5-Series (E12)
1972–1981

ENGINE:
Four cylinders in line, iron block, alloy head/six cylinders in line, iron block, alloy head

Capacity	1,766cc/1,990cc (4-cyl), 1,990cc/2,494cc, 2,693cc, 2,788cc (6-cyl)
Maximum power	90bhp at 5,500rpm to 184bhp at 5,800rpm
Valve gear	Two valves per cylinder, single overhead camshaft
Fuelling	One downdraught Solex carburettor/two downdraught Solex carburettors/Bosch fuel injection

TRANSMISSION:
Four-speed manual, all-synchromesh/five-speed manual, all-synchromesh; optional automatic transmission

SUSPENSION:
Front: Independent, coil springs, MacPherson struts, anti-roll bar, telescopic dampers
Rear: Independent, coil springs, anti-roll bar, telescopic dampers

STEERING:
Worm-and-roller (with power assistance, most models)

BRAKES:
Hydraulic, front disc/rear drum, or front disc/rear disc

WHEELS/TYRES:
Steel disc; 175-14in radial-ply

BODY/CHASSIS:
Unit constriction, pressed-steel four-door saloon

DIMENSIONS:

Length	15ft 1.9in
Width	5ft 6.5in
Height	4ft 8.1in
Wheelbase	8ft 7.8in
Track, front	4ft 7.4in
Track, rear	4ft 8.8in

WEIGHT:
2,778lb–3,197lb

PERFORMANCE/ECONOMY:

Max speed	101–129mph depending on engine fitted
Acceleration	0–60mph in 14.5–8.7sec, depending on engine fitted
Fuel consumption	typically 21–24mpg to 18–21mpg depending on engine fitted

UK PRICE WHEN NEW incl. tax:
From £3,199

NUMBER BUILT:
699,094

M5 (E34) (3.8-litre in brackets)
1988–1995

ENGINE:
Six cylinder in line, iron block, alloy head

Capacity	3,535cc (3,795cc)
Bore x stroke	93.4mm x 86mm (94.6mm x 90mm)
Compression ratio	10.0:1 (10.5:1)
Maximum power	315bhp at 6,900rpm (340bhp at 6,900rpm)
Valve gear	Four valves per cylinder, twin overhead camshafts
Fuelling	Bosch Motronic fuel injection

TRANSMISSION:
Five-speed manual, all-synchromesh (six-speed from mid-1994)

SUSPENSION:
Front: Independent, coil springs, MacPherson struts, anti-roll bar, hydraulic dampers
Rear: Independent, coil springs, semi-trailing arms, anti-roll bar, hydraulic telescopic dampers

STEERING:
Recirculating ball, with power assistance

BRAKES:
Hydraulic, front disc/rear disc, with servo assistance and ABS

WHEELS/TYRES:
Alloy disc; 235/45-17in radial-ply

BODY/CHASSIS:
Unit-construction, pressed-steel four-door saloon

DIMENSIONS:

Length	15ft 6in
Width	5ft 8.9in
Height	4ft 6.8in
Wheelbase	9ft 0.7in
Track, front	4ft 10in
Track, rear	4ft 10.9in

WEIGHT:
3,682lb (3,801lb)

PERFORMANCE/ECONOMY:

Max speed	157mph (170mph)
Acceleration	0–60mph in 6.4sec (6.4sec)
Fuel consumption	typically 18–20mpg (16–19mpg)

UK PRICE WHEN NEW incl. tax:
£43,465 (£48,950)

NUMBER BUILT:
12,249 (3,905 with 3.8-litre engines)

The vast majority of 5-Series cars would be four-door saloons, with the only alternative style ever put on sale being the five-door Touring (estate car), which arrived on the third-generation platform in 1991. As with all BMW saloons of this period, each generation had a long and very successful life (nearly three-quarters of a million of the first type were produced), each new generation growing ever so slightly larger, more capable, and faster than before, with each one setting standards that most of the world struggled to match.

Even at this stage, it is instructive to see just how much the 5-Series benefited from 'technology creep' in its first 30 years. In 1972, the very first (E12) type 5-Series started life with a 115bhp/1,990cc four-cylinder engine; by the early 2000s the 'entry level' fifth-generation car had started with a 177bhp/2,497cc engine. The most powerful early-type 5-Series engine was the 176bhp/2,788cc version, whereas in the 2000s this had progressed to 507bhp (and a mighty 4,999cc V10!) from the latest M5.

Yet, over the years, the 5-Series has rarely been seen as being at the cutting edge of technology – not even at the cutting-edge of BMW technology – for the company has usually preferred to offer the best interpretation of what they already knew, carefully developed and beautifully built, but all put together in a very integrated manner.

And so it was with the original 5-Series cars, which appeared in

The 5-Series took over from the last of the long-established 'New Class' saloons, and soon built up its own pedigree. Early 5-Series cars were either 520s (with a carburettor-equipped engine) or 520is (with fuel injection).

The original 5-Series appeared in 1972, and was a rather angular but undoubtedly capable machine. Along with the parallel 3-Series family, it became one of the cornerstones of BMW's output in the next decade. (LAT)

September 1972, in the same month that BMW's home city, Munich, hosted the Olympic Games, and in the same year that BMW's futuristic 'four-cylinder' HQ building took shape outside the older, historic, factory at Milbertshofen in central Munich.

Except in their style (and, of course, in their title), by 1970s standards these were utterly predictable BMWs – which, as it happened, made them all the more saleable. In their basic layout – front engine/rear drive, overhead-camshaft engines, independent rear suspension by semi-trailing links – they were close relatives of the '02-Series' which carried on for another three years, and of the 'New Class' cars which they displaced. Some observers called the new cars 'evolutionary', others 'conventional' but, mercifully, no-one seemed to call them boring.

Larger, smoother and altogether more modern than the 'New Class', the 5-Series was what the advertising industry might call an 'aspirational car' for the middle classes, as it offered more – that important bit more – than ever before. Although the first cars carried 1,990cc four-cylinder engines, and the related transmissions, which had powered the definitive 'New Class' cars, every other aspect was new – a brand-new

platform, new four-door saloon style, and new chassis engineering. It was only when the media got behind the wheel that they also realised that BMW had softened up the cars' character quite considerably, this time going for comfort and luxury rather than sporty handling and performance.

There was more space, too. Compared with the 'New Class' cars, the wheelbase was up by 3.4in, the wheel tracks by 3.0in, the overall length by 4.7in – and the unladen weight by 200lb. Even though the name of Mercedes-Benz was not often mentioned in Munich (not out loud, anyway…) the evidence was that BMW was trying to position its larger cars alongside the rival ranges from Stuttgart, and to grab every possible 'conquest' sale that was available.

In nine years, this, the E12 5-Series saloon, may not have been technically exciting, but it was extremely successful. For the first year, only the 2-litre carburetted 520 and injected 520i were available, then

the first of the six-cylinder derivatives, *and* the 'economy' models began to appear. The 525 of 1973 was a carburetted 145bhp/2,494cc car, while the 528 of 1975 had 165bhp/2,788cc. At the other end of the range, the 90bhp/1,766cc-engined 518 appeared, and although it was no tyre burner, nearly 150,000 would be sold.

The second wave of models included the 176bhp 530i (sold only in North America) and, from 1977, the 520/6 (with the brand-new 122bhp six-cylinder 2-litre power unit), then the fuel-injected 528i, which had the 176bhp/2,788cc 'six'. Finally, and this was very much toe-in-the-water engineering compared with what was to follow, for 1980 BMW announced the M535i, which was based on the 528i, but was fitted with the same 218bhp/3,453cc twin-overhead-camshaft engine as the contemporary 635CSi coupé (see Chapter 11). Fast (139mph), smart (it had a transverse boot-lid spoiler), and very competent, it was a good opening to the M5

pedigree, although with only 1,650 cars built in less than two years, it was always something of a rarity.

E28 – the second-series 5-Series (1981–1988)

When the E28 took over from the E12 in 1981, the big surprise was…that there was no big surprise. The new car looked so much like the old car that it was simply not easy to tell the two cars apart. As with the 3-Series re-style, which would follow in 1982, the changes were evolutionary, rather than radical. BMW didn't mind the waves of disappointment which greeted the new E28 – they were confident that the clientele, and the

Expansion of the 5-Series range began in 1973 with the launch of the 525, which used the rather bulky but very effective 145bhp/2.5-litre six-cylinder engine.

The M535i of 1980 was one of the first BMW road cars to carry an 'M' (for Motorsport) title. This pedigree evolved steadily over the following decades, to the extent that the M5 of the early 2000s had a V10 engine developing more than 500bhp!

dealer chain, would like what they were offered – and they were right.

Under the skin, the platform, chassis, engine and transmission options were all either carryover items, or lineal derivations of what had gone before. Not only that, but much of the interior body structure was also the same as before, including the same doors and roof panels. BMW claimed that changes to the overall shape, which were as concerned as much with improving aerodynamic performance as providing a new-look, had reduced the drag. The drag

coefficient (Cd), it was claimed, had come down from 0.44 to 0.384, which was a considerable improvement for what appeared to be minor visual adjustments.

All cars now had a nose with a layout of two large and two smaller headlamps, and there were changes to the bonnet opening and structure, so that BMW stated there was a weight saving of 64lb. Not only that, but a 53lb saving was claimed for the running gear. Technically, the patented 'double link' front suspension was from the latest 7-Series cars, but there was disappointment that the ageing semi-trailing link rear suspension geometry had been retained. No matter how often BMW huffed and puffed about the simplicity and great packaging of such a layout, the fact is that these cars suffered

from rather disturbing final oversteer when cornered hard.

Over the next seven years, the E28 kept the Munich assembly lines very busy, with more than 2,000 such cars being produced every week: 722,328 in all. One in five of every BMW built at this time was a 5-Series, and there was never any doubt that it was a profitable programme. Right from the start there was a six-car range which looked (and was) much like that of the superseded E12 variety. The entry-level car was the 90bhp/1,766cc 518, the most powerful was the fuel-injected six-cylinder 184bhp/2,788cc 528i, while the 121bhp/2,693cc 528e was a 'de-toxed' model built specifically for sale in North America. All except the very cheapest models were fitted with five-speed gearboxes. At that stage, though, there was no M5-type, but this would follow.

Then, and although it was almost unthinkable to many BMW enthusiasts, in 1983 BMW launched its first-ever diesel-powered car, this being the normally-aspirated 524d – the engine being a new design manufactured at the Steyr premises in Austria. Looking back from the new century, the 86bhp output of the six-cylinder 2,443cc engine appears risible. BMW was defensive about its prospects (there were several whispered mentions about the opposition, Mercedes-Benz, and the 'Stuttgart taxis' which it sold so well…) but it made haste to do better, and from 1986 it launched the 524td, where the 't' denoted 'turbocharger', as well as previewing a 122bhp version of the same 2,443cc engine.

M5 twins – 1984–1988

Not even BMW, though, could bring every planned derivative to market at the same time, which explains, perhaps, why the next M-for-Motorsport model was not launched until the end of 1984. But the wait was worth it. From that point not one, but two different M-badged four-door saloon cars were launched – one called M535i, the other the altogether more purposeful M5.

This, incidentally, was the moment when the company made the following statement: 'The M symbol can now be used to express what a number of very different products have in common: Grand Prix engines and a collection of sportswear fashions, high-performance, top-of-the-range vehicles in the individual BMW series, and one-off sports jobs built by BMW Motorsport GmbH, such as the M1…'

Although the 218bhp/single-cam/3,430cc M535i was extremely well equipped, its specification including ABS braking, uprated suspension, alloy wheels and a limited-slip differential, together with a body kit including spoilers and skirts, all for a UK launch price of £17,950, it was the M5 which was much more special.

Here was a more purposeful (and, as it transpired, rarer) derivative of the E28. This time around the 24-valve 3,453cc twin-overhead-camshaft engine (compared with the M535i, the new M5 had a larger cylinder bore) produced 286bhp, and

had to be canted over by no less than 30° in the engine bay to provide space around the inner wings and bonnet panel. Backed by the Getrag 280/5 five-speed gearbox, with larger brakes and firmed-up suspension, but without overblown side skirts, this ferocious projectile could reach 153mph, and was thus the fastest mid-1980s BMW in production. It was always exclusive, and expensive (costing £31,295 when launched in the UK in 1986), so it came as no surprise to learn that only 2,145 such machines were ever built.

E34 – a new-generation and a new-style (1988–1996)

The third-generation 5-Series, known internally as E34, not only looked much more modern than the E28 which it replaced, but was the first of its type to include an estate car ('Touring'), and it sold remarkably

well, with 1,333,438 built in eight years. Larger, smoother, and ever-more versatile than previous mid-large-sized BMWs, it was an evolutionary technical generation ahead of the E28 which, frankly, seemed only to have been marking time in the 1980s.

With a smoothed-out style, and running on a 108.7in wheelbase, its drag coefficient had been reduced by 18 per cent, although its chassis and running gear were still very much as before, but with refinements. BMW, stubbornly it seemed to many observers, had stuck to its independent semi-trailing link, although the links were now only skewed at 13°, and both anti-dive and anti-squat geometry were featured. For this generation, each and every car initially had a fuel-injected six-cylinder engine, one of BMW's two types, ranging from 129bhp/1,990cc all the way to 211bhp/3,430cc, with the still-rare

This was the M5 of 1984, outwardly a standard-looking BMW saloon car, but one which had 286bhp and 3,453cc. All that power and torque on snow? Oooerr!

Way back in the 1970s, BMW said they would never produce estate versions of their cars. Commercial realities then took over, and by the 1990s, both the 3-Series and (here) the 5-Series models, included estate cars, called 'Touring' models, in their range.

The early 1990s 5-Series were much larger and more impressive than the original car of the early 1970s. This is one of the first V8-engined models, and was registered in 1993.

2,443cc turbo-diesel engine now rated at 115bhp.

Although it would be quite wrong to suggest that this 5-Series was a boring product – with such looks and such a choice of running gear it could never be that – but there is no doubt that initially it was almost exactly as expected by the media, the clientele, and of course by the company's rivals.

BMW, however, richened the mix

considerably, first by introducing a graceful and completely practical five-door 'Touring' model in 1991, then making a four-wheel-drive chassis available for certain models. This was like that offered under the 325i of the period, which was quite expensive, and rare, although popular in regions such as Scandinavia and Central and Southern Europe, where winters could be severe, and ultimate traction is a real benefit. From October 1992 530i/540i twins were introduced, with a new generation of 32-valve, twin-cam-per-bank V8 power units. The 540i unit produced a very torquey 286bhp at first – and this was only the beginning for a V8 engine family which would be used in many more new BMWs (including the Z8 sports car) in the years which followed.

None of those cars, however, was as delectable as the second-generation M5…

E34 M5 – 1988–1995

Here is a dream project for an enthusiast: think of a 1990s type 5-Series saloon, add every desirable

M-for-Motorsport feature, call it M5 and put it on the market? Only a dream, right? No, not at all – for this is what BMW actually achieved at the time. Until it was displaced by an even more extraordinary Type E39 in the late 1990s, no BMW was ever praised like that. In a seven-year life, no fewer than 12,249 such cars were sold, every one of them going to someone whose life was changed, for ever. BMW even made a few Touring versions for those who wanted to tie incredible performance to a load-carrying role.

Because BMW knew that the chassis was good (although the rear semi-trailing suspension put limits on the total capability) it could produce an extremely rapid machine without making major changes to the chassis. However, by comparison with the earlier M5, the big six-cylinder engine was enlarged slightly, with a 2mm longer stroke, to 3,535cc. Along with revised valve timing and a different crankshaft, peak power was pushed up to 315bhp at 6,900rpm. Backed by a five-speed gearbox, big brakes, big tyres, and revised suspension settings, here was a super-fast five-seater which could rush up to 157mph in double-quick time – and do it in great style.

All this, incidentally, was with full luxury equipment – ABS, electric windows, on-board computer, electric sun-roof, air conditioning, and self-levelling rear suspension. The only detail which stopped this being too good to be true was the selling price – a whopping £43,465 in the UK at launch time in 1990 which, in round figures, made it 50 per cent more costly than the contemporary 535i.

There were two major up-dates of this model, these being done to meet the challenges from competitors, particularly Mercedes-Benz's 500E. After much careful development, BMW Motorsport produced the final 'stretch' of this now ageing engine. By increasing the bore by 1.2mm, and the stroke by 4mm, the capacity was pushed up to no less than 3,795cc – which was a long way from the 2,494cc engine initially seen back in

1968! Peak power went up to 340bhp at 6,900rpm.

Three years later, in May 1994, the M5 got a six-speed transmission (automatic transmission, by the way, was never available), and the top speed became 170mph. Acceleration figures of 0–60mph in 5.4 seconds, and 0–100mph in a mere 13.6 seconds was quite astonishing for such a substantial machine.

The last of these amazing cars was built in July 1995, just before the E34 range was displaced by a new-generation 5-Series, the E39 type.

E39 5-Series – fourth-generation (1995–2003)

Appearances can certainly be deceptive. Although the fourth-generation 5-Series, launched in September 1995, looked much like the third-generation E34 it displaced, it was new from end to end, with a larger cabin and – most importantly – all-new suspension and revised

The M5 of 1995 was a simply phenomenal machine, with no less than 340bhp on offer from its 3.8-litre, six-cylinder engine. This was the largest and most powerful iteration of that long-lived straight 'six'.

engines. This time around, the wheelbase measured 111.4in, it was 70.8in wide, yet extensive use of light-alloy components, especially in the engine blocks and the suspension members, brought the unladen weight down by 55lb to 88lb. BMW was proud to boast that the new bodyshell was 80 per cent stiffer than the one it superseded, and made no secret of the fact that they intended the 5-Series to fight, head-on, with the latest Mercedes-Benz E-Class range.

The drag coefficient had been further reduced, to a best figure of 0.27 on the 520i models, and there was a radically changed chassis. Not only had rack-and-pinion steering finally been adopted on the 5-Series (six-cylinder cars only; for packaging reasons recirculating ball steering was retained with V8 engines), but this was also the first 5-Series to use the advanced Z-axle independent rear suspension.

In the mid-1990s, many motoring pundits voted the 5-Series as the best all-round BMW of all – and the sales figures proved it.

By the fourth generation, the 5-Series had grown up even further. Big, fast, and very roomy, its cabin was almost as large as that of the original 7-Series, a type with which it shared factory space at Dingolfing. The two ranges also shared some components including the new 4-litre V8 engine.

Initially, the engine line up was much like that of the E34, starting with a 150bhp/1,990cc 'six', and topping out with a 286bhp/4,398cc V8, but now there was also a 184bhp/2,926cc 'common rail' diesel power unit which brought new meaning to the phrase 'economical performance'. Five-speed manual or optional automatic transmissions were available on all types, with a six-

speed manual available on the 4.4-litre V8 model.

With an interior trimmed and equipped up to the best Mercedes-Benz standards, this was a formidable range which succeeded even beyond BMW's expectations – it was not until 2003 that yet another generation of 5-Series, this time with Chris Bangle-inspired styling, would take over.

In the meantime, BMW had done the seemingly impossible – by producing an even better M5…

E39 M5 – 1998–2003

Mission impossible, some called it. How on earth could BMW improve on the phenomenal M5 of 1984–88, with its 340bhp engine and a 170mph top speed. Rumour mongers suggested that BMW Motorsport was in trouble because there was a delay in launching a replacement.

Far from it. In fact, they were taking pains to make a new M5 as fast, as different, and as accomplished as possible. How to make a new car faster than the old, when the six-cylinder engine had finally run out of potential? Answer: evolve a white-hot V8-engined version instead.

Evolved – quite a long way evolved, in fact – from the contemporary 540i, the new M5 used a monumentally powerful 400bhp/4,941cc version of the modern V8 engine, and matched it to the usual six-speed Getrag manual transmission. Allied to the new-generation suspension there were completely redeveloped spring, damper and steering settings, alloy wheels (9.5 rims at the rear) were 18in in diameter, and there were carefully aero-tested front spoiler and side skirts to complete the handling balance.

So what if its UK price in May 1999 was £59,950 (not quite Porsche 911 levels, but in the same marketing slot) – it was an utterly phenomenal machine, that was not only rapid but extremely comfortable, as much a 'businessman's express' as an out-

Buying 5-Series – first and second generations

1. Big, solid, always four-door saloon types, the 5-Series were conventional by BMW standards. Once again, there are huge numbers to choose from, although proportionately, fewer have survived than have early 3-Series. Second-generation cars looked very similar to original types, so don't be put off by greater age. No question, though, that six-cylinder-engined types – 520i, 525, and 528 – were more favoured than the 'entry-level' four-cylinder 518/520s.

2. M535i and M5 (M = Motorsport) were rarities, more powerful than mainstream 5-Series types, but have higher 'classic' worth for those very reasons. Well thought of today, and not surprisingly, they are much more costly to maintain and restore.

3. Because of handling differences, it is easy to recommend second-generation (E28) types over the original (E12) variety. The original types had the same basic semi-trailing arm rear suspension as earlier 3-Series (see Chapter 7 and 'Buying'), so more powerful types suffer oversteer and sudden tail-end breakaway in slippery conditions: this can be entertaining if expected, but potentially disturbing if not.

Much-changed rear suspension geometry improved things for second-generation cars (E28s), but this is still not a patch on the Z-axle layout of later 3-Series cars.

4. Dodgy handling may not be endemic, but can be worsened by generally worn suspension bushes and mountings, particularly at the rear. If when test-driving a car before purchase this is found to be the case, consider renovating the chassis, as it will be an investment which will give you more driving pleasure for a finite cost. Not only will the car feel better, but the chances of a tail-slide, spinning accident may be much reduced. Badly worn joints, in any case, give cause for an MoT failure.

5. In spite of its solid-looking structure, these bodyshells used 1960s anti-corrosion technology. The good news is that surviving cars have usually been restored at least once, and rendered rust-proof for years to come. Corrosion appears in conventional monocoque places, including the rear suspension sub-frame, spring and rear damper mountings (where stress reversals have given the joints a hard time), and especially under the sills.

Other corrosion horror-spots included the base of the front bulkhead, rear wheelarches, inner and outer rear wheelarches, and around the edges of doors.

6. Big six-cylinder engines live longer in these cars than in the 3-litre coupés, and were better developed. Look for smokey exhausts and oil consumption, which may indicate worn valve seals and guides, and deteriorating piston rings. Four-cylinder engines (518 and early 520)

aged in the same way as in 02 and early 3-Series models (see previous chapters).

7. Be prepared for the high cost of buying replacement parts. The 5-Series might not cost too much to buy as a useable classic, but genuine factory parts (as opposed to those of unknown origin) are invariably quite costly. It is impossible to restore, maintain and run a middle-sized, middle-aged BMW for the same price that you could operate a fast Ford, or even an Alfa Romeo. And if you cut corners, the car will inevitably deteriorate.

8. Some E28s have ZF power-assisted recirculating-ball steering, which wears and feels sloppy as it ages. By the same token, their mounts (to the front subframe) may crack, and idler bushes may also have developed play, and lost precision. Although not cheap to restore, the result is often a transformation of the car's feel.

9. Remember, above all, that an early 5-Series was never a particularly glamorous car (only the M5 types truly qualify for that description) which means that surviving cars may not have had enough attention bestowed on them as they got older. A good basic design, with high engineering standards, may not have been enough to stave off cost-cutting neglect over the years, for some of these machines are now well over 20 years old.

and-out performance machine.

Road test figures told only part of the story, for BMW had provided an electronic limiter to the top speed (*Autocar* quoted it as 161mph, which was a touch higher than the 'theoretical' 155mph limit). Even so, 0–100mph acceleration in a mere 12.7 seconds, the ability to pull away

smoothly and strongly from 30mph in sixth gear, the 155mph maximum in fifth gear, 135mph in fourth gear and even 99mph in third gear, had all the testers gasping.

We are privileged to quote from the summary: 'Quite simply, the new car is the most impressive high-performance luxury saloon we've ever

driven… It achieves this accolade because of the thoroughness of its development and the fact that in not one area could it be significantly improved…'

Maybe not, but when BMW produces the next iteration on the M5 theme, we might all have to think again.

M1 – *the mid-engined 'supercar'*

If Jochen Neerpasch had not been a founder-member of BMW Motorsport GmbH, and if he had never had an ambition for BMW to win the FIA Group 5 race car series, the fabulous mid-engined M1 would never have gone on sale. Specifically designed as an 'homologation special', it also turned out to be a magnificent road car too.

The story really began in 1972. Having built up Ford-of-Germany's successful Capri RS2600 race-car programme, Neerpasch was then head-hunted by BMW, specifically to revitalise their own racing programme. The result, in 1973, was the all-conquering 3.0CSL (already described in Chapter 6), but this was merely an overture.

Along with his chief design engineer, Martin Braungart (another defector from Ford-of-Germany), Neerpasch began to formulate a scheme for a limited-production 'Supercar' which in race-car form, would be a potential Porsche-beater in Group 5 ('silhouette') sports car racing, and which should win the Le Mans 24-Hour race. In some ways, although not at all in detail, he was thinking about a practical evolution of the BMW Turbo which had already been shown in 1972.

Porsche, at that time building the all-conquering turbocharged 935s (these being very loosely based on the 911 Turbo) were formidable competitors, but not invincible. A properly engineered mid-engined car, Neerpasch reasoned, should be able to compete successfully with a converted rear-engined car, especially if it could be made lighter too.

Maybe this was not the ideal time to invite his bosses to spend a truck-load of money on an indulgence (at best, such a programme could only be a flag-waver, at worst it could be a real money pit). Also, they would have

As far as most snobbish supercar customers were concerned, the BMW M1 had only one failing – that it did not carry a different badge. To some, the M1's style, performance, stability and its good breeding wasn't quite enough. They were all wrong. (LAT)

to build 400 cars to gain Group 5 approval. As there was now no way BMW might get away with promising to build the cars, but only completing a few of them – such cheating had been tried before, by their rivals, and most of these loopholes had been closed.

Even so, Neerpasch and Braungart went ahead, and sketched out a new car, postulating that it should have a brand-new, 3-litre V10 engine, and that resident genius Paul Rosche's small department should design it for them.

A V10? Was there a hidden agenda? Indeed there was – for in 1975 Neerpasch and BMW also had ambitions to start building 3-litre engines for F1. But why a V10? Simple really: the all-conquering Ford-Cosworth DFV was a V8, while Ferrari used a V12. To quote Rosche: 'We had the idea of a V10 which would combine the best of both units. But in the end it made sense to go with the existing "six" – all we needed to develop for that was the 24-valve head…'

BMW's board gave its approval in 1976, although it was convinced that much of the expertise in conceiving a mid-engined two-seater would have to be bought in, and it was also sure that there was no section of BMW which could efficiently build a mere 400 cars. BMW, at this time, could understand the problem of building a handful of cars, or of building 400 cars a day, but 400 in total?

According to the original master plan (which was prodded along by Neerpasch himself) the new car, coded M1 (Motorsport GmbH, Project No. 1), would have to be engineered by Lamborghini of Sant' Agata, Italy, with style by Ital Design's Giorgetto Giugiaro. Then, when the prototypes of the car had proved themselves, Lamborghini would build all the cars on BMW's behalf.

A good plan, to be sure, but within a year it all fell to pieces. Although Lamborghini got on rapidly with the job by engineering the chassis, and liaising with Giugiaro, and had a handful of prototypes up and running by the end of 1977, the Italian

M1

1979–1981

ENGINE:
Six cylinders in line, iron block, alloy head
Capacity	3,453cc
Bore x stroke	93.4mm x 84mm
Compression ratio	9.0:1
Maximum power	277bhp at 6,500rpm
Valve gear	Four valves per cylinder, twin overhead camshafts
Fuelling	Kugelfischer-Bosch fuel injection

TRANSMISSION:
Five-speed manual, all-synchromesh

SUSPENSION:
Front: Independent, coil springs, wishbones, anti-roll bar, telescopic dampers
Rear: Independent, coil springs, wishbones, anti-roll bar, telescopic dampers

STEERING:
Rack-and-pinion

BRAKES:
Hydraulic, front disc/rear disc

WHEELS/TYRES:
Alloy disc; 205/55-16 front; 225/50-16in rear; radial-ply

BODY/CHASSIS:
Separate multi-tubular chassis, with tubular cross-bracing, with glass-fibre two-seater sports coupé body

DIMENSIONS:
Length	14ft 3.7in
Width	5ft 11.8in
Height	3ft 8.9in
Wheelbase	8ft 4.8in
Track, front	5ft 1in
Track, rear	5ft 2in

WEIGHT:
2,867lb

PERFORMANCE/ECONOMY:
Max speed	162mph
Acceleration	0–60mph in 5.5sec
Fuel consumption	typically 17–20mpg

UK PRICE WHEN NEW incl. tax:
£37,570

NUMBER BUILT:
450

concern's finances were in a parlous state. Even though they had secured Italian government money to fund the project, they missed several BMW-imposed deadlines, so that in April 1978, BMW was forced to announce that: 'Unhappily, BMW find themselves forced to terminate the agreement in order not to endanger the M1 project...'

The solution was complex, but ruthlessly efficient, but first I should describe the layout of the car, which

The 2000 Turbo Coupé of 1972 was strictly a one-off, with a transversely mounted four-cylinder engine behind the cabin, but there were some styling 'cues' which would influence the M1 that followed several years later.

had already settled down, and was proving to be promising.

Between them, BMW and Lamborghini had settled for the classic two-seater coupé/mid-engine/rear-drive (as found on several other Supercars of the period). Lamborghini's own expertise then produced a very strong square-section multi-steel-tube chassis frame which was reinforced in strategic places by sheet steel, and superstructures in tubular steel. It was, and still is, the only mid-engined BMW road car ever to have been put on sale.

The body style by Giugiaro (and, yes, there were certain similarities with the DeLorean DMC12, which the

Italian genius had shaped at around the same time) featured a low, wide and slightly angular closed coupé shape, with flared wheelarches, with slats over the engine bay, and with the 'signature' BMW twin-kidney grille up front. This was to be fashioned entirely in glass-fibre, and was totally unstressed.

Mounted in-line immediately behind the cabin, and directly evolved from the existing six-cylinder road-car unit, the 3,453cc engine gained a four-valves per cylinder/twin-cam, cylinder head. It was conservatively rated at 277bhp, although up to 470bhp was available in full racing tune, and was mated to a twin-plate clutch and a sturdy five-speed ZF transaxle.

That engine conversion sounded simple enough, but also involved a stronger crankshaft, and different connecting rods and pistons, along with a sophisticated dry-sump lubrication system. Bosch-Kugelfischer fuel injection was used, with a Magneti-Marelli electronic ignition system. It was an all-encompassing reworking of a strong basic engine, and would be extremely useful in future BMW models including M5 and M6 types.

Lamborghini had laid out the suspension and steering which, like other Italian supercars of the day, featured coil spring/independent suspension at each corner, and unassisted rack-and-pinion steering, with servo-assisted four-wheel disc brakes. Road cars were to be fitted with 16in Campagnolo alloy wheels – 7in at the front, and 8in at the rear.

Complex assembly lines

No sooner had BMW pulled the M1 project away from the moribund Lamborghini concern, than it had to make decisions about the entire project. Should it cancel it completely (and lose face?), should it attempt to have it built at Munich, or should it get involved in something far more complicated?

It was Giorgetto Giugiaro himself who used his already renowned 'Mr Fixit' charms, to make sure that the cars *would* be built, although not in a way that made BMW's accountants totally happy. First of all, Marchesi of Modena (who were used to that sort of contract) would build the chassis frames and suspension units, which would then be transported to Ital Design of Turin (Giugiaro's own company) who would take in ten-section moulded GRP bodyshells from Transformazione Italiana Resina, build them up, bond and rivet them to the chassis, then paint and glaze the assembly.

Recognisable but far from complete, the structures would then be transported (by truck) to Baur of Stuttgart (Baur was one of BMW's most favoured suppliers). Baur would undertake complete and final assembly, using engines from BMW of Munich, transmissions from ZF, many other components from the BMW parts bin, and other items from suppliers all over Germany.

Then, and only then, were M1s finally ready to be road-tested, before being sent to BMW Motorsport for final 'snagging' and pre-delivery work. Because of the complicated nature of the build process, it was not surprising that much tweaking often had to be done before the cars were finally sold!

BMW rapidly began to run out of time because such a complex manufacture/supply/assembly process took time to set up. Although the car was officially previewed in October 1978 at the Paris Salon, there were still no cars ready for sale – and by this time the whole reason for the machine (Group 5 racing) had been killed off. Like other car-makers before and since – Porsche's 959, Ford's RS200 and Audi's mid-engined Quattro projects all spring to mind – by the time the product was mature, BMW found that they had commissioned ambitiously engineered cars for a formula which no longer existed.

In the end, the first deliveries were not made until February 1979, with just 144 cars produced in that year, followed by 251 in 1980, while the last 55 road cars were built in the first months of 1981. Of that total, at least 50 were modified and sold by BMW Motorsport as specialised race cars, for when his Group 5 ambitions were frustrated, the inventive Jochen Neerpasch had come up with a one-make formula – the Procar series – which would provide mountains of publicity (see *The Racing M1s* sidebar) at a time when sales were still going ahead.

In the meantime, the road cars were seen as very expensive. Originally listed at no less than 100,000 Deutschmarks – twice the price, for

example of the current 635CSi coupé – the few which were sold overseas cost even more than that. When the British magazine *Autocar* tested an M1 in 1980, it quoted a price of no less than £37,570 (at the time a 300bhp Porsche 911 Turbo cost £27,950 and a Ferrari 512BB Boxer was 'only' £35,100).

But what wonderful road cars they were. These were not cheap-and-cheerful bodged-up competition cars, but were expected to pass each and every one of BMW's high standards. As Paul Rosche later reminded us: 'It was the first car that BMW Motorsport made. There were so many issues – emissions controls, safety regulations and ergonomics – that we'd never come up against with race cars… We have a motto at BMW – "we don't make rubbish" – so we did it properly and in the end we got everything under control.'

During this period of intensive development, M1s were covering

Pure, beautiful, supercar styling, 1978 period – this being the mid-engined M1 as shaped for BMW by Giorgetto Giugiaro of Ital Design. Before then, no BMW road car had ever looked like this. Maybe the M1's general proportions were similar to those of other mid-engined supercars of the period, but the double-kidney grille and the famous 'spinner' badge, which was prominently displayed on the tail, made its parentage unmistakable.

The racing M1s

For BMW it was all very embarrassing. The mid-engined M1 had originally been intended for Group 5 racing, but that category was killed off. The fall-back position was that it could qualify for Group 4 racing, but not

An extra front spoiler, additional rear wing, special wheels and tyres, and a load more horsepower, all helped to turn the M1 into a magnificent 'Procar' race car in 1979 and '80.

until 400 cars had been produced, and carefully counted by FIA inspectors. This wasn't going to be possible until 1981, by which time the M1 might have been obsolete.

It was at this point that Max Mosley of FOCA (the Formula One Constructors' Association) proposed a solution, which was to run a Procar series for the M1s, as supporting events for F1 races held in Europe. Cynics suggested this offer was made

as an enticement to get BMW to enter F1 racing – and as a ploy it worked!

The original plan, in 1979, was to run M1 Procar races after the last practice session of each of the eight Grands Prix during the European season. The first five grid positions

How to make an already rare M1 even more exclusive – invite a world-famous artist to add his own colour scheme to a race-prepared Procar. Like it?

Procar M1s were in action at Monaco, as a support race for the 1979 Formula 1 Grand Prix.

would be reserved for the top five F1 drivers in the appropriate practice session, the remainder of a 25-car field being made up of private owners.

This might have worked perfectly if BMW had not signed up with Goodyear for a control tyre, for F1 teams contracted to Michelin would not allow 'their' drivers to compete. As it transpired, Mario Andretti,

Jacques Laffite, Niki Lauda, Nelson Piquet and Clay Regazzoni took part regularly, and in 1979 the series was won by Lauda in one of Ron Dennis's Marlboro-backed Project 4 machines.

Procar racing, however, was very expensive – it could cost £40,000 to build a car, and another £120,000 to race it for a full season. Even so, the series ran again in 1980, this time with Brabham driver Nelson Piquet picking up the title. That, however, was the end of a two-year episode, which at the end of 1980 left many

private owners with worn-out M1 race cars which were unsuitable for any more motor racing.

BMW themselves developed a one-off Group 6 car with an 800bhp twin-turbocharged engine, which competed at Le Mans in 1979 and amazingly, managed to finish sixth overall. A year later, Group 6 M1s took sixth place in the Mugello Six Hours, came third in the Nürburgring 1,000km, and 14th at Le Mans, but that really brought down the curtain on the M1's competition period.

Maybe the M1 didn't look quite as sleek with the headlamp pods flipped up, but this was still a formidably fast car, with a 160mph-plus top speed.

more than 900 miles a day, often on unrestricted German autobahns, and at very high speeds indeed.

It was, as everyone surely expected, a magnificent, beautiful, and well-equipped supercar, which did everything remarkably well, although BMW was apparently ashamed of the cockpit noise levels. They had never before had to develop such a machine however, and if they had spent any time driving a few Ferraris, Maseratis and Lamborghinis they would surely have changed their minds about the supposed noise problem.

Not only did the M1 look fabulous – even today, after nearly 30 years, an M1 still looks great, timeless, and distinctly purposeful. BMW, for sure, could allow itself to boast a little, which may explain why there is not just one spinner badge, but two on the moulded tail!

The M1 was (need one emphasise this?) not only searingly fast, but well equipped too. As you might expect with such a layout, where the front wheels and arches were tucked back

close to the cabin, the foot-wells were quite restricted (Lamborghini laid out the original chassis package, don't forget…), but the seating package was otherwise very comfortable, with snug leather or (to choice) cloth-covered bucket seats from Recaro, a carpeted and completely trimmed interior, and a four-spoke steering wheel.

Nitpickers used to play games, trying to identify some switches and controls which had been lifted from other BMW mass-production cars (notably from the 5-Series and 02 cars) – but such people forget that this was also a project which had to be completed quickly, and on a strictly limited investment budget.

Although the Procar variety (with 470bhp) were out-and-out racers, the road cars were as flexible as one had come to expect from BMW. Britain's *Autocar* magazine dubbed it a 'A Supercar with Class', and '…possibly the best mid-engined road car yet', and added these comments: 'Engineering and management were agreed that in road-going form the M1 was to be as refined as possible and, equally important, have BMW's usual high standard of trim and build quality.

'At 3,000rpm [the engine] is pulling like a lion…the induction and exhaust

notes have become more purposeful. By the time you reach 4,500rpm the car is pushing forward hard, induction and exhaust notes blending into a beautiful howl.'

In general, overall noise levels were described as 'high but acceptable – but sometimes delightful…', while the roadholding was called 'leechlike'. It was that characteristic, not merely the performance, which endeared owners to their M1s. 'The rearward weight bias and those wide-section Pirelli P7 tyres give the M1 superb grip and traction,' continued the magazine. 'Perhaps the car's greatest joy is being able to consistently use its huge reserves of power to rocket out of corners and past others…'

Although the test was unsigned, the illustrations show that it was ex-Lotus Grand Prix driver John Miles who had been involved in all the hard driving, so his great experience shone through, and his analysis was sound. Nothing, according to the writer, could destroy the excellent, soft-sprung, balance of this 2,867lb machine.

The performance was absolutely as startling as expected, for the 162mph top speed was matched by 136mph being available in fourth gear, 0–100mph acceleration in a mere

13.0 sec, and the ability to cruise indefinitely at 120mph wherever conditions (and the law) allowed it.

The M1, too, was clearly a car which could go on delivering over high mileages, as Marc Surer confirmed in *Classic & Sports Car* in recent years. Having owned two standard road cars, he completed more than 100,000km in the first car (before it was damaged in someone else's accident), and still owned a second car which had already completed more than 60,000km.

'You can buy much more powerful cars today, but the problem with them is that they're so much heavier,' said the former F1 driver. 'The M1 is direct: it has no ABS, no power steering and you hear the engine scream behind – it's a real driving machine. You'd have to go a long way to find a car that goes like it on a mountain road…'

When the very last M1 was completed in July 1981, BMW drew a line under their first and – as it transpired – only mid-engined supercar project. For sure this had been a loss maker (although the company never admitted how much that figure was) but it must have paid for itself many times over in terms of favourable publicity. Because the chassis was relatively simple to restore, and because the bodyshell was in rot-proof GRP, many of the production run survived to become much-admired classic cars. By the mid-2000s, the value of a really nicely presented car had risen to more than £50,000, maybe not enough to take account of inflation since the late 1970s, but enough to show that the market place treats these cars with great respect.

Viewed from any angle, the mid-engined M1 was an impressive, purposeful and above all distinctive two-seater machine. Although BMW had great trouble in urging it into production, the effort was surely worth it. (LAT)

Neatly packaged with an engine behind the cabin, the M1 was an excellently presented, very well-equipped car. (LAT)

7-Series
– the company flagship

The late-model 7-Series cars, like this 1999 model with a Sports Pack, are now seen as the most elegant and visually pleasing of all the big BMWs, for the machine which took over two years later, styled under the direction of Chris Bangle, was a much more controversial design.

It wasn't until 1977 that BMW announced the original 7-Series saloon, but when it arrived this signalled the completion of a coherent product range which would be built for the next 30 years. From that date, 3-Series BMWs catered for the 'small-medium' market, 5-Series cars were true medium-sized cars – and the 7-Series was the large car of the range.

It may be heretical to suggest that the 7-Series, in all its many forms, has never been the most exciting of BMWs, but there's evidence to back this up. In almost every case, the 7-Series has been large and carefully engineered, but (by BMW's evolving standards) conventional. Visual innovations were usually previewed on smaller BMWs, as was the introduction of new engines and transmissions.

First 7-Series (E23 type)
1977–1986

ENGINE:
Six cylinders in line, iron block, alloy head

Capacity	2,495cc/2,788cc 2,986cc/3,210cc 3,430cc/3,453cc
Bore x stroke	86mm x 71.6mm to 93.4mm x 84mm
Compression ratio	9.0:1 to 10.0:1
Maximum power	150bhp at 5,500rpm to 218bhp at 5,200rpm (plus 252bhp at 5,200rpm for turbocharged 745i)
Valve gear	Two valves per cylinder, single overhead camshaft
Fuelling	One Solex carburettor – Bosch fuel injection; KKK turbocharger on 745i model)

TRANSMISSION:
Four-speed manual or five-speed manual, all-synchromesh; optional automatic transmission

SUSPENSION:
Front: Independent, coil springs, MacPherson struts, anti-roll bar, telescopic dampers
Rear: Independent, coil springs, semi-trailing arms, (anti-roll bar on 745i), telescopic dampers

STEERING:
Recirculating ball, with power assistance

BRAKES:
Hydraulic, front disc/rear disc

WHEELS/TYRES:
Steel disc or cast alloy disc; 195/70-14 to 205/70-14in radial-ply

BODY/CHASSIS:
Unit-construction pressed-steel four-door saloon

DIMENSIONS:

Length	15ft 11.3in
Width	5ft 10.9in
Height	4ft 8.3in
Wheelbase	9ft 2in
Track, front	4ft 11.4in
Track, rear	4ft 11.9in

WEIGHT:
3,418lb to 3,594lb

PERFORMANCE/ECONOMY (typical):

Max speed	127mph (732i); 129mph (735i)
Acceleration	0–60mph in 8.9sec (732i); in 7.5sec (735i)
Fuel consumption	typically 19mpg (732i); 22mpg (735i)

UK PRICE WHEN NEW incl. tax:
From £8,950

NUMBER BUILT:
285,029

Third-generation 7-Series (E38 type)
1994–2001

ENGINE:

Petrol:	Six cylinders in line; V8 and V12, iron or alloy block, alloy heads
Capacity	2,793cc to 4,398cc
Maximum power	193bhp at 5,500rpm to 286bhp at 5,400rpm
Valve gear	Four valves per cylinder, twin overhead camshafts per head
Fuelling	Bosch or Bosch-Siemens fuel injection
Diesel:	Six cylinders in line; V8, iron block, alloy head
Capacity	2,497cc/2,926cc/3,901cc

TRANSMISSION:
Five-speed manual or six-speed, all-synchromesh, or optional automatic transmission

SUSPENSION:
Front: Independent, coil springs, MacPherson struts, anti-roll bar, hydraulic telescopic dampers
Rear: Independent, coil springs, Z-axle multi-link location, anti-roll bar, hydraulic telescopic dampers

STEERING:
Recirculating ball, with power assistance

BRAKES:
Hydraulic, front disc/rear disc, with servo assistance and ABS

WHEELS/TYRES:
Cast alloy disc; From 215/65-16in radial-ply

BODY/CHASSIS:
Unit construction, pressed-steel four-door saloon; two wheelbase lengths

DIMENSIONS:

Length	16ft 1.3in
Width	6ft 1.3in
Height	4ft 8.5in
Wheelbase	9ft 7.3in and 10ft 0.9in
Track, front	5ft 1in
Track, rear	5ft 1.8in

WEIGHT:
3,682lb to 4,322lb

PERFORMANCE/ECONOMY:

Max speed	141mph (730i) to 155mph (750iL)
Acceleration	0–60mph in 10.3–6.3sec
Fuel consumption	(petrol engined cars) typically 23–27mpg to 22–24mpg

UK PRICE WHEN NEW incl. tax:
From £39,800

NUMBER BUILT:
327,599

No matter, BMW, after all, was not in existence to provide a continuous talking point to the media, but to operate as a business. After the traumas of 1959 and '60, it was a relief to see profits being consistently made, and there is no doubt that the production of more than one million 7-Series cars by the early 2000s helped to make that certain.

The original E23 7-Series was, in almost every way, a direct successor to the six-cylinder types which had been on sale since 1968 and, as ever, BMW had carefully analysed that car's success before signing off the new (E23) 7-Series. Even so, because those early E3-type cars had been a resounding success (217,645 were sold between 1968 and 1977), there was little hesitation. The big change, though, was that the 7-Series went into production at Dingolfing, rather than in Munich.

Original 7-Series (E23) 1977–1986

Looking back, it is clear that BMW must have taken a very large 'Brave Pill' when evolving this new series, for styling and project work must have gone ahead in 1973 and '74 – in the very depths of the original Energy Crisis. They were braver than some.

In the late 1990s, BMW showed off the lineage of the 7-Series, starting with the 335 of the late 1930s, and moving up through the 501 types, the 2500/2800 saloons, and three generations of 7-Series.

The original 7-Series saloons, known internally as the E23 model, appeared in 1977 as a direct replacement for the 2500/2800/3.0S saloons which had sold so well.

Although companies like Fiat slashed their new-model spending, and Ford-Europe considered factory closures at this time, BMW, it seems, never had any doubts. Prototypes were on the road by 1974/75, and the new model was launched in April 1977.

BMW did not have far to look for inspiration. The E3 range had been such a success that it was really only necessary to provide a thorough up-dating of the layout, and so it was. Parking a new E23 type alongside an old E3 showed that the new car was slightly larger than the old, but that it had very similar proportions. It needed to be larger, incidentally, because the original 5-Series (E12) had been so carefully packaged that its cabin was almost as large as that of the original six-cylinder cars! By modern standards (and BMW was not about to shout this one too loudly), the drag coefficient of 0.452 was mediocre in the extreme.

The choice of four doors, full five-seater accommodation, and a variety of six-cylinder engines, plus manual or automatic transmissions, were all as expected – except that BMW hoped the new models would be even bigger and better competition for Mercedes-Benz, no more was needed. The Mercedes in question was the S-Class, which was even larger and, no question, was neither as fast nor as nimble. In the years which followed, this was going to be a fascinating sales battle.

The new 7-Series was, indeed, only slightly larger than the old E3 – 4in longer in the wheelbase and 4in longer overall, with 2in wider wheel tracks. This time round, though, BMW did not plan to make a longer-wheelbase version of its new car, which might have made good production-engineering sense, but slightly irritated the sales force. Although that decision was never rescinded, when the next 7-Series (E32 of 1986) came along, a choice of wheelbase/cabin lengths would always be available.

The style of the new cars was almost exactly as forecast, with that characteristic lean-forward front end, the kidney grille, and four headlamps – and, as you might expect, there were definite styling 'cue' similarities with the original 3-Series, which had progressed through the same styling studios only two or three years earlier.

Technically, there were no major innovations, but attention had been paid to every detail. MacPherson strut front suspension now featured 'double joint' links to the lower wishbones, the independent rear suspension was still by coil springs and semi-trailing links, the steering

featured power assistance, and servo-assisted disc brakes were now used at all four wheels.

So far, so predictable, and it was the same story with the engines, which were all derivatives of the well-established 12-valve/single-overhead-camshaft 'six' first seen on the old E3 models. At first there were three derivatives – 170bhp/2,788cc, 184bhp/2,985cc, and (fuel injected) 197bhp/3,210cc. For some markets (Italy, notably) there was also a 150bhp/2,494cc model, which was very rare – all of these engines were

canted over towards the right side of the engine bay, and backed by Getrag (four-speed manual) and ZF (automatic) transmissions.

Although BMW did not make a single important style change to these 7-Series cars in the next nine years, every year there seemed to be a reshuffle, an upgrade, or an additional model of some sort.

In late 1979 the 730i was replaced by the 3,453cc 735i, and fuel injection standardised across the range. The resultant 728i disposed of 184bhp, the 732i had an output of 197bhp,

Alpina

Originally an independent tuning shop, Alpina was set up by Burkhard Bovensiepen in Buchloe (south-east Germany) in 1963. By the 1970s, not only was the company specialising in BMW work, but it was actually supplying race-tuned engines to BMW's own 'works'-backed teams.

Alpina tuning was profitably applied to every BMW range at this time, and was so competently carried out that BMW began to take the company into its confidence when

evolving new models. By the 1990s, Alpina was so closely linked to BMW that it could almost be assumed that the arrival of a new BMW would soon be followed by an Alpina-derivative.

As an example, the Alpina B10 of 1984 was a much-modified version of the 735i, with no less than 260bhp and, as an Alpina company spokesman claimed with glee: 'that's five more horsepower than the 745i, and our car doesn't suffer turbo lag…'

The B11 which followed in 1987 performed similar miracles on the second-generation (E32) type – and there would be similar upgrades on all future BMW cars, large or small.

Alpina started up as an independent concern, which soon began to concentrate on BMW models. Before long, BMW was happy for Alpina to apply its tuning-magic to any of their models – including this early 1970s 3.0Si saloon. (LAT)

and the 735i delivered an impressive 218bhp.

At the same time, an exciting new 745i model was previewed (sales beginning in mid-1980), this having a turbocharged 252bhp/3,210cc engine. Self-levelling rear suspension was standardised on that car. Although 16,031 such cars were built, they suffered from serious turbo lag, and it was never marketed in the UK.

Five-speed manual transmissions became available at the same time, as did ABS anti-lock braking, which would be standardised in 1981.

From late 1982, the front-end style was slightly changed, with BMW claiming a nine per cent reduction in drag, the largest of the engines was reduced to 3,430cc, and Bosch Motronic fuel injection was standardised. In addition, there was a ZF four-speed automatic transmission option (it had previously been three-speed), and a modified type of semi-trailing link rear suspension.

From 1984, BMW's South African subsidiary started building its own version of the 745i, which was normally aspirated, but with the M-Type 24-valve twin-cam cylinder head

The 750iL, which appeared in 1987, was the first BMW production car to use a V12 engine. With 300bhp, this provided a top speed of at least 150mph.

– and 286bhp! Only 192 such cars were ever produced, but with a 149mph top speed they were the most exciting of all E23s.

Second generation 7-Series (E32) 1986–1994

For the E23, maybe a production rate of 30,000–35,000 cars a year doesn't sound all that high, but BMW found this highly profitable, and had no hesitation in commissioning a replacement model, the E32. Four years in the making, this new car looked very different from its predecessor, and had many visual similarities to the next-generation 5-Series which would arrive two years later.

For once, BMW gave advance notice of a change-over. In August 1985 they announced that a new-generation 7-Series would appear in September 1986, and so, with Germanic precision, it did. Production was, in fact, well under way by that time, as the first cars had rolled off the Dingolfing assembly lines in June 1986.

This, the second type of 7-Series, had a style which caused a real stir, for BMW was under increasing criticism for the mundane style of its

existing, older models. Here, though, was the first of a new model line up (the next 5-Series would appear in 1988, and the E36 3-Series would follow in 1990) where all the cars would be smoother in detail, more aerodynamically efficient in service, and altogether more rakish than their predecessors.

Although the two families looked very different in profile and in detail, there were some similarities between the two platforms, although BMW claimed that there were absolutely no carryover panels. They also said there was a 50 per cent increase in torsional stiffness, and a massive two-thirds improvement in beam strength.

Even so, the new (E32) 7-Series was slightly larger in all dimensions *except* height than the original (E23) model – with a 1in longer wheelbase, 2in longer overall, and with 0.7in wider wheel tracks. The new car was heavier than before, by about 110lb, but none of that mattered as the drag coefficient was well down – from 0.42 to an extremely creditable 0.32. Not only that, but BMW made it clear that this time around there would eventually be a longer-wheelbase version too.

At first there was little obvious improvement to the chassis and running gear, even if BMW claimed to have worked over and improved, every

component which merited attention. Interestingly enough, at first only two six-cylinder engines were on offer – 197bhp/2,985cc, and 220bhp/3,430cc – although BMW made it clear that they had a new V12 engine under development. We did not know this at that time however, but V8 power units would also figure in the 1990s.

As with the previous 7-Series, the latest car was sumptuously specified and equipped, so much so that it is not really necessary to point out features like full air conditioning, squashy interiors, fascia panels stuffed with instruments and controls, a soft ride, self-levelling to order and efficient Bosch fuel injection, on all types. The real news, as it unfolded, was in the ever-widening choice of engines.

Starting in 1987, BMW introduced its first-ever automotive V12 engine, a 60° unit with light alloy block and heads. To keep the heads compact, and the width of the engine right down, there were only two valves per cylinder, both nearly vertical to the cylinder alignment (the opposed angle was only 14°), and operated by rockers from single overhead camshafts.

This was an engine which had been under development for some time, and was the first of the family which BMW went on to use in cars like the forthcoming 8-Series, and in later 7-Series types. Sensibly, the bore and stroke dimensions, plus modified versions of pistons and connecting rods, were those of the existing 2,494cc straight-six power unit.

Fitted to the E32 7-Series, in a model known as the 750i, the first V12 was a 300bhp/4,988cc power unit, which was always matched to automatic transmission. It provided the Bavarian concern with a magnificently smooth, silent, but extremely powerful company flagship, for the top speed was an utterly effortless 155mph, although the fuel consumption could sometimes be as awful as 16mpg.

At the same time the promised longer-wheelbase model arrived, with the platform and cabin both stretched by 5in, providing much more space in

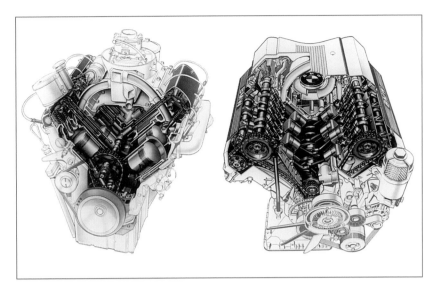

Two V8s are compared, although they have no common points except the 90° vee angle. On the left is the engine first seen in 502, 503 and 507 models in the mid-1950s while on the right is BMW's modern V8 of 1992, complete with twin overhead camshafts per cylinder head, and four valves per cylinder.

the back seat area. At first this fully-tooled 'stretch' cabin was only available on the V12-engined car, and carried the title of 750iL, but by the early 1990s it became available with any of the E32 engine/transmission combinations already on offer.

Sales of this rather exclusive V12-engined duo would naturally be limited by the high price (the first UK-market 750iL cost £53,750) but even so, before the E32 was dropped in 1994, no fewer than 48,559 cars had been sold.

From 1991, BMW added double-glazing to all door windows, following the pioneering example of Mercedes-Benz, and one year later the company then launched a completely new M60 family of 90° V8 engines. Before long, it was planned, these would replace all the ageing straight-sixes, originally in 3.0-litre and 4.0-litre varieties, but with quite a lot of built in 'stretch' to meet future power and torque requirements. Like the venerable 'sixes', the new V8s were absolutely vital 'building blocks' for BMW's planners, for they would eventually find use in the 5-Series, 6-Series, 7-Series, 8-Series, the Z8 and the X5 4x4 models too.

Developed versions of this engine would not only be fitted to the new, limited-production, Morgan Aero 8 in the 2000s, but for a short time they were used in turbocharged form in the Bentley Arnage of the late 1990s.

There was, of course, absolutely no

technical connection with the earlier V8s of the 1950s, for these were high-tech units with four-valve cylinder heads and twin overhead camshafts per bank of cylinders. Cylinder blocks were cast in aluminium, with no cylinder liners, but with nickel dispersion coatings in the cylinder bores.

For the E32 7-Series, there were 218bhp/2,997cc or 286bhp/3,982cc versions of the V8, the two cars logically being badged as 730i and 740i respectively. Both these cars were equipped with the latest five-speed ZF automatic transmission (its use would eventually filter down to be used in 5-Series and even 3-Series cars in the 1990s) – and clearly there was much more to come in the future.

Over the next two years, therefore, E32s were built with engines spanning 197bhp/2,985cc ('six') to 300bhp/4,988cc (V12), for the range had reached full maturity. In summary, from 1986 to 1994 there had been no fewer than ten different models in the 7-Series family – four of them with six-cylinder engines, four of them with V8s, and two with the monumental

The first 286bhp V8-engined 740iL went on sale in 1992. This is a 'ghosted' view of the running gear which, in this case, still featured semi-trailing link rear suspension.

V12. Well over 300,000 of all types were eventually produced. In May 1994, however, the E32 bowed out, and a like-for-like replacement, the E38, took over.

By 1999, when this 740i was built, the majority of 7-Series had V8 or V12 engines.

Third generation 7-Series (E38) 1994–2001

By the early 1990s, BMW had spent much time, and invested 'squillions' of Deutschmarks, in bringing forward new-generation 5-Series and 3-Series ranges. Well over half-a-million of the first two 7-Series had been sold since 1977, so the company knew exactly what it wanted the next-generation 7-Series to achieve.

Almost every BMW-watcher therefore, could have forecast the form and make-up of the car which BMW always knew as E38. It would have a style which was strictly evolutionary from the E32, it would be powered by V8 and V12 petrol engines, diesel-power would figure for the very first time on these large cars, and it would be fitted with yet another iteration of the multi-link independent rear suspension which had first been seen under the Z1 sports car of 1988.

BMW spent six years getting the E38 range ready for production, although at first glance little of that time had gone into the styling, which was a completely evolutionary update of that used so successfully on the E32, albeit with a drag coefficient that dropped from 0.32 to 0.30. As ever, there were to be standard and longer-wheelbase versions of the four-door saloon shell, but no other variations were ever planned.

Yet again, this was a new 7-Series with its own unique platform. It was a range which had put on size – and weight. With a 4in longer wheelbase, it was an inch wider than previously.

Most of the extra space was in the rear seat, which became very roomy indeed if the longer-wheelbase version was chosen. Because of all the extra safety gear now compulsorily fitted the car was also a whopping 342lb heavier. The shell itself was 100 per cent stiffer in torsion than the E32 had been. No wonder this new-generation machine was chosen to star in the latest James Bond film, *Tomorrow Never Dies*, when it ended a multi-storey car park 'chase' sequence by diving across the street into a shop window.

Early cars had a choice of V8 and V12 engines – from 218bhp/2,997cc to 326bhp/5,379cc, but from 1996 a 197bhp/2,793cc 'six' and a 143bhp/2,497cc straight-six overhead-camshaft turbo-diesel option were added while the V8s were enlarged to 236bhp/3,498cc and 286bhp/4,398cc respectively.

Later still, as the range developed, the diesel became a 184bhp/2,926cc/twin-cam, while from 1998, the

In 2001, BMW signalled the end of 'traditional' 7-Series styling, by releasing this view of the last E38 leaving the assembly line at Dingolfing, with the first of the new-type cars behind it.

company even produced a limited-production 245bhp/3,901cc V8 turbo diesel too. Customers of the 7-Series really had no excuse for complaining about a lack of choice, for each and every one of these cars could beat 130mph, and beat-up their deadly rivals from Mercedes-Benz with some ease.

Even when the new century opened, this 7-Series was still selling at the rate of 40,000 cars every year, the range now comprising ten different sub-

When the new-generation 7-Series saloon appeared in 2001, its overall appearance was, to say the least, controversial. Although the nose was well-integrated, the tail was criticised by many style-conscious pundits. BMW reacted to this, and developed a face-lifted model (i.e. 'smoothed-out') in 2005.

types, although about one-in-two sales were achieved by the 740i model. It was no wonder that yet another new type, this time styled by Chris Bangle's team, would take over in 2001.

6-Series
and 8-Series
coupés

Not the lightest of cars, but the 24-valve M635CSi was nevertheless an exciting car to use on long, fast journeys. (LAT)

Once the 'New Class' saloons had been dropped, the sleek 3.0-litre CS and 3.0 CSi coupés were effectively living on borrowed time, for they had used the same platform, suspension and running gear. If there was ever to be a new range of coupés, therefore, was it not obvious that they would be based on the new 5-Series types?

And so it was. Launched in March 1976, the new generation 'E24' coupés – the 6-Series – were originally built by Karmann at Osnabrück, but by the late summer of 1977 the company's role was reduced to that of bodyshell suppliers only. BMW never likes to admit their cars ever experience quality problems, but these had apparently appeared at Karmann, so henceforth final assembly was centred at Dingolfing, alongside the 5-Series range.

As with the old-type 3.0-litre coupés, the new 6-Series models were based on the very lightly-modified platform, chassis components and all the running gear of the original 5-Series saloons. Although suspension changes were made to suit the new car's characteristics, and only two types of six-cylinder engine were initially offered, the 'oily bits' were all familiar to enthusiasts, technicians and mechanics who had already experienced the new 5-Series cars. In the beginning there was no ultra-high-performance 'M' model – although such a car would eventually be launched, but not until 1984.

The new 6-Series cars – 630CS and 633CSi at first – were smoothly styled 2+2-seater coupés, and were aimed at virtually the same market sector as the cars they had replaced, but they were larger, heavier and inevitably more expensive. Since this was also a period of high cost inflation (which had been brought about by the after effects of the Arab-Israeli War, the Energy Crisis, and the massive hoist in oil prices of 1973/74), 6-Series cars looked expensive when they were launched, and increasingly more so in the next few years.

Technically the interest was in the engines and transmissions. Although the badging of the '633CSi' suggested that a 3.3-litre engine was to be fitted, in fact it was yet another novel derivative, actually of 3,210cc. This was about to be available in BMW's larger saloons too, and would become a standard size in future seasons. The 630CS had a carburetted 185bhp/2,985cc 'six', while the new 3,210cc unit had 200bhp, and was

M635CSi
1984–1989

ENGINE:
Six cylinders in line, iron block, alloy head
Capacity — 3,453cc
Bore x stroke — 93.4mm x 84mm
Compression ratio — 10.5
Maximum power — 286bhp at 6,500rpm
Valve gear — Four valves per cylinder, twin overhead camshafts
Fuelling — Bosch L-Jetronic fuel injection

TRANSMISSION:
Five-speed manual, all-synchromesh

SUSPENSION:
Front: Independent, coil springs, MacPherson struts, anti-roll bar, hydraulic telescopic dampers
Rear: Independent, coil springs, semi-trailing arms, anti-roll bar, hydraulic telescopic dampers

STEERING:
Recirculating ball, with power assistance

BRAKES:
Hydraulic, front disc/rear disc, with servo assistance and ABS

WHEELS/TYRES:
Cast alloy disc; 220/55-390mm radial-ply

BODY/CHASSIS:
Unit construction, pressed-steel two-door coupé

DIMENSIONS:
Length — 15ft 7.2in
Width — 5ft 7.9in
Height — 4ft 5.2in
Wheelbase — 8ft 7.3in
Track, front — 4ft 8.3in
Track, rear — 4ft 9.70in

WEIGHT:
3,329lb

PERFORMANCE/ECONOMY:
Max speed — 150mph
Acceleration — 0–60mph in 6.0sec
Fuel consumption — typically 19–22mpg

UK PRICE WHEN NEW incl. tax:
£32,195

NUMBER BUILT:
5,855

8-Series
1989–1999

ENGINE:
V8, iron block, alloy heads/V12, iron block, alloy heads
Capacity — 3,982cc/4,398cc (V8) 4,988cc/5,379cc/ 5,576cc (V12)
Maximum power — 286bhp at 5,800rpm to 380bhp at 5,300rpm
Valve gear — Four valves per cylinder, twin overhead camshafts (V8), two valves per cylinder, single overhead camshaft (V12)
Fuelling — Bosch fuel injection

TRANSMISSION:
Six-speed manual, all-synchromesh: optional automatic transmission

SUSPENSION:
Front: Independent, coil springs, MacPherson struts, anti-roll bar, telescopic dampers
Rear: Independent, coil springs, multi-link location, anti-roll bar, telescopic dampers

STEERING:
Recirculating ball, with power assistance

BRAKES:
Hydraulic, front disc/rear disc

WHEELS/TYRES:
Cast alloy disc; 235/50-16 to 265/40-18 radial-ply

BODY/CHASSIS:
Unit construction, pressed-steel two-door, 2+2-seater saloon

DIMENSIONS:
Length — 15ft 8.2in
Width — 6ft 1in
Height — 4ft 4.7in
Wheelbase — 9ft 9.6in
Track, front — 5ft 1.2in
Track, rear — 5ft 1.5in

WEIGHT:
From 4,035lb

PERFORMANCE/ECONOMY:
Max speed — 155mph (electronically speed limited)
Acceleration — 0–60mph in 6.5 to 5.5sec
Fuel consumption — typically 18–20mpg to 15–18mpg, depending on engine

UK PRICE WHEN NEW incl. tax:
From £59,500

NUMBER BUILT:
30,621 (7,803 with V8 engines, all others with V12s)

fuelled by Bosch's latest L-Jetronic fuel injection system. Manual transmission cars got a four-speed Getrag, while automatic transmission machines had a newly developed ZF three-speeder.

These were coupés which would have a 13-year life (the last of all were produced in April 1989, just ahead of the launch of the 8-Series coupés which replaced them), during which no fewer than 86,216 had been produced; at the peak, in 1985, more than 9,600 were made in one calendar

The original 6-Series coupé of 1976 took over from the long-running, earlier-generation 3.0CS types. This is the 630CS model.

year. This covered a career in which there were virtually no style changes, but a great deal of modernisation to the engines and suspension.

The 630CS lasted only until 1979, and from that year the first of the 635CSi types (with 218bhp/3,453cc) appeared. Meanwhile, and to spread the appeal of the family, the injected 628CSi (184bhp/2,788cc) came on stream in 1979, although this type rarely sold more than 1,000 units a year, and in 1982 a corporate reshuffle led to the big engine being reduced very slightly in capacity, to 3,430cc.

Under the skin, from 1982 the 6-Series fell in line with the second-generation 5-Series saloons, picked

up a modified independent rear suspension (only a 13° skew angle of the wishbones, to try to improve the grip), and was also given the latest option of a four-speed automatic transmission.

The most exciting 6-Series of all was the M635CSi (1984–89) of which no fewer than 5,855 cars were sold. This was BMW Motorsport's way of producing the ultimate in 6-Series coupés, not by making it lighter, but by making it more powerful, faster and more distinctive.

Naturally, the entire chassis was reworked, with Bilstein dampers and larger-capacity front brakes, and there were effective (and visually obvious)

The M635CSi was a very popular, long-lived derivative of the 6-Series coupé, last made in the late 1980s.

Same badge, same six-cylinder twin-cam engine, but an entirely different chassis. The M635CSi (closest to the camera) had its engine up front, while the M1 had its engine located behind the two-seater cabin.

front and rear spoilers, plus a set of sexy, exclusive, split-rim cast alloy wheels, but the real advance was up front, under the bonnet. Somehow or other, BMW Motorsport managed to squeeze in the four-valves per-cylinder/twin-overhead-camshaft M1 power unit (as described in Chapter 9), this now being rated at 286bhp/3,453cc, but for it to fit at all, it had to be canted well over, at 30°, towards the right side of the engine bay. A five-speed gearbox was standard, and automatic transmission was never available.

(Such an engine tilt, incidentally, became almost standard practice on later M models, such as the M3 and the M5 saloons.)

Even though BMW made no attempt to take weight out of the bodyshell –

The 635CSi featured a fuel-injected 3.5-litre straight-six engine, and was the backbone of 6-Series sales in the late 1970s/early 1980s as well as being the fastest of the 6-Series coupés. (LAT)

The BMW 850CSi of the early 1990s used the company's magnificent 5-litre V12 engine.

indeed this was the best-equipped of all 6-Series types at the time – and from 1987 air conditioning, leather-covered seats and electrically-actuated front seats were all standardised. At 3,462lb unladen, the new model was no lightweight, yet the result was an extremely capable, albeit expensive machine. Customers had to weigh the balance between a 150mph top speed, with 0–60mph in a mere 6.0 seconds, against a very high price – £32,195, for instance, when launched in Britain in 1985.

Although there was never any question of the M635CSi being used in motorsport (it was too large and too heavy – the near-contemporary M3 saloon being much more suitable), it was certainly the most sporty of a range which had grown up a long way from the coupés originally launched in the mid-1970s. If only we had known this at the time, but the 8-Series which took over would be even larger, heavier and less sporting than that.

8-Series coupés – 7-Series relations

Smooth, wickedly fast, technically advanced – and expensive! That was the way to summarise the 8-Series coupé, which went on sale in 1990. It was always a controversial car, not always admired, and often criticised.

The new 8-Series could never be considered a direct replacement for the 6-Series, for there was no carryover of the bodyshell or the underpinnings from that car. Not only that, but new-generation V8s would take over. Accordingly, the new 8-Series became a close relation of the second-generation 7-Series of 1986 and at that time the 'rumour factory' forecast the use of V12 engines and a six-speed manual transmission.

The new coupé was shaped by an in-house team led by Klaus Kapitza, a graduate of London's Royal College of Art. It was big and impressive, and boasted a drag coefficient (Cd) of only 0.29. Always planned as a 2+2 seater,

it was 5.6in shorter than the 6-Series cars, and rode on a 105.5in wheelbase. It was much wider – 5.1in wider – than the 6-Series. The result was a squat, wedge-shaped fixed-head coupé and only delicate use of detail saved it from being described as 'brutal'. The headlamps were hidden away behind pop-up flaps (BMW claimed only moderate interference with overall air-flow when they were erect), this giving the front of the new car a rather anonymous aspect.

The timing of the 8-Series was important – and significant. The second-generation 7-Series dated from 1986, the third-generation car arrived in 1994 while the 8-Series appeared in 1990, neatly, halfway between the arrival of the two 7-Series types.

At the front end, the floorpan, front suspension, steering, the V12 engine, and the automatic transmission were shared with that of the current 750iL. Around the rear of the 'chassis', though, there was novelty all around. Following the introduction of the Z1 model (described in the next chapter), which proved the layout, the 8-Series coupé was the first series-production BMW to use the compact, but highly effective Z-axle layout of independent rear suspension. This signalled to the world that BMW had concluded that this should be their new 'standard' rear suspension of the future – and so it was.

Because this was almost a cost-no-object project, the 8-Series also included features like ABS (this was expected, anyway), automatic electronically monitored Boge damper adjustment, and ASC (automatic stability control) which controlled power output on slippery surfaces.

Inside, the 8-Series was rather wasteful of space, for in spite of its size, the rear seats had so little legroom as to be virtually useless. It was extremely well-equipped, however, and because everything was power-assisted, and the steering column even had electrical 'default' positions so that the wheel moved out of the way of the driver's legs when

the ignition was switched off this was an extremely easy and effortless car to drive.

Like all such high-performance BMWs, there would eventually be an extensive line-up of engines and transmissions. Initially, though, the new car was badged as an 850i, using a lightly tuned version of the new corporate single-overhead-camshaft 5.0-litre V12 engine which had already appeared in the 750i saloons of the period. (Looking back now, 'only' 300bhp from 4,988cc looks positively de-tuned, but think about the torque delivery!)

The first cars were delivered in 1989, and in 1991 no fewer than 9,517 were delivered but, amazingly, after that, demand fell away, and settled to between 1,500 and 3,000 cars a year: in the key US market the car simply didn't sell. This was not at all profitable to BMW, yet because this was a company flagship, the 8-Series had to be kept going.

To maintain the interest, therefore,

BMW added the 850CSi from late 1992, this having a 380bhp/5,576cc version of the colossally capable V12 engine, matched to a new type of Getrag six-speed gearbox, which would eventually be shared with the M3 and M5 models.

'If BMW's 5.6-litre 380bhp version of the 850 coupé wore M8 badges instead of the CSi label, no-one would complain…' wrote one pundit at the time, so maybe the problem was just one of perception.

Elegant, for sure, and beautifully engineered, the 8-Series lacked the spacious cabin which would have perhaps helped it sell better in the 1990s. But why was it not a commercial success? It was very fast, it was very capable, and it also looked extremely stylish. On the other hand, it was always very expensive, and offered only 2+2 seating. Developed under what BMW later admitted was almost a limitless budget, the 8-Series coupé, launched in 1989, used all the most modern technology. If only it could have been lighter, and not as costly… (LAT)

This was the fascia/instrument panel of the 840Ci model. Like most such large-engined BMW models of this period, the V8 engine was backed by automatic transmission.

Reminding us all that BMW not only built smart coupés in the 1970s and '80s, but a series of impressive motorcycles too. (LAT)

range still further in 1993, BMW introduced what we might call an 'entry-level' 8-Series (but at £52,950 that was a high 'entry fee' to pay, by any automotive standards): the 840i. This combined all the virtues of other 8-Series types, but without the use of the massive V12 engine. In its place, instead, the very new 286bhp/3,982cc 90° V8 (as used in the latest 7-Series and 5-Series saloons), complete with four-valves per cylinder, and twin-overhead-camshaft cylinder heads, took over, and had oceans of engine bay space in which to spread itself. It was only made available with ZF automatic transmission but was to give a temporary boost to 8-Series sales, which rose above 3,000 per annum in 1993.

BMW had done its best to upgrade the rest of the specification, for the CSi had fatter tyres on 17in wheel rims, a new front spoiler, a rear diffuser, drive-by-wire accelerator control, a fold-flat rear seat/platform, and a re-trimmed interior.

Soon after this, and to broaden the

Mid-life changes

Once the new-generation E38 7-Series saloons had appeared in 1994, it was almost inevitable that the closely

Buying 6-Series coupés

1. In production for more than a decade, this design improved with age. The 635CSi was a better car in all respects than the original 630/633CSi types. Many of the 86,000 built up to 1989 have survived, and have a considerable 'classic' reputation. The later 628 models were, theoretically, more economical than 3.3-litre or 3.5-litre types, but this does not necessarily make them more desirable today. The fastest, most prestigious examples cost the most to purchase as modern classics – that investment is surely worth it.

2. The motorsport-intended M635CSI, built from 1984, is a special case, with the more complicated 24-valve twin-cam engine. Buy it for its image and reputation, but be prepared to spend much more to keep it in good condition.

3. Smart it may be, but this bodyshell can rust severely, especially inside the engine bay, in the region of the inner front wing panels, particularly where they join up to the cross panel in the nose and meet up with the outer wings.

As ever on these BMWs, you will also need to check very carefully for corrosion around all the bushes and mountings which connect the rear suspension/rear axle sub-frame, springs and dampers to the under/rear-end of the bodyshell itself.

4. Other endemic rust spots include passenger footwells, especially where they join up with the structural sills, door skins at heavy stress points (including the wing mirror supports), and the surrounds to the quadruple headlamp fixings.

5. By this time in its career, the first-generation six-cylinder engine was well-sorted. Well-maintained examples last for more than 100,000 miles – except that camshafts and their valve followers tend to wear out at about that time. Rattly engine noises (the timing chain is a culprit) may not mean an engine about to fall apart, but be prepared for a big bill when the time comes to rebuild it.

6. As with other BMWs of this period, rear suspension bushes and mountings tend to wear badly after 50,000 miles – and restoration (although not cheap) is always recommended to bring the roadholding precision back. The handling of these cars improved after an early 1980s redevelopment exercise, when the semi-trailing arm angle was reduced. As with all such BMWs, it helps to have the very best tyres fitted that you can afford.

7. Although all the trim and decorative items are still available, the prices of authentic factory items are high. Come to terms with the fact that this BMW was always a costly car to buy – and the same applies to its maintenance and repair.

related 8-Series would soon be rationalised to suit. Although there would be no style changes – in 1999 the final 8-Series cars looked almost exactly the same as those when the series was launched a decade earlier – the same modern series of engine and transmission changes which benefited the E38 were phased in.

The first important change was that the original 5-litre V12-engined 850i was allowed to die off – the last cars actually being built in October 1994. In its place there was a car badged 850Ci, this time with a 326bhp/5,379cc V12 engine (exactly as found in the new 7-Series saloons), this type only being available with ZF automatic transmission.

That transmission, of course, pioneered BMW's use of Steptronic control, where the change-speed lever could be used, effectively, as a manual change, although the torque converter always remained in use.

It made a car into a smooth, effective and very purposeful vehicle, even though it could still be used as a no-fuss machine to crawl along in heavy traffic. In this regard, the 8-Series proved to be a useful test-bed for the same transmission which was to be used in later 7-Series and 5-Series models.

The final product move, which was made early in 1986, was to change the 840i into the 840Ci, this principally meaning dropping the original 4-litre V8, in favour of a 286bhp/4,398cc unit. Although there was no more peak power than before, there was a useful torque increase (to a peak of 310lb ft instead of 295lb ft), which made the car that much more flexible to drive. At the same time, the Steptronic automatic transmission control was made standard.

Even so, all this product activity came to be seen as a way of whistling to keep up the spirits of the 8-Series range, as sales did not perk up at all. Only 9,517 cars had been sold in 1991, 3,099 in 1993, and then just 2,177 in 1995, yet a miserable 663 cars was the best that could be managed in the whole of 1998. The last cars were produced in May 1999, after which the 8-Series was quietly allowed to die away.

It is easy to be wise after the event, but perhaps the car was always too bulky and not at all agile enough to take the fancy of clients who might otherwise be tempted to sell off their Porsches or their Mercedes-Benz coupés. It must surely have been a loss-maker as far as BMW's accounts were concerned, and there were never any signs that it would be replaced.

The Z1 & Z8
– extrovert
two-seaters

Every engineer who has worked in the motor industry can tell the story of projects which were conceived, engineered, and developed to the point of prototypes being built, only for those cars to be cancelled. For the romantics, this can be like suffering a death in the family, but for the pragmatists it is merely time to shrug, sigh deeply, and move on to the next challenge.

It isn't always like this. Although BMW has suffered such cancellations many times (maybe more than we think, for some projects are kept behind closed doors and never, ever, mentioned), but just occasionally, the company allows its engineers to go their own way, to pursue a concept, then to show it to the public. In effect, it allows them to 'think aloud'. On such occasions the company, by judging public reaction to what they see, may learn something for the future.

Two such projects – Z1 and Z8 – show that BMW is always ready to take a risk, always ready to push out its own technical boundaries, and is willing to take notice of public reaction.

Z1 – what, no doors?

Here was an otherwise innocuous-looking open two-seater which had the rather startling visual feature of drop-down, slide-away doors. That, though, was not the most important aspect – for the body also hid BMW's first-ever use of the multi-link independent rear suspension, which would be adopted on many subsequent BMWs.

In the beginning, the Z1, they say, was authorised to counteract a slump in BMW's sporting image. In the early 1980s, it was pointed out, the big 6-Series coupés had put on weight

All the pundits suggested the Z1 could have used a lot more power, one reason being that the new suspension layout provided such excellent handling.

Z1
1988–1991

ENGINE:
Six cylinders, iron block, alloy head
Capacity   2,494cc
Bore x stroke   84mm x 75mm
Compression ratio   8.8:1
Maximum power   170bhp at 5,800rpm
Valve gear   Two valves per cylinder, single overhead camshaft
Fuelling   Bosch fuel injection

TRANSMISSION:
Five-speed manual, all-synchromesh

SUSPENSION:
Front: Independent, coil springs, MacPherson struts, anti-roll bar, telescopic dampers
Rear: Independent, coil springs, multi-link location, anti-roll bar, telescopic dampers

STEERING:
Rack-and-pinion, with power assistance

BRAKES:
Hydraulic, front disc/rear disc

WHEELS/TYRES:
Cast alloy disc; 225/45-16in radial-ply

BODY/CHASSIS:
Unit construction, pressed-steel/composite two-door, two-seater sports car, with slide-down doors

DIMENSIONS:
Length   12ft 10.5in
Width   5ft 7in
Height   4ft 1.0in
Wheelbase   8ft 0in
Track, front   4ft 8.0in
Track, rear   4ft 9.0in

WEIGHT:
2,948lb

PERFORMANCE/ECONOMY:
Max speed   136mph
Acceleration   0–60mph in 7.9sec
Fuel consumption   typically 26mpg

UK PRICE WHEN NEW incl. tax:
£36,925

NUMBER BUILT:
8,000

Z8
2000–2003

ENGINE:
V8, alloy block, alloy heads
Capacity   4,941cc
Bore x stroke   94mm x 89mm
Compression ratio   11.0:1
Maximum power   400bhp at 6,600rpm
Valve gear   Four valves per cylinder, twin overhead camshafts
Fuelling   Bosch fuel injection

TRANSMISSION:
Six-speed manual, all-synchromesh

SUSPENSION:
Front: Independent, coil springs, MacPherson struts, anti-roll bar, telescopic dampers
Rear: Independent, coil springs, multi-link location, anti-roll bar, telescopic dampers

STEERING:
Rack-and-pinion, power-assisted

BRAKES:
Hydraulic, front disc/rear disc, with ABS

WHEELS/TYRES:
Cast alloy disc; 245/45-18 front; 275/40-18 rear radial-ply

BODY/CHASSIS:
Separate aluminium tubular/fabricated chassis frame, with steel/aluminium two-door two-seater sports body

DMENSIONS:
Length   14ft 5.2in
Width   6ft 0.4in
Height   4ft 3.8in
Wheelbase   8ft 2.6in
Track, front   5ft 1.1in
Track, rear   5ft 1.3in

WEIGHT:
3,495lb

PERFORMANCE/ECONOMY:
Max speed   155mph
Acceleration   0–60mph in 4.7sec
Fuel consumption   typically 18mpg

UK PRICE WHEN NEW incl. tax:
£80,000

NUMBER BUILT:
5,703

Even in 1986, BMW showed off the unique construction of the new Z1 two-seater. The doors were arranged, not to hinge outwards, but to slide down into recesses in the deep side sills.

and lost some of their character, while the M3 saloon (which would do great things for BMW's motor racing image) was still under wraps. For too long, critics said, BMW had been making only mildly exciting products for trendies and company executives.

BMW Technik GmbH was set up as a specialised technical division, with a hundred-strong staff in early 1985,

The Z1's front-end style was at once bland, but wind-cheating. Like the M1 model which had preceded it, this was a BMW with retractable headlamps, which were rare at the time for the Bavarian concern.

and encouraged to think laterally. At the time the group leader was Ulrich Bez, who had once been a top engineer at Porsche – and who would go on to be the charismatic boss of Aston Martin in the early 2000s. His style leader was ex-Ford stylist Harm Lagaay.

The first job tackled was christened Z1, a machine eventually previewed in 1986. Why Z1? Because this was a product of a new operation known as *Zentral Entwicklung* (Central Development). It was the first of a series of 'Z-cars', and was also BMW's first open two-seater since the charismatic 507 of the 1950s.

To get their show on the road as rapidly as possible, BMW Technik decided to use as much of the existing 325i model's running gear as possible, although this did not constrain the

style. It was the style, more than the running gear, which first caught the public's attention. In proportion, the Z1 was quite a bland machine, even if the wedge-shaped nose included headlamps housed behind sloping covers, but the major novelty was the inclusion of doors which did not open outwards as usual, but slid downwards into the ultra-deep, ultra-wide sills of the monocoque. Operation was by electric motors and toothed belts, these components being in the car's structure rather than in the doors themselves.

This was a fascinating innovation (never before seen on a production car or, as far as is known, on a commercial vehicle), for at the touch of a button (in each case on the body flank immediately behind the door pillars) this changed the aspect of the Z1 from conventional two-seater roadster to something related to a rather up-market buggy. Dozens of road test pictures showed the car being driven around at high-speed with the soft-top furled and the doors stowed downwards, but practical experience showed that this could be a very draughty business: it was not a feature of the Z1 which ever found a use on any other BMW.

Although shorter in the wheelbase, and with considerable stiffening around the tunnel, and truly massive

sills, much of the floorpan, the front suspension, steering, engine and manual transmission were lifted from the best-selling 325i saloon. However, the rear suspension (still kept under wraps for some time) was all-new. Relative to the front wheels, the engine had been moved several inches backwards, and was directly linked to the differential at the rear by a stout aluminium torque tube; it was surely no coincidence that Bez had come from Porsche, where the torque tube layout was a feature of the latest 924, 944 and 928 sports coupés.

The bodyshell was manufactured from plastic laminate, and the fold-back soft-top used exactly the same mechanism as that of the 325i Convertible. Although BMW stated they had harnessed ground effect knowledge from F1 cars, they nevertheless only claimed a drag coefficient figure of 0.32 with the soft-top erect, or 0.44 with it stowed away.

When BMW revealed the project in mid-1986, only two Z1s had been built, and at that precise moment there were no committed plans to put it on sale. After that decision was made, much prototype development, testing, proving and tooling-up would be needed before deliveries could begin. In the event, this explains why the first cars did not reach their customers until 1988, with only 58 such cars delivered before the end of the year.

Although the Z1's initial reception was warm enough, it took time for BMW to decide to put the car into production, and car build would be at a very leisurely rate. At first, BMW planned to produce no more than 2,000 cars a year, though they doubled this by 1990. The front end of the body, and the interior, were both restyled and re-equipped during the winter of 1986–87 and, so that management could keep a close eye on progress, final assembly was to be at the main Munich plant, hard by the 'four-cylinder' building.

It was only when deliveries began that BMW was finally ready to show off all the new technical features. To add stiffness to the much-modified

325i steel platform, a composite-fibre sandwich enhanced torsional rigidity by 10 per cent, while tubes around the windscreen pillars, and across the shell behind the fascia all helped. Apart from some changes to the type of composite used in the unstressed bodyshell (front and rear side panels were in Xenoy, a high-tech thermoplastic), the original concept was carried forward.

The impact of the new independent rear suspension, however, was quite another matter. Hung from a sturdy steel cross-beam/subframe, which also supported the differential and the tail of the torque tube, this was a layout never before seen under any BMW.

Here, for the first time since the mid-1950s, was a new type of rear suspension, and one which would eventually be adapted for every future new BMW model line. As already noted, during the 1980s the traditional type of semi-trailing link suspension had come in for more and more criticism – this centring on the unavoidable camber change as the rear wheels rose and fell.

Accordingly, the engineering team was set free to find a real and uncompromising solution, where performance was always to take precedence over cost control. The result, which BMW called the Z-axle,

looked (and in some ways was) very complex. Although coil springs and telescopic dampers were retained, these were the only obvious links between new and old, for the rear wheel movement was now controlled by what was described as a 'centrally guided, spherical double wishbone system'. It would be as difficult to describe the layout, and the nuances, in print as it would be to describe the intricacies of an integrated circuit, or an advanced knitting pattern!

Not only did this system constrain the wheel attitudes very accurately, but (like the Porsche 928 before it) there were ways of controlling toe-in and toe-out too. Apart from offering outstanding control of the wheel angles, along with 'anti-squat' and 'anti-dive' measures, it was claimed to be lighter than the old-type semi-trailing-arm layout.

It took time, even for the most seasoned motoring writers, to get used to this, a distinctly new type of BMW. Mel Nichols, writing in *Autocar*, summed up the Z1's unique character: 'Refinement is a strong early message from the Z1. At first, it seems an incongruous partner for the sheer

Details varied considerably from model to model, but BMW's famous Z-axle (this shows a typical layout) was first seen under the Z1 roadster, which went on sale in 1988.

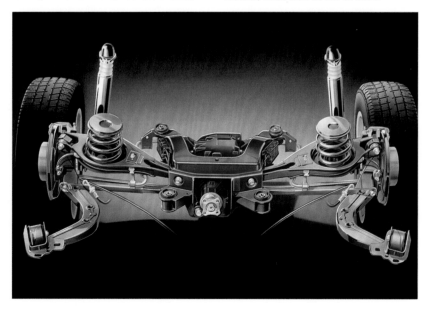

open-air feeling of driving with the doors down. The only cars previously offering such exposed motoring have been things like Morgans and Caterhams – and they come with hard suspensions and a rortiness that's a million miles away from this silken BMW. This is more like a Mercedes SL with the doors missing, but then it has the nimbleness and light feeling of a roadster, so it doesn't fit the mould there either.'

BMW now struck the usual motor industry 'chicken-and-egg' situation. If they limited production then, by definition, selling prices would be high, but if they spent more money on reducing unit costs, and brought down the selling price, was there a big market for this car?

In the end, and after much deliberation, BMW opted to make the Z1 exclusive, but freely available at

The Z1 was really a rolling test bed for new engineering (some people said it was 'BMW engineers thinking aloud...'), so there was little attempt to provide an arresting style as well. Although much of what went into the Z1 of 1986 was later seen under the Z3/Z4 models of the 1990s and 2000s, every detail of their application was different. There was never, incidentally, any sign of a Z2 model.

the right price – their own high price. In this way, it was always going to be an expensive car – when launched it cost the equivalent of £25,000 in Germany – but BMW stuck to their policy, and it paid off.

Although the Z1 was never astonishingly fast – with a top speed of 136mph and 0–60mph acceleration in 7.9 seconds, it was no faster than the mass-production 325i range on which it was based – it was still a sports car that developed its own exclusive market. Exclusive? Of course, for this was not a BMW which could be sold in the USA, and in any territory it was always an expensive BMW – an expensive car by any contemporary late-1980s standards, for the German price was set at 85,000 Deutschmarks (about £26,500).

By the time official Z1 imports to the UK began, the concessionaires had set an ambitious price of £36,925, although customers were not deterred. In those days, in the UK, a BMW 325i Convertible (a close relative, but an open-top four-seater) cost £21,225, a TVR 350i cost £19,350 and – to bring the Z1 into favourable focus – a Porsche 911 Carrera cabriolet was £41,711.

Naturally there were criticisms, but not of the main concept. Several pundits suggested that the Z1 deserved a more powerful engine, some thought that a hard-top version should be available in addition to the drop-top, and naturally there were those who wanted to see the price reduced.

BMW listened politely, said nothing, took no action, and carried on building Z1s, at peak, at the gentle rate of about 15 cars every day. As a publicity tool, as an image raiser, and as a way to gain in-service experience of the new Z-axle, the Z1 did a great job. When it reached the end of its 'sanction' of 8,000 machines in 1991 (of which about 140 came to the UK), it was quietly retired.

Z8 – big bruiser

Eight years after the sleek Z1 was discontinued, in 2000 BMW produced another 'why don't we...?' roadster, the Z8. In their design, their engineering, and their intention, the two cars could not have been more different. Where the Z1 had been neat, understated, and silky-smooth, the Z8 was big, brassy, very powerful and altogether

Sliding doors before the Z1

To use sliding instead of swing-open doors might look attractive, neat even, but it was never going to be easy to engineer. Panel vans had used sliding doors for years, although most rattled, all were difficult to seal, and awkward-looking channels were needed to support them.

All over the world, prototypes were built, some were exhibited at motor shows, but almost none got further than the press viewings. Soon after the Second World War, however, Kaiser allowed the designer 'Dutch' Darrin to indulge himself with the two-seater sports car that bore his name. Reputedly, its sliding door mechanism worked well, but this was an expensive machine which sold only slowly.

Few other attempts (at least, in production-ready form) were made

to improve on this installation, so when the BMW Z1 Roadster was launched in 1988, it caused a real stir. Even then, of course, this was not really a sliding door installation, but one where the doors actually slid downwards into pouches in the sills.

Since the demise of the Z1, only Peugeot, with its 1007 city car, has been brave enough to put a model with sliding doors onto the market – MPVs excepted, of course.

It was typical of BMW that, even when the Z1's doors were slid down, the cockpit/cabin still looked neat, tidy and integrated. If only BMW could have had a lower price for the Z1, many more would surely have been sold. And with looks like that, some supercar performance would also have been appreciated. (LAT)

more 'in your face'. The inspiration, they say, came in 1993 when BMW's 'terrible twins' – Wolfgang Reitzle and Bernd Pischetsrieder – had attended rather a bibulous party at the factory in which an old 507 was on display, liked

it all over again, and decided that one day – one day – they would try to repeat the trick.

Like the Z3 before it (which is described in the next chapter), this was a car chosen to star in a James

Bond Film (*The World is Not Enough*), where it met a very unseemly end, by

To test the public's reaction to a possible Z8 sports car, BMW produced the ZO7 'project' coupé, and exhibited it at the Tokyo Motor Show.

being cut in half, lengthways, by circular saws dangling from helicopters being flown against it by anti-Bond villains! The cut-in-half car (or, should I say, more accurately, *a* 'cut-in-half' car) was later seen at a 'Bond cars in films' exhibition at the National Motor Museum at Beaulieu.

(There are stories, incidentally, that in spite of signing a very lucrative contract to supply cars, that BMW was slow in supplying pilot-production Z8s to the film company, which resorted to building some lookalike prototypes of their own – based on replica AC Cobra chassis!)

Conceived under the code ZO7, and evolved by the resourceful BMW Technik GmbH team-within-a-team, a concept car was revealed at the Tokyo Motor Show of October 1997. The definitive machine was then shown off in 1999, a few months before deliveries could begin.

Once again, this was going to be a test-bed for new engineering techniques, although the sheer glamour of providing a V8-engined

Was the Z8 styled by the advance project team in California? One look at this rear view, surely, tells us that the shape was influenced by other V8-engined drop-tops which thunder up and down the freeways of Los Angeles! So can this really be the same company which launched the Isetta bubble car in the 1950s?

400bhp monster also had its attractions. Only a very profitable, very self-confident, and very ambitious company could have tackled such a car – and BMW was all of those. It was, after all, producing about 800,000 cars a year at the time, and was looking to push this up further in the years which followed.

Amazingly, the style seen as a concept in Tokyo was carried forward, virtually unchanged to the real prototype of 1998, although the streamlined hump behind the driver's seat did not survive the transition, nor did the alternative fastback style, for in production this was to be no more than an open-top two-seater. It was a car which faced up, head-to-head, with cars such as the Chrysler Corporation's Viper, and to make a real impact on the market place it would need all the performance and all the sheer pizzazz of cars like the latest Ferraris and Aston Martins.

Although the Z8 could not possibly be a direct replacement for the 8-Series cars (the character of the two cars was widely different), there were some technical similarities – in particular in the use of BMW's latest, much-lauded, 4.9-litre V8 engine, which was backed by a six-speed manual transmission.

The style, so startling 'retro' in 1997, was preserved in almost every

detail, with rounded lines, with no front or rear bumpers (merely large swollen mouldings to take impacts – one shuddered at the price of renewing these after an accident), with a big and solid windscreen and surround, and of course with electrically-powered soft-top actuation.

The real technical advance in this car was hidden away from view – an advanced form of welded and extruded aluminium spaceframe chassis construction. At the time, and even later, BMW was not at all anxious to show off this chassis, although experience showed it to be such a success (but at high cost) that the same constructional methods were used to underpin the BMW-engineered Rolls-Royce (the new Phantom) which appeared four years later. BMW had always aimed to keep this car down to an un-laden weight of 3,087lb (1,400kg), but by the time every safety regulation and crash test had been satisfied, and all the expected equipment added, this had risen to 3,495lb (1,585kg) – still creditable, but no longer sensational.

This structure was clothed in a smooth aluminium-skinned body style, which definitely had cues and artistic images which looked familiar when viewed alongside the old 507. For this, credit mainly went to Henrik

Fisker, a Dane who was then heading up BMW's 'Designworks' studio in California. Compared with the concept car, the road car was provided with twin safety hoops behind the two seats, and at one time it was suggested that a removable aluminium hard-top would also be provided, but this feature does not seem to have made it into the showrooms. Like the Z1, because this was a car which was going to need a lot of personal attention from top management, they arranged for structures to be built up at the Dingolfing plant, but for all final assembly to be concentrated in dedicated workshops in the Munich plant, close to the HQ building.

The running gear – engine, transmission, and chassis – was a clever amalgam of current and proposed BMW volume-car hardware, with the hottest versions of the 5-Series and 7-Series range providing most of it. The big, 4.9-litre V8 power unit, with aluminium castings, four-valves per cylinder and twin overhead camshafts per bank, had double Vanos variable valve timing, and produced no less than 400bhp at 6,600rpm.

This was quite enough to guarantee a top speed of an electronically limited 155mph (175mph would have been possible if that limiter had been

immobilised), and it perfectly justified the brawny, M5-type Getrag six-speed gearbox. The same top speed, incidentally, was available in fifth gear, and no less than 139mph came up in fourth before the 7,000rev-limiter cut in!

The rest of the chassis was predictable enough – BMW's latest take on a MacPherson strut front suspension, but this time allied to power-assisted rack-and-pinion steering, the very latest iteration of the Z-axle rear end which had made its debut under the Z1 in the late 1980s, and massive four-wheel disc brakes, ABS-equipped, and all.

What a remarkable picture, showing that the general proportions of the Z8 (furthest from the camera) were very close to those of the 507 style of the 1950s. Perhaps BMW cheated here, by using exactly the same paint colour, but it emphasises just what a sleek car the 507 was, for its time.

Big, impressive, brutal rather than elegant, the Z8 was a commanding two-seater of the early 2000s. BMW took great care to make sure it looked different from other roadsters. The front end featured a horizontal interpretation of the traditional 'twin-kidney' grille style because a big air intake was needed to get enough cooling air into that packed-with-power engine bay.

Technik city cars – E1 and Z13

Like most long-established car makers, in the 1990s BMW spent some time studying the idea of producing small 'city cars' – the sort of small, under-powered, machines that the 'green' lobby would foist upon the motoring public if they got the chance. In this case, the impetus was a far-fetched USA threat of imposing a 'zero-emissions' quota on car makers by the end of the century.

BMW went through the motions, and although there was little evidence that they ever intended to put such machines into series production, at least they were able to learn more about packaging and alternative power plants.

The first such car to meet its public was the E1, of which several versions were made between 1991 and 1993. The original car was a cute and stubby little four-seater, with a dry-battery electric power pack and a 44bhp electric motor in the tail. The structure was based around a light aluminium chassis frame, and with a claimed top speed of only 75mph drum brakes were considered adequate. This car was eventually destroyed in a fire – which apparently started in its electrical propulsion system.

The E2 followed in 1992, this being a longer-wheelbase development of the E1, with a more powerful (55bhp) electric motor package and a bigger cabin.

In the meantime, BMW also developed the Z13 project, which was another aluminium-framed city car. Announced in March 1993, this was a compact little rear-engined two-door/three-seater machine (the driver's seat was in the centre of the car), and it was a really high performer, for the engine was an 895bhp/1,100cc water-cooled four-cylinder as used in the contemporary BMW K1100RS motorcycle, this driving through a CVT transmission. This was an appealing little pocket-

rocket, which caused some BMW personalities to ask: 'Why don't we. . ?' – but like the other prototype city cars, it came to nothing.

The final E1 project car appeared in September 1993, with styling related to the Z13, but with yet another variation on the aluminium structure concept. This time there were two power plants – the 82bhp K1100 motorcycle engine and CVT transmission up front, with a totally separate 45bhp electric motor and

E1 was a small hybrid-powered saloon dating from 1993.

massive rechargeable battery pack in the tail, driving the rear wheels.

Like most such concept 'city cars', this final E1 type went straight from press launch to obscurity, and seems to have been abandoned soon afterwards.

Z13 used a rear-mounted BMW motorcycle engine.

Although BMW strove to keep down the weight, the Z8 nevertheless adopted huge cast-alloy 18in road wheels, with 8in rims at the front of the car, and 9in rims at the rear.

When the Z8 went on sale in 2000, there was never any doubt that it would be an expensive – very expensive – machine, and with that in mind BMW had already settled for producing only 1,500 cars a year. This equated to only six cars a day, peanuts by volume car-makers' standards, and certainly a rate at which hand-assembly was justified and seen to be so. All cars produced had left-hand-drive.

Even by BMW's 2000 standards, the Z8's original UK price of £80,000 caused a few eyebrows to be raised. In that sort of stratospheric bracket, clients could buy a Porsche 911 (two-wheel-drive) for £55,950, a Jaguar XK8 Convertible for £57,955, a Mercedes-Benz SL500 for £63,940 and (by digging deep into financial reserves) a Ferrari F355 Spider for a whopping £105,439; no other BMW car came close in price – for even the V12-engined 750i saloons were between £5,000 and £10,000 cheaper.

The Z8, in other words, was being asked to sell as a real Supercar, where buyers' opinions can be fickle, and where expectations of performance, build quality and individual character levels are very high indeed, and up to a point, the new BMW succeeded.

Yet the fact is that the Z8 was more of a bruiser, more of a cruiser in some ways, than an ultra-high performance sports car. Once fired up, there were spine-chilling rumbles from the big V8 engine – not the singing sound of a Ferrari, or the staccato bark of a flat-six Porsche – which was bound to appeal to wealthy Americans used to similar domestic V8s. Like many other open-top two-seaters, its structure was not really stiff enough, there was more understeer than a quick driver would have wanted, and the ride quality was a touch hard for the image required.

The road-testers of *Autocar* summarised the Z8's muddled character: 'All the ingredients are in place, but the finished product lacks the cohesion we'd expected… It's too wide, heavy and, critically, fails to involve its driver as any car must before it can be labelled a great driving machine… The Z8 is a great-looking base for a world-class engine,

A Z9 derivative of the Z8? This was a one-off concept showing how BMW might have wanted this pedigree to develop. Other priorities got in the way however, and the Z9 remained as a 'might-have-been'.

but merely a good rather than a great sports car.'

BMW, to their credit, took such criticism to heart, and did their best to improve the cars in detail as production ran on, but the end came gracefully in 2003. By that time the specialised facilities at Dingolfing and Munich were getting in the way of preparations to build new cars (like the 1-Series), so the project was closed down after 5,703 cars had been built, a total only slightly below what one would have expected in a three-year career.

One great bonus came out of this programme – the sheer know-how gained in the development and manufacture of complex aluminium spaceframe structures. It was no coincidence that Z8 manufacture was winding down at precisely the time that production of aluminium-spaceframed Rolls-Royce Phantoms was building up.

The Z3 & Z4
– the North American connection

Z3

1995–2002

ENGINE:
Four cylinders/six cylinders in line, iron block, alloy head, or six-cylinder, light-alloy block, alloy head

Capacity	(4-cyl) 1,796cc/1,895cc (6-cyl) 2,171cc/2,494cc/ 2,793cc/2,979cc/3,201cc
Maximum power	116bhp to 321bhp
Valve gear	Two valves per cylinder, single overhead camshaft (1,796cc); all other engines four valves per cylinder/twin overhead camshafts
Fuelling	Bosch Motronic fuel injection

TRANSMISSION:
Five-speed manual, all-synchromesh, or optional automatic transmission

SUSPENSION:
Front: Independent, coil springs, MacPherson struts, anti-roll bar, hydraulic telescopic dampers
Rear: Independent, coil springs, semi-trailing arms, anti-roll bar, hydraulic telescopic dampers

STEERING:
Rack-and-pinion, with power-assistance

BRAKES:
Hydraulic, front disc/rear disc, with servo assistance and ABS

WHEELS/TYRES:
Alloy disc; from 205/60-15in radial-ply

BODY/CHASSIS:
Unit-construction, pressed-steel two-seater open sports car, or (Z3M only) hatchback coupé

DIMENSIONS:

Length	13ft 2.5in
Width	5ft 3.4in
Height	4ft 2.8in
Wheelbase	8ft 0.2in
Track, front	4ft 7.5in
Track, rear	4ft 8.1in

WEIGHT:
from 2,558lb

PERFORMANCE/ECONOMY:

Max speed	123mph (1.9-litre); 155mph (Z3M)
Acceleration	0–60mph in 8.4sec (1.9-litre); 0–60mph in 5.1sec (Z3M)
Fuel consumption	typically (1.9-litre) 28–32mpg, (Z3M) 19–22mpg

UK PRICE WHEN NEW incl. tax:
from £19,950

NUMBER BUILT:
297,082

Z4

2002–

ENGINE:
Four-cylinder, alloy block, alloy head/six-cylinder, light-alloy block, alloy head

Capacity	(4-cyl) 1,995cc, (6-cyl) 2,171cc/2,494cc/2,979cc
Maximum power	From 150bhp/1,995cc to 231bhp/2,979cc
Valve gear	All engines, four valves per cylinder/twin overhead camshafts
Fuelling	Seimens fuel injection/engine management

TRANSMISSION:
Five-speed or six-speed manual, all-synchromesh, or optional automatic transmission

SUSPENSION:
Front: Independent, coil springs, MacPherson struts, anti-roll bar, hydraulic telescopic dampers
Rear: Independent, coil springs, semi-trailing arms, anti-roll bar, hydraulic telescopic dampers

STEERING:
Rack-and-pinion, with power-assistance

BRAKES:
Hydraulic, front disc/rear disc, with servo assistance and ABS

WHEELS & TYRES:
Alloy disc; from 205/55-16in radial-ply

BODY/CHASSIS:
Unit-construction, pressed-steel two-seater open sports car

DIMENSIONS:

Length	13ft 5.0in
Width	5ft 10.0in
Height	4ft 3.2in
Wheelbase	8ft 2.2in
Track, front	4ft 10.1in
Track, rear	5ft 0in

WEIGHT:
from 2,756lb

PERFORMANCE & ECONOMY:

Max speed	134mph (2.0-litre) 155mph (3.0-litre)
Acceleration	0–60mph in 8.2 secs, (2.0-litre); 0–60mph in 6.2 secs (3.0-litre)
Fuel consumption	typically (2.0-litre) 26–32mpg, (3.0-litre) 25–28mpg

PRICE NEW incl. tax:
From £22,755

NUMBER BUILT:
On going

First seen in 1995, the Z3 roadster was BMW's first-ever mass-market two-seater, and was built only at Spartanburg, USA.

Although the sales figures tell another story, there's no doubt that BMW's Z3 sports car was initially disappointing to the technology-hungry media. Even though it looked sleek by contemporary mid-1990s standards, there was nothing startling about the running gear: indeed, the entire platform was based on that of the 3-Series Compact.

No matter. Following up on a corporate decision made in the early 1990s, BMW wanted to get established in the sports car market, and to start building cars in the USA, where sales were booming. The combination of E36-style 3-Series engineering, bland styling (safe, that is, for American customers), and assembly in South Carolina ticked all the boxes in that frame. Announced in

In the first year of Z3 production, 1996, most cars were built with this 1.9-litre four-cylinder engine.

The Z3 was smooth and practical, if not sensationally beautiful, from any angle. It was designed with North American sales in mind and built in BMW's modern South Carolina factory.

Porsche Boxster in all markets, sometimes by a factor of two to one. What was that about 'give the public what it wants…'?

A great burst of favourable pre-launch publicity undoubtedly helped. On reflection, in 1995 BMW chose an unbeatable way to launch their new sports car – by making sure that it appeared in a much-hyped James Bond film – *Goldeneye* – well before there were any cars in the showrooms. Maybe the Z3's appearance in that film was fleeting, and there was no death-defying stunt driving to sear it into the enthusiast's subconscious, but BMW's subliminal point was made: 'If this car is good enough for James Bond, it *must* be good enough for you!'

Rumours of a new BMW two-seater had begun to spread in 1993, and later in the year BMW confirmed its intention to build the new car at a brand-new factory in South Carolina, USA. Not only would this be BMW's first American-built car, but apart from the Z1 (which was purposely a short-term product) it would be the company's first-ever volume-production open two-seater. The 328 of the late 1930s, the 507 of the 1950s, and the mid-engined M1 of the 1970s were all too exclusive, and (by the standards of the day) too expensive to qualify.

late 1995, and with deliveries to the USA, and back across the Atlantic into Europe, beginning in 1996, the Z3 surged smoothly up the charts. Although only 2,060 cars were built in 1995, by the end of 1997 nearly 110,000 had been produced. To BMW's joy, and Porsche's lasting chagrin, it outsold the mid-engined

This was a major change in corporate policy, but the decision was made for very good commercial reasons, following a lot of careful analysis. Not only had Mercedes-Benz made a great deal of money out of open-top two-seaters (the SL family) in recent decades, but they were also known to have a new and much smaller type (the SLK) under development.

Other rivals, such as Mazda (with the MX-5/Miata) were also sure that open-top two-seaters were commercially viable. And, purely by chance, once BMW took control of the Rover Group in 1994, they discovered that Rover was also proposing to revive the MG brand with the launch of the MGF! To match, and hopefully to out-do, such cars, BMW therefore commissioned a two-seater called the Z3. It would pick-up major components from other cars in the company's range, and would be intended for sale in the popular/mid-price bracket.

As an aside, the Z1 had been on sale from 1988 to 1991, so whatever happened to 'Z2', which we never saw? Some say that it never

progressed beyond exploratory discussions and BMW was tight-lipped about that at the time, and remains so, to this day.

For very good commercial reasons, the new sports car, soon christened Z3, would not run on a brand-new platform, for the investment burden, and timescale involved, could not be

From mid-1999, the Z3 was slightly restyled, with more bulbous rear wings and bumper. This is the 2.8-litre six-cylinder derivative, with the optional 'Speedster cover' behind the seats.

Z3s were always very well and comfortably equipped two-seaters. This is the fascia layout of the revised model of mid-1999.

The combination of Z3 structure and the
ultra-powerful engine of the M3 produced the
late-1990s M Roadster. Its sister car, the M
Coupé, was not attractive enough, and was
not a success.

Based closely on the Z3, the M Roadster had
flared wheelarches to accommodate the fatter
tyres, and revised front lower body panels to
help provide high-speed stability. Other give-
away features were revised sills, different
wheels and four exhaust outlets.

justified. Instead, BMW had to choose
one or other versions of the E-36/
3-Series platform – and soon settled
on the Compact layout, rather than
the more modern version also
available. This was not only done for
cost-saving reasons, but because the
Compact's old-type semi-trailing-link
rear suspension took up less space in
the tail than did the Z-axle of other
3-Series types.

In fact, the Compact platform/
floorpan/running gear could not be
used without some significant
redevelopment. Whereas the

wheelbase of the E36 Compact was
106.3in, that chosen for the two-seater
Z3 was only 96.2in. This was effectively
done by cutting-and-shutting the
floorpan where the rear seat footwells
were located on the Compact – yet
even so, the Z3 seats were significantly
further away from the front axle line
than before. Some observers even
went as far as to compare the Z3 with
British sports cars of old, pointing out
the long bonnet/short tail packaging,
and the fact that the seats were almost
as far back towards the line of the back
axle as possible.

Spartanburg, USA

Early in the 1990s, BMW decided to start building cars in North America, mainly to serve that market. After a lengthy search, which involved trawling every state in search of labour availability, planning permissions, and financial incentives, the company settled on a green-field site at Spartanburg, South Carolina.

This city, which is about 60 miles west of Charlotte, offered

everything except car-building expertise. Shrugging this off, BMW presented its new constructional team just 23 months to get a brand-new plant up, running and building cars. To 'shake down' the facility, BMW first arranged for some USA-market E36 3-Series cars to be assembled there, but the new Z3 sports car, for which Spartanburg's facilities had always been intended,

finally broke cover in November 1995.

After that time, Spartanburg was expanded steadily, first by also becoming the home of the new X5 4x4 model, and later by the assembly of Z4 sports cars, which took over from the Z3 in 2002. By 2003, annual production had exceeded 165,000 units a year – and BMW had further plans to expand this in the future.

The 3.2-litre M Coupé launched in 1999 was very powerful, but not as elegant as many of its customers would have liked.

Shaped in BMW's new Design studios in California, the style of the original Z3 is best described as conservative. Although there's no doubt that it would be attractive to Americans, and pleasing to almost everyone, it was bland, and the passage of time has not been kind to it. However, as with the Porsche 911 in the 1970s, the need to fit wider wheels and tyres for high-performance models meant that the rear wheelarches needed to be flared even more – and that helped.

For traditionalists, the good news was that it still retained the double-grille front end – and was positively plastered with 'spinner' badges, one on the nose, one on the tail, and one on each flank behind the front wheel-arches. Even on the first cars, the wheelarches were somewhat flared, and the cockpit was up to the standards expected of this type of BMW.

As far as the soft-top was concerned, BMW had played safe, by consulting a specialist concern known as the American Sunroof Corporation. For sure, this was a fold-back top, but it was as well-engineered as any in the

Like the Z3 which it replaced, the Z4 two-seater had its cabin set well-back towards the rear wheels, this time with a very sharp cut-off to the tail contours.

First and second thoughts compared – the original Z3 of 1995 had a more rounded and rather bland style, while the Z4 of 2002 has a much more aggressive, more cultured shape.

The Z4's sculpted sides and strange headlamp contours are typical of the new 'flame-surfacing' BMW styling. The Z4 is powered exclusively by one of BMW's celebrated in-line six-cylinder engines.

world, and would remain so during a long life. It was not power-assisted, of course, but was as good a manual assembly as could be arranged – and a lift-off hard-top was to be optional.

Looks, style and equipment were all well and good, but the Z3's original problem was that it simply wasn't fast enough, and it didn't handle very well. There were only two engine choices in early Z3s: a 118bhp/1,796cc unit with a single-overhead-camshaft head, and a 140bhp/1,895cc engine with twin

overhead camshafts. Brisk by contemporary standards, for sure, but not outstanding, and some critics openly yawned. During 1996, though, the frowns only turned into smiles when a much more meaty version with the six-cylinder 192bhp/2,793cc engine was launched – for that car could reach 135mph and felt more competitive, even though the semi-trailing-arm rear suspension often limited fast cornering.

Over the next two years, BMW then continued with its familiar mix-and-match policy of shuffling four- and six-cylinder engines to cover the entire market with 2.0, 2.2, 2.5 and eventually 3.0-litre versions of the 'six' eventually coming on stream, but that was not all. In the face of the evidence that semi-trailing arm rear suspension would not really suit such enterprise, the company also launched a 321bhp M Roadster.

Seasoned BMW fanatics can now write their own specification for this car. Into the familiar Z3 structure, but with even wider wheelarches to cover 245/40-17in tyres, the team crammed the 321bhp/3,201cc engine and six-speed gearbox of the existing M3, while, for sale only in the USA there was a 243bhp/3,154cc derivative of the same power unit.

Starting at the end of 1998, BMW also launched the Z3 coupé, which featured a rather gawky three-door hatchback body. Elegant it was not, and although it was undoubtedly a practical, very high-speed load-carrier, it never really hit the spot. Available only with six-cylinder engines, including the full-house M3 power units, it was one of the less happy shapes to come out of the Spartanburg factory.

Z4 – starting over

Seven years after the Z3 had been introduced, BMW finally replaced it with a totally different two-seater – the Z4. No matter what criticism had been thrown at the Z3 (and, especially in later years, there had been a lot), BMW could always say – and did so –

that they had sold nearly 300,000 of them, and that it had already been a very profitable programme, 'thank you very much'.

Even so, the world saw the Z4, which took over at the end of 2002, as a much more serious contender. Not only did it look more distinctive, but it was totally based on the modern 3-Series platform, this time with the Z-axle independent rear suspension. Cannily, too, BMW had moved it further up-market, by launching it only with six-cylinder engines, and at a higher price. Compared with the 3-Series on which the running gear was based, the power-assisted steering was electrical, the wheel tracks were wider, and the ride/handling balance had been redeveloped.

Although the company had always been slightly cautious about the image of its Z3, there was no need for any defensive talk concerning the Z4. This time around, the new car ran on a 98.2in wheelbase (a shortened version of the E46 3-Series family car platform, whose wheelbase was 107.3in), and looked more chunky and more purposeful than before. Significantly, BMW also claimed that the new shell was more than twice as torsionally stiff as the Z3 had been.

The exterior design was yet another interpretation of the Bangle 'flame surfacing' theme, for there were sharp edges atop the front wings, and a very noticeable swage across the doors. The difference compared with the Z3 was remarkable – it had sometimes been possible to ignore the Z3, but a Z4 seemed to be much more visually obvious than that. The shape now included more stylised headlamp pods, and a rather humped tail, sharply cut off to enclose the high-level brake light. There were now two separate safety roll hoops behind the high-back seats, and the soft-top had optional, electrically actuated power assistance.

When first launched, there were 192bhp/2,494cc and 231bhp/2,979cc six-cylinder engines, but by 2005, 150bhp/1,995cc four-cylinder and 170bhp/2,171cc six-cylinder power units had been added to fill out the

Under the skin, much of the running gear of the Z4 is an evolution of the 3-Series, complete with in-line six-cylinder engine and the celebrated Z-axle independent rear suspension.

range. Most cars had five-speed gearboxes, but a six-speed Getrag 'box was available with the most powerful engine. There are no diesel-engine alternatives as yet, nor a second-generation hatchback/hard-top type – but with BMW it is never wise to say that such things will never appear.

In the first ten years, indeed, the Z3/Z4 range had come a long way at BMW. Originally a fringe player, it had become an established model, and in production terms it was certainly an important cornerstone of the Spartanburg operation in the USA. More derivatives, and yet more generations, seem sure to follow.

While taking a sabbatical from F1 racing, BMW also found time to develop V12-powered racing sports cars. This V12LMR model won the prestigious Le Mans 24-Hour race in 1999.

BMW
today

By ruthlessly paring off as much weight as possible, and by edging up the 3.2-litre engine's power output to 360bhp, BMW made the M3 CSL of 2003 the fastest 3-Series of all time.

Today BMW is an industrial colossus. There is truly no comparison between 21st century BMW, a group which produces well over a million cars every year (and does that on three continents) with the car-making company which stuttered back into life in the 1950s.

Once the company had faced down imminent bankruptcy in 1959, recovery, expansion and increased profitability was steady, and relentless. Year after year, it seemed, the limit to the company's size had been reached – and year after year the pundits were proved wrong.

1–Series
introduced in 2004

ENGINE:
Four cylinders/six cylinders in line, alloy block, alloy head

Capacity	1,596cc to 2,996cc petrol; 1,995cc diesel
Maximum power	115bhp at 6,000rpm to 258bhp at 6,600rpm
Valve gear	Four valves per cylinder, twin overhead camshafts
Fuelling	BMW/Siemens fuel injection, with turbocharger on diesels

TRANSMISSION:
Five-speed or six-speed manual, all-synchromesh; optional automatic transmission

SUSPENSION:
Front: Independent, coil springs, MacPherson struts, anti-roll bar, hydraulic telescopic dampers
Rear: Independent, coil springs, multi-link Z-axle, anti-roll bar, hydraulic telescopic dampers

STEERING:
Rack-and-pinion, with power-assistance

BRAKES:
Hydraulic, front disc/rear disc, with servo assistance and ABS

WHEELS/TYRES:
Cast alloy disc; from 185/60-16in radial-ply

BODY/CHASSIS:
Unit-construction, pressed-steel five-door hatchback

DIMENSIONS:

Length	13ft 0.5in
Width	5ft 10.9in
Height	4ft 8.3in
Wheelbase	8ft 8.7in
Track, front	4ft 10.5in
Track, rear	4ft 10.9in

WEIGHT:
from 2,657lb

PERFORMANCE/ECONOMY:

Max speed	121mph to 155mph
Acceleration	0–60mph in 10.0 to 6.0sec
Fuel consumption	typically 36–45mpg (diesel); 30–35mpg (petrol)

UK PRICE WHEN NEW incl. tax:
from: £15,690

M6 coupé
introduced in 2005

ENGINE:
V10, alloy block, alloy head

Capacity	4,999cc
Bore x stroke	92mm x 75mm
Compression ratio	12.0:1
Maximum power	500bhp at 7,750rpm
Valve gear	Four valves per cylinder, twin overhead camshafts
Fuelling	BMW/Siemens fuel injection

TRANSMISSION:
Seven-speed manual, all-synchromesh

SUSPENSION:
Front: Independent, coil springs, MacPherson struts, anti-roll bar, hydraulic telescopic dampers
Rear: Independent, coil springs, multi-link Z-axle, anti-roll bar, hydraulic telescopic dampers

STEERING:
Rack-and-pinion, with power assistance

BRAKES:
Hydraulic, front disc/rear disc, with servo assistance and ABS

WHEELS/TYRES:
Cast alloy disc; 255/40-19in front; 285/30-19in rear, radial-ply

BODY/CHASSIS:
Unit construction, pressed-steel two-door fixed-head coupé

DIMENSIONS:

Length	15ft 11.7in
Width	6ft 1.0in
Height	4ft 6.2in
Wheelbase	9ft 1.5in
Track, front	5ft 1.7in
Track, rear	5ft 2.4in

WEIGHT:
3,770lb

PERFORMANCE/ECONOMY:

Max speed	155mph
Acceleration	0–60mph in 4.5sec
Fuel consumption	typically 18–22mpg

UK PRICE WHEN NEW incl. tax:
£79,760

X5 4x4 (SUV)
introduced in 1999

ENGINE:
Six cylinders in line/V8 petrol; six cylinders in line diesel, alloy block, alloy heads

Capacity	2,979cc/4,398cc/ 4,619cc/4,799cc petrol 2,993cc diesel
Maximum power	231bhp at 5,900rpm to 360bhp at 6,200rpm (petrol); 184bhp to 218bhp at 4,000rpm (diesel)
Valve gear	Four valves per cylinder, twin overhead camshafts
Fuelling	Bosch/Siemens fuel injection, plus turbocharger for diesels

TRANSMISSION:
Four-wheel-drive. Five-speed/six-speed manual, all-synchromesh; optional automatic transmission

SUSPENSION:
Front: Independent, coil springs, MacPherson struts, anti-roll bar, hydraulic telescopic dampers
Rear: Independent, coil springs/air suspension, self-levelling, multi-link Z-axle, anti-roll bar, hydraulic telescopic dampers

STEERING:
Rack and pinion, with power assistance

BRAKES:
Hydraulic, front disc/rear disc, with servo assistance and ABS

WHEELS/TYRES:
Alloy disc; from 235/65-17in radial-ply

BODY/CHASSIS:
Unit construction, pressed-steel five-door estate/SUV

DIMENSIONS:

Length	15ft 3.6in
Width	6ft 1.6in
Height	5ft 7.7in
Wheelbase	9ft 3.0in
Track, front	5ft 2in
Track, rear	5ft 2in

WEIGHT:
from 4,400lb

PERFORMANCE/ECONOMY:

Max speed	126mph to 153mph
Acceleration	0–60mph in 8.8 to 6.0sec
Fuel consumption	typically 20–24mpg to 18–22mpg

UK PRICE WHEN NEW incl. tax:
from £33,000

One image tells two stories – first, BMW's Regensburg factory had produced its three millionth car in March 2005, and second that the range now included the 1-Series.

The fifth generation 3-Series (this is the Touring/estate version) featured a toned down interpretation of the Bangle-generation styling theme. Like all previous 3-Series models, the new type was expected to sell in huge quantities.

Not only that, but the company's product range never seems to have stopped growing either. At the time of writing, in the mid-2000s, there were eight distinctly different models in the BMW range – including one sports car, and two four-wheel-drive SUVs. In addition, BMW controlled the fast-selling Mini marque through a factory in England, and made the Rolls-Royce Phantom at Goodwood in Sussex. It

also produced motorcycles in Berlin, and had a high-tech civil aero-engined gas-turbine factory in Germany too.

By the end of the 20th century, BMW was already producing more than 750,000 BMW-badged cars a year, and at the same time controlling the British Rover Group, which at that time made another 300,000 vehicles per annum. Three final assembly plants in Germany were operating along with those in the USA and in South Africa, which were fed by engine plants in Austria and the UK.

That, of course, was only a snap shot, for within five years Rover had been discarded, USA assembly had rocketed, the New Mini had been established in the UK, Rolls-Royce had been annexed, X3s were being built in Austria, and no fewer than a million BMW-badged cars were being built in one year.

All this, of course, made it impossible to describe BMW as a steady, established, business – for that business was changing every time one looked at it. In the 1980s, for instance, when there were only three separate ranges of closed cars in the lists – the 3-Series, 5-Series and 7-Series – together with one or other of

The Rover affair

The Rover Group, the battered remnant of the troubled British Leyland colossus, came to BMW's attention in 1993. British Aerospace had owned the company since 1988, and having spent years knocking down old factories and contracting the business, was now ready to bail out.

Rover embraced three other active makes – Land Rover, MG and Mini – and other once-famous names (including Triumph and Austin-Healey) were also in the trademarks locker. There was also a valuable technical and financial link with Honda of Japan.

With three large and under-used factories to support – Longbridge (Birmingham), Solihull (near Birmingham) and Cowley (Oxford) – Rover was still a loss-making conglomerate, and could not hope to survive on its own, but BMW was happy to buy it all from BAe for £800 million. From March 1994, Rover therefore became a wholly owned subsidiary of BMW, and the Honda connection was unceremoniously ended.

For the next six years, BMW invested hugely in Rover, and as an example of good faith a vast new corporate engine plant was built at Hams Hall, just a few miles from Solihull. BMW petrol and diesel engines were earmarked for future Rover models, BMW tapped into Land Rover's 4x4 expertise for its own purposes (X5 and X3 both benefiting), Rover 75s appeared on BMW company fleets in Germany, and small Rovers were used as courtesy cars in British BMW dealerships.

Unhappily (and especially in Munich), Rover became known as the 'English patient', for profits were never made. Even though important new models like the Rover 75, the MGF sports car, the Land Rover Freelander and the new-type Discovery were all brought forward, and the Rover design, engineering and development HQ was relocated to Gaydon, sales lagged, and the balance sheet was still red.

Even while a totally new Mini project was being engineered (see New Mini sidebar), BMW's patience finally snapped, and from 1999 more and more German managers were drafted in to impose change. That, though, was only a short-term strategy, for in March 2000 BMW decided to get rid of most of its British investments.

After an industrially turbulent period one potential buyer (Alchemy Partners) came and went, and then Ford-of-Europe offered to buy the entire Land Rover business, with a deal finally done in May 2000.

Following the sale of Land Rover to Ford, BMW kept the Mini brand (and the new model, which was almost ready for launch), retained many of the trademark rights to dormant brands – and then 'sold' the remainder of the Rover Group to a management buy-out team for the princely sum of £10.

Rover (soon to be renamed MG Rover) would retain the Rover and MG brands, Rover 75 assembly would be transferred to Longbridge, while BMW completed work on the Mini project and put it into large-scale production at Cowley, which they soon renamed BMW Oxford. A £427 million 'soft' loan, which did not have to be paid back for many years, was provided to Rover, so that the still loss-making business could stay afloat until it became profitable.

Within months, BMW had expunged the Rover experience from its image as though it had never been there. Even so, five years later, the MG Rover business was still losing money, had not been able to afford to introduce any important new models, and eventually ran out of cash in April 2005, before another saviour could be found. After that, BMW gritted its corporate teeth and wondered if any of that £427 million loan would ever be re-paid…

---

the coupés (such as 6-Series or 8-Series), it was possible to forecast which might be updated, and even when. In the 2000s, with no fewer than eight different ranges, plus New Mini, all clamouring for attention and renewal, and the logical evolution of so many different factories and engine plants to be considered, this was a much more complex business.

Here, it is only possible to give a snapshot of what has been done in recent years, and to make a guess as to where BMW might be aiming its future:

Passenger cars

In the early part of the new century, not only did BMW renew the 3-Series (in 2004), the 5-Series (in 2002) and the 7-Series (in 2001), but it also introduced an entirely fresh entry-level range, the 1-Series of 2004. Each and every one of these cars used a front-engine/rear-drive layout with MacPherson strut front suspension, and Z-axle rear suspension. BMW had tested front-wheel drive on many occasions, and in spite of finding packaging advantages, decided that for them it was only appropriate for use in the New Mini, which was not badged as a BMW!

All these cars had radically different styling from those of previous BMWs, using shapes which were dictated by Chris Bangle's design team, the details of which caused a great deal of controversy by their sometimes exaggeratedly shaped 'flame surfacing'.

In each and every way, there was a strong family resemblance between the types – four headlamps in the

New Mini

When BMW bought the Rover Group in 1994, the assets included the Mini name, for the legendary Issigonis-designed car, although already 35 years old, was still in production at Longbridge.

Although Rover no longer believed in the Mini, BMW most certainly did, and instructed that an all-new model be developed. Design/styling began in 1995, Longbridge-based engineering followed in 1996, and the first Fiat-powered 'skin' prototypes were completed in 1997.

As with the original type, the New Mini was still a transverse-engined

From the wreckage of its six-year ownership of Britain's Rover Group, BMW salvaged the Mini brand, introducing the new version of this amazing little front-wheel-drive car in 2001.

front-wheel-drive car, but every single component was changed, and this was a much larger car than before. Power came from an engine developed jointly with Chrysler-USA (to be manufactured in Brazil), and the style would be a three-door hatchback built around the front-seat 'package' of a BMW 3-Series.

Original planning saw the new car engineered at Longbridge, developed at Gaydon, and to be produced at Longbridge, but from 1999, BMW took detail control themselves. As a consequence of the Rover 'divorce' of March 2000, BMW retained the Mini project, uprooted the all-new production machinery already being installed at Longbridge, and transferred it all to Cowley (later rechristened BMW-Oxford).

Although BMW would then have liked to have airbrushed out Rover's contribution to the New Mini project, the fact is that this input was considerable. However, sorting out production, re-establishing the brand, installing fabulous, state-of-the-art production machinery at Oxford, and selling the new model all over the world, was totally to BMW's credit.

By mid-2005, the 500,000th new-generation Mini had been built, with production edging up towards 4,000 cars every week, the success of the project looked assured. BMW assured everyone that the Mini was a unique project, and that it had no intention of introducing other front-wheel-drive cars, but rumours persist that some sort of 'cross-over' engineering might follow the appearance of the second-generation models in the late 2000s.

From 2001, BMW's *brand-new flagship was the 6.0-litre V12 engined 760Li, the basic four-cam engine of which was also fitted to the new Rolls-Royce Phantom.*

For 2005, BMW *gave the 7-Series a cosmetic makeover, although the basic proportions were not altered.*

The massive and commercially successful 7-Series model which was launched in 2001. The first 7-Series types had been put on sale in 1977.

nose, one or other versions of the 'kidney' grille, and remarkably similar lines and proportions concerned with door shut lines, window profiles, and fascia layouts.

To cater for this very large range, BMW evolved a master plan for engine design, development and production, and today there are petrol and diesel engines to suit every eventuality, all of them with four valves per cylinder, twin overhead camshafts per bank, and all with BMW-inspired fuel injection.

To cover this range, there were four-cylinder petrol engines (many of them built at a brand-new factory at Hams Hall, not far from Birmingham Airport in the UK), other four-cylinder engines built in Germany and Austria, straight-six and V8 petrol engines produced in Germany, along with the (relatively)

BMW's first contender for the vast SUV (sports utility vehicle) market was the X5, which went on sale in 1999. The basic four-wheel-drive layout was an obvious descendant of the 325iX system of the 1980s. Petrol and diesel, six-cylinder and V8-engined types were all produced with the petrol-engined 3.0i being one of the most popular.

more exclusive 60° V12 petrol engines. Four-cylinder and straight-six turbo-diesel engines were mainly made at Steyr in Austria. By 2005, there was really only one, dedicated, stand-alone engine – the magnificent, high-revving, 90°, 507bhp V10/5.0-litre ultra high-performance engine which was reserved for use in the M5 saloons and the M6 coupés.

These mass-produced petrol engines, of course, covered an enormous range – from a 115bhp/1.6-litre 'four' powering the 'entry-level' 1-Series, to a 445bhp/6.0-litre V12 for the 7-Series (and, in modified form, the British-built Rolls-Royce Phantom).

In their own way, though, the turbo diesels were even more astonishing, for BMW had become a world leader in using 'common rail' fuel injection, and in reducing the units' weight as much as possible. Once again there were closely related four-cylinder and six-cylinder types, spanning 115bhp/1,995cc 'four', all the way to 231bhp/2,993cc 'six' – and for the 7-Series only, there was a limited-production 300bhp/4,423cc V8 turbo diesel.

Getrag supplied all-synchromesh manual transmissions – with five, six

or (for the M5/M6 models only) seven forward speeds, while ZF was responsible for automatic transmissions, with five or six forward ratios. One excellent feature, fitted to most automatic-transmission models, was the Steptronic control of ratios, which effectively allowed the driver to use the same gearbox as a clutchless manual transmission.

With each car reaching the showrooms in a variety of styles – 3-Series cars, for instance, were invariably available as saloons, convertibles, estate cars, coupés or short-tail hatchback 'Compacts' – and an impressive and beguiling options list, it made the customer's *and* the salesman's job very demanding.

X5 and X3 – four-wheel-drive BMWs

When BMW opened up a brand-new factory in South Carolina, USA, and then only built Z3 sports cars in it, we all wondered what was afoot. It wasn't until 1999, when the first X5 was unveiled, that the penny finally

dropped: BMW wanted to break into the growing, and profitable market for SUVs (sport utility vehicle) in North America. The most efficient way to develop such a project, they concluded, was to complete all the engineering in Europe, but to build the cars in the USA.

Although concept work had already begun it was, of course, no coincidence that the original BMW SUV – later badged X5 – was mainly developed after the company had taken control of the Rover Group (see sidebar The Rover affair). Before 1994, BMW had no experience of building off-road (not even 'soft-road') vehicles, for their only four-wheel-drive vehicles had been the converted 3-Series and 5-Series machines of the 1980s and '90s. Absorbing Rover (and therefore, Land Rover) changed all that, for BMW was immediately able to tap in to the half-a-century of expertise held at Solihull.

When the X5 was still under wraps, but known to be on the way, many cynics suggested that it might be no more than a BMW-ised Land Rover Discovery or Range Rover, but as soon as it broke cover they were proved wrong. BMW made it clear that they had learned much from Land Rover, but that the X5 was a unique design – unique, that is, except for using as much 5-Series and 7-Series hardware as possible. The platform and five-door SUV superstructure, was all-new, but the engines (four different six-cylinder and V8, petrol and diesel types), main transmission (manual or automatic), and front and rear suspensions were all derived from those of BMW's existing cars.

As on Ford's and BMW's earlier 4x4 cars, there was a transfer box behind the main transmission, with a propeller shaft to the front differential installed neatly alongside the engine sump. The normal torque split was biased towards the rear – 38 per cent/62 per cent. Even more complex than existing Discoveries, the X5 had 7-Series self-levelling of the rear suspension in the Z-axle.

It was, however, not an out-and-out off-roader, for BMW did not provide a

low-range/high-range transmission choice. BMW made no bones about this, making it clear that its competitors were the Mercedes-Benz ML class and the Lexus RX300, but not big bruisers like the Discovery/Range Rover, or the Jeep Grand Cherokee. With that in mind, they aimed to sell up to 50,000 units a year, and build them at Spartanburg. This was false modesty: before long, annual sales were almost double that, and the X5 had become the standard-setter in its class.

BMW's second four-wheel-drive machine, this time dubbed an SAV (sport activity vehicle), was the X3 of 2003, which looked similar to the X5, but was a very different machine, lighter, smaller, with a shorter-wheelbase platform, narrower wheel tracks, and a different cabin. As *Autocar* so wisely commented: 'The X3 is to the 3-Series as the X5 is to the 5-Series…' This time around, too, BMW decided to have the car engineered and assembled by Magna at that company's factory at Graz, in Austria, for both the German and

BMW's second-generation SUV/4x4 was the X3, a vehicle significantly smaller than the X5, although engineered in the same basic manner.

North American facilities were approaching full-capacity.

In its technical capabilities, the X3 was more of a 'school run'/weekend leisure carry-all than a true off-roader, and initially came in for a rough ride from critics who had expected more. BMW, counting up the orders (more than 100,000 in the first year), seemed to be relaxed about this, and rapidly built up the list of optional engines. By 2005, BMW had made two different petrol and two different diesel engines available, ranging from 150bhp to 231bhp.

The 6-Series – reborn in 2003

Over the years, BMW coupés have come and gone in the popularity stakes. In the 1970s the six-cylinder-

Rolls-Royce – another modern BMW brand

Until the 1970s, Rolls-Royce led a famous, stable and gilded existence. First of all it built cars ('The Best Car in the World'), then it began making superb aircraft engines, and in 1931 it absorbed the Bentley brand. From 1939 Rolls-Royce built thousands of the legendary Merlin aircraft engine, after which car manufacture was always secondary. Post-war car production was at Crewe.

After the company plunged into receivership in 1971 (jet engine problems were to blame) the car-making operation was hived off, and eventually purchased by Vickers in 1980. All was well until 1998, when Vickers then decided to sell off its car-making interests.

A squalid bidding battle then developed, with VW thinking they had secured the Bentley *and* Rolls-Royce brands, before Rolls-Royce plc, the aero-engine concern (legally separate, but still holding trademark rights) pointed out that under an agreement made in 1973, it had the power to veto the sale of the Rolls-Royce name and trademarks, and could effectively choose the new owner of the car concern – and that this would *not* be VW. Having enjoyed aero-engined co-operation with BMW for at least a decade, they offered the car-making brand to Munich instead, and it was instantly snapped up.

A deal was struck whereby the new masters at Crewe (VW), would continue making Rolls-Royce cars until 2002, after which BMW would start all over again with its 'own-brand' Rolls-Royce. From 1 January 2003, therefore, BMW officially opened up a new factory at Goodwood (close to the world-famous house in Sussex, and one-time motor racing circuit), launched a magnificent new Phantom which was

BMW took control of the Rolls-Royce brand in 2003, its first new model being the massive Phantom. Up front, the car looked as traditional as ever, but it was built around an ultra high-tech aluminium structure and had a BMW 6-litre V12 engine.

based on V12 engines and other related 7-Series running gear, and began to build a new image.

At such rarefied price levels, this was never going to be easy. With annual production measured only in hundreds, BMW would need patience, and a wider product range, before it made any money from this highly prestigious business.

The Rolls-Royce 100EX was a one-off cabriolet built to celebrate the centenary of the marque in 2004. The reception was so favourable that BMW decided to develop a production version, to be built at the Goodwood facility from 2007.

The new-generation 6-Series coupé – badged as a 645Ci – was based on 7-Series engineering and was launched in 2003.

The cabriolet version of the 645Ci coupé followed on in the summer of 2004. As with the coupé, this model was built alongside the 7-Series models at the Dingolfing factory.

engined cars had won many hearts (and hundreds of 'saloon' car races), while in the 1990s the larger, heavier V8/V12-engined 8-Series machines had not been a commercial success. Indeed, after 8-Series assembly ended in 1999, some BMW-watchers thought it might be all over.

BMW, however, would not give in. Once the new-generation 5-Series saloons had been signed off, a separate team set about the development of a pair of new 6-Series cars – originally there was to be a four-seater coupé, and a swish, up-market convertible derivative would

Chris Bangle

From the mid-1990s, the shape and design of all new BMWs was strongly influenced by American Chris Bangle, whose approved style definitely fell into the 'love-it-or-hate-it' category. One phrase – 'flame surfacing' – which described the sculpted appearance of some new BMWs, became controversial in the extreme.

Before becoming Chief of Design in the BMW Group in October 1992, Ohio-born Bangle had attended the Art Center College of Design in Pasadena, California. Within the motor industry from the end of the 1970s, he completed significant assignments at Opel in Germany, then moved to Fiat, where he eventually became Head of Exterior Design, then Director of Design at the Italian concern.

Bangle himself knew that his approved designs were not at all conventional and would not appeal to everyone, but he was always very robust in defending his ideas, pointing out that the cars were best seen in the flesh, rather than being judged from photographs. Cars like the early-2000s 1-Series were noticeably more flamboyantly shaped than their ancestors.

Nevertheless, by the early 2000s, he had been further promoted, effectively being moved a little away from the cutting edge of design, and several of his earlier 'shapes' had already been face-lifted to make them more generally acceptable.

Designer Chris Bangle's career at BMW inspired some bizarrely-detailed styles.

follow. As with previous coupés of this size and type, the new 6-Series was based on a saloon car platform – that of the new-type 5-Series. Except that the wheelbase of the platform was cut-and-shut by just 4.3in, the underpinnings of the new 6-Series were almost pure 5-Series.

Considering that the style was by Chris Bangle's controversial team, here was a surprisingly sleek, if large, coupé. Spacious (except for its rear headroom – this was a full four-seater), and extremely well-equipped, it was the sort of two-door model which advertising agencies like to show swishing down an Italian autostrada, parking serenely outside the casino in Monaco, or attracting all the glossiest and most desirable girls at an up-market horse-race meeting.

The M6 version of the 6-Series coupé, complete with 507bhp/5-litre V10 engine, made its bow in 2005, using the same engine and transmission as the latest M5 saloon.

Price reduction was never a factor – when the 645Ci went on sale in the UK in 2004 it cost no less than £50,450 – for a high specification, with sumptuous equipment, was everything. It would eventually be possible, of course, to go 'slumming' with the 630, where the entry-level 3-litre six-cylinder engine produced 258bhp, but the majority of sales were actually for the 333bhp/4,398cc V8-engined 645Ci.

Formidable new M-badged cars

BMW had never produced a predictable, let alone a boring, M-badged car. Somehow, too, they always manage to surpass the previous model with more novelty that is truly exciting. Even so, in 2004 the company astonished everyone – not merely by launching a new-generation

M5 and an M6 in the same calendar year – but by equipping both cars with a brand-new V10 engine!

Although V10 layouts were already well-known in F1 racing, and in the layout of large diesel-engined trucks, in road cars they are very rare. When BMW started work on their own engine, neither Lamborghini's Gallardo, Porsche's Carrera GT, nor VW's 4.9-litre turbo diesel had broken cover – and American engines like the Dodge Viper V10 were really civilised derivatives of a light-truck engine.

In modern industry parlance, BMW decided to design a new very-high-performance V10 'because we can...' – in other words, because they were capable of doing so, because the company was highly profitable and could afford such indulgencies, and because they were already building up experience with the (entirely different) Formula One engines being supplied to Williams.

Even so, when the 507bhp 4,999cc V10 road car finally appeared in mid-2004, it was not merely another 'me-too' engine. Not only did this particular design feature a 90° vee-angle (which was not as expected – 72° being thought more 'normal' for this layout), but it featured BMW's celebrated 'double Vanos' control of the camshaft timing.

This was the very first normally-aspirated BMW engine which produced more than 100bhp/litre – it was only as recently as the mid-1980s that Ford had startled everyone by breaching the same 'barrier' with a *turbocharged* engine! For use in the M5 and M6 models, BMW matched it with a new Getrag seven-speed sequential-change manual transmission.

In the 1990s, building massively powerful V12 engines for fitment to the McLaren F1 road car was a profitable diversion for BMW. This was the GTR version of the F1 three-seater, which proved to be very successful on the race track.

Thus equipped, and with the usual careful attention to roadholding, braking and full equipment, it was no

High-output F1 V10 engines

Although BMW withdrew from F1 in 1986 when rule changes made the turbocharged 1½-litre engines obsolete, the engineers never lost touch. Normally aspirated 3½-litre V12s were developed in the late 1980s, but were never raced. Larger V12s were not only supplied for the McLaren F1 road car, but for use in other racing sports cars of the late 1990s.

The design of a brand-new 3.0-litre V10 F1 engine began in the late 1990s, and BMW re-entered F1 by supplying these engines to Williams F1 from 2000. Competitive from the very beginning, these units were soon rated as among the most powerful in F1, and it was no fault of the engines that more victories were not achieved. By 2005, when BMW was also thought to be ready to start up their own team, the engines were rated at more than 900bhp, and on-screen TV telemetry showed that they were peaking at 19,000rpm.

BMW re-entered Formula 1 motor racing in 2000 by supplying V10 3-litre engines to the Williams team: the driver here is Ralf Schumacher.

Modern F1 engine builders are notoriously secretive – so this example of the BMW V10 of 2001 was not shown until it had already been superseded by an even better version.

wonder that the media gushed praise all over these two new cars. Although, as ever, BMW electronically limited the top speed of both cars to 'only' 155mph, it was thought likely that they might reach nearly 200mph if that limiter could be disengaged.

Engines – BMW, the universal provider

Motor industry economists now talk in millions when analysing just how many engines need to be made before a new project makes money. As an aside, therefore, it is worth summarising just how heavily BMW were committed in the mid-2000s, and how much variety they wrung out of so few basic designs:

Petrol engines

Four cylinders: 115bhp/1,596cc to 150bhp/1,995cc
Six cylinders: 170bhp/2,171cc to 258bhp/2,996cc
V8: 333bhp/4,398cc and 367bhp/4,799cc
V10: 507bhp/4,999cc (M5/M6 only)
V12: 445bhp/5,972cc and (for Rolls-Royce) 460bhp/6,749cc

Diesel engines

Four cylinders: 122bhp and 163bhp/1,995cc
Six cylinders: 204bhp to 231bhp/2,993cc
V8: 300bhp/4,423cc (7-Series only)

All these engines have twin overhead camshafts, four valves per cylinder, light-alloy cylinder blocks (magnesium in the case of the sixes), and Valvetronic variable valve timing/ valve lift.

Typical, modern BMW power/running-gear engineering – the 6-cylinder, 3-litre common-rail turbo-diesel engine and automatic transmission.

Spartanburg – the North American dimension

As noted earlier, in the 1990s, BMW made a strategic decision to open up a new production plant in one of their most important export markets, the USA. Once Spartanburg had settled down and matured, with most of the Z4 sports cars and X5 SUVs being sold in the same continent, the USA almost began to count as a new 'home territory'.

Ten years on from the building of the first Z3, Spartanburg was regularly producing more than 3,000 private cars every week, which put it right up there, on a par, with some of BMW's European assembly plants. Already there were signs that, one day and not too far distant, BMW might want to push up that production rate even further. Rumours that it might revive

one or other of the brand names that it retained after abandoning Rover – Triumph was an obvious favourite – were linked to the possible demand for such cars in the USA. And would BMW's other major brand, Mini, always be content with one assembly plant, at Oxford?

In summary, when writing about a complex and actively changing business like BMW, it is impossible to round off a history without leaving any number of loose ends. Ten years down the road, I am sure that the entire product range will have been renewed, from 1-Series to X5, I suspect that new ranges will have been added, and that annual production will still be accelerating, well beyond the one million mark.

BMW's future, like its past, looks fascinating...

index